Falling for
London

Falling for
London

A Cautionary Tale

Sean Mallen

DUNDURN
TORONTO

Cover design: Laura Boyle
Cover illustration: Farida Zaman (faridazaman.com)
Cover art direction: Isabella Cairess Favaro
Printer: Webcom

Library and Archives Canada Cataloguing in Publication

Mallen, Sean, author
    Falling for London : a cautionary tale / Sean Mallen.

Issued in print and electronic formats.
ISBN 978-1-4597-4194-2 (softcover).--ISBN 978-1-4597-4195-9 (PDF).--
ISBN 978-1-4597-4196-6 (EPUB)

    1. Television journalists--Canada--Biography. 2. London (England)--
Description and travel. 3. Mallen, Sean--Family. 4. Mallen, Sean.
5. Mallen, Sean--Travel--England--London. I. Title.

PN4913.M285A3 2018   070.4'3092   C2018-900475-4

 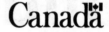 Canada

C2018-900476-2

1 2 3 4 5   22 21 20 19 18

We acknowledge the support of the **Canada Council for the Arts**, which last year invested $153 million to bring the arts to Canadians throughout the country, and the **Ontario Arts Council** for our publishing program. We also acknowledge the financial support of the **Government of Ontario**, through the **Ontario Book Publishing Tax Credit** and the **Ontario Media Development Corporation**, and the **Government of Canada.**

Nous remercions le **Conseil des arts du Canada** de son soutien. L'an dernier, le Conseil a investi 153 millions de dollars pour mettre de l'art dans la vie des Canadiennes et des Canadiens de tout le pays.

Care has been taken to trace the ownership of copyright material used in this book. The author and the publisher welcome any information enabling them to rectify any references or credits in subsequent editions.
— J. Kirk Howard, President

Printed and bound in Canada.

VISIT US AT

 dundurn.com | @dundurnpress | dundurnpress | dundurnpress

Dundurn
3 Church Street, Suite 500
Toronto, Ontario, Canada
M5E 1M2

For my parents, Joanne Mallen and Ed Mallen, who always believed in me. Wish they were here so I could present them with the first copy.

Endless thanks to Isabella (who insisted I make the dedication to Ed and Joanne) and to Julia (who wanted me to dedicate it to our dog, Oreo). I always listen ... except when I get a London job.

When a man is tired of London, he is tired of life.
— Samuel Johnson

The whirligig of time brings its revenges.
— William Shakespeare, *Twelfth Night*

This melancholy London — I sometimes imagine that the souls of the lost are compelled to walk through its streets perpetually.
— William Butler Yeats

Chapter One

This ... is London.
— Edward R. Murrow

Murrow was the prototype for a foreign correspondent. From a distance, his heyday during the war seems hopelessly romantic. Under fire with the rest of London, living intensely, drinking, smoking, working all hours. He drank with Churchill and romanced the PM's daughter-in-law. His resonant voice and powerful words evoked all the life-and-death drama of a struggle for existence. His brow seemed permanently furrowed in passionate commitment to his calling.

What young broadcast reporter would not want to be Murrow?

Many apply, but few are called.

After more than twenty years of local and national TV reporting in Canada, I had thought my time had passed. Overlooked several times for foreign postings, I was resigned to a comfortable and largely satisfying job covering the Ontario legislature, complete with my own modest, no-budget, political affairs talk show, which had won a few awards.

As I approached my midfifties, it seemed that my next move would be into public relations — perhaps making a bit more money than my journalism career had ever offered.

I would think sometimes that maybe it was time to grow up and get a real job before some new boss young enough to be my kid called me into his office to advise that he did not like my face on TV anymore and was calling security to escort me to the door.

Then the lightning bolt struck.

In early 2011 our London correspondent departed in favour of an anchor job back home. *Do I apply one more time*, I wondered?

"Okay," said Isabella. "But I'm not promising to go."

We'd been married almost sixteen years, grateful to have found each other after many romantic misadventures. She knew I dreamed of living and reporting from abroad, preferably in London — she never liked it, but equally never wanted to be an obstacle.

When I announced that I was going to Kosovo for a week in 1999 to report on the aftermath of the war, she wept fearful tears when I left for the airport.

When it seemed I was headed to Pakistan in the weeks after 9/11, she was inconsolable. As it turned out I never went anyway.

That was before Julia brightened our lives — a bubbly, happy kid, now in Grade 1, attached to her friends and daycare. We had a circle of close friends and relatives. Isabella had a job she loved, producing and directing an online design show. We had just committed to a major kitchen renovation, adding enormously to our debt, but finally finishing off our house.

Life was pretty good.

I sat at my desk at Queen's Park, staring off through the window. My stomach contracted.

Should I do this? If I get it, how will we do it?

Am I just too old for this?

Time to grow up and get a real job?

Fuck it. Not going to get it anyway. Give it one more chance and then give it up.

I applied, pouring my heart into the email to the show's producers, just as I had for so many other jobs before where I came close but missed.

The job interview was by phone, with me sitting in a deserted hallway of the legislature on a quiet day when most of the politicians were away. They asked me how I would get into Libya to cover the civil war.

"Well, I would just go to the border and start asking people for advice," I said confidently.

I had absolutely no bloody idea how I would ever get into Libya if the time ever came. And Isabella would certainly hit the roof if I ever tried.

The producers were kind and genial. I respected and liked them both. But this felt different from all the job interviews I had had before — all those times when I knew I came close but was not the choice.

They clearly wanted someone younger, more ready to go into war zones. Someone more conversant with Twitter (I would tweet once a week to a tiny list of followers to advise them of the subject of my talk show).

That's it, game over, I thought. In a way, it was a relief.

At least I tried.

A federal election was looming and I was angling to turn my provincial program into a national talk show during the campaign. But I was about to be banished to an early morning Sunday time slot that would make it impractical.

The producer who did the London job interview was among the executives I was lobbying to win a Saturday evening time. He sent an email asking me to give him a call. It was mid-March 2011.

"Hi. So, do you think we can find a time for this show?" I asked when he picked up.

"Well, we're going to take it off your hands because I want to send you to London."

A beat. I was the speechless broadcaster.

"Well … uh … good thing I'm sitting down," I finally mumbled.

"I feel really good about this decision," he said. "I've advised the vice-president and your boss that I'm making the offer and frankly they were both surprised, but also happy for you."

Naturally they were surprised. I'm the one who never got these jobs.

My head was spinning. I looked out the window that overlooked the front lawn of the legislature from our fourth-floor perch. The red-tailed hawk that nested in the tree at our level was ripping apart a small animal that had made the mistake of straying into its territory.

The producer went over the offer: a three-year contract, with both a much-higher salary and a living allowance to compensate for the cost of living in London. They wanted me to go as soon as possible because the Royal Wedding of William and Kate was just over a month away.

"Okay, then. I guess I'd better talk to my loved ones," I said, thinking that if it were fifteen years earlier I would already be calling a taxi to the airport.

I took a deep breath and called Isabella.

"Do you have bad news?" she asked, sensing the tension in my voice.

"Depends on how you look at it. They've offered me the London job."

Now it was her turn to be stunned into mumbling.

"Oh … well, I'm glad you finally got it. I'm really, really proud of you."

"We need to figure out how we're going to move there … how to get Julia into school."

"Oh … well … it's about time they recognized you, Sean."

I said I would be home early and we could start to plan. We hung up.

The news was slowly sinking it, causing a mixture of euphoria and terror.

The cellphone rang. Isabella. In tears.

"I'm sorry, but I just can't do this! I can't tear Julia out of school … can't leave my mom and dad … can't leave my job. WE'RE DOING A KITCHEN RENOVATION!

"HOW COULD YOU THINK WE COULD JUST GET ON A PLANE AND GO TO LONDON? WHAT WOULD JULIA DO? I'm so sorry, but you can't do it."

As she wept, I knew every point she made was utterly pertinent. Here I was, finally offered the job I always wanted, but to take it I'd be hurting the two most important people in my life.

I stalled, telling her to wait until I got home and we could speak about it in person.

"You would have to just go yourself and maybe we could come in the fall. Julia can't just leave her friends behind," she said, tears abating a bit.

It was a slight opening.

"Okay. You make a good point," I said. "I haven't really thought it all through yet. I didn't expect this to happen."

Thus began two weeks of intensive research, bargaining, pleading, raging, calculating, and soul-searching.

Isabella called her mother, who enthusiastically told her, "Go, go!"

Her sister, a former colleague of mine, was sympathetic to both of us — understanding Isabella's fears and my ambitions.

"Well, he is a reporter boy," she observed to Isabella — i.e., he has always had these dreams, and they are hard to abandon.

We did not tell Julia yet.

I pulled out a yellowed map of London from my backpacking trips thirty years earlier and tried to visualize the location of the bureau — a place called Camden Lock. Could not find it.

We started looking online for apartments to try to get an idea of the costs. Whole notebooks were filled with calculations. I was going to be paid almost double what I had ever made in my life. But we would be losing Isabella's substantial salary.

Within hours it became clear: we could not afford it.

"We'd be $50,000 in debt after one year," Isabella observed in a prediction that proved eerily accurate.

"Maybe you should just go on your own and Julia and I will stay here."

It was not a good scenario as either a spouse or parent. I insisted that they come, that it was a once-in-a-lifetime opportunity.

"I've already lived and worked in other countries. I don't need to do it again," she said.

"But it's London! The world's greatest city! Open your mind to the possibilities," I pleaded.

"It's another city."

Isabella had danced as a ballerina in Winnipeg, then Montreal, lived in Japan and Europe, where she modeled, and made wonderful documentaries, before finding success with the design show. She had found a creative, satisfying niche. She genuinely wanted me to succeed, but I was asking her to turn her life upside down.

My ambitions demanded a wrenching and unwanted change.

This was going to be rough.

I reached out to Tara, the previous correspondent, who had returned to Canada to take an anchor job. She was both kind and informative — patient with my repeated phone calls asking for information and advice.

"It was a great experience," she said. "But we lived modestly."

On days when she was filing a story, she generally got out of the office at around 8:00 p.m. On average she was on the road once every six weeks.

"So, you'll work late every night and then travel regularly, leaving Julia and me alone in London where we know nobody," said Isabella in a fearful tone. "You're wrecking our lives."

Our days settled into a dreary routine. I would go over the numbers for the umpteenth time. Isabella would offer the possibility of acceptance, only to then withdraw it.

She was a complex person. She loved adventure, but feared change. Just as she was feeling secure and settled, she was faced with a leap into the unknown.

I put off giving my response, saying it was more complicated than I had expected.

Meanwhile, the government in Ottawa was poised to fall and I was dispatched to cover the confidence vote — a historic moment, but my head was spinning between London and Toronto and an angry, hurt wife.

I declined a chance to go out for dinner with my Ottawa colleagues and stumbled back into my room at the Château Laurier. There was a voice mail message on my phone. It was my brother Eddie, voice grim.

"Hi, Sean, sorry to tell you this in a voice mail but Aunt Sheila passed away this morning. Give me a call."

She had been our mother's companion for many years in retirement. Mom had died three years earlier and Sheila's condition had been in steady decline. She had no children. Eddie and my sister, Theresa, had been overseeing her affairs and care.

It was a sad moment, but in a way a relief. Her last days had not been pleasant.

I stretched out on the hotel bed, closed my eyes, tried to breathe, and wondered what could be next.

But as the days unfolded, it seemed my dear aunt, in passing, had opened a door for me. She left what she had to my sister, two brothers, and me. A small inheritance that could help finance my London project.

Isabella was still adamant, still saying no. My tactic was to listen, commiserate, and stall. In the morning I would think it was never going to work and resolve to say no. During the day I would have moments of optimism, where I pictured my saying yes.

I confided my dilemma to my officemate, Randy, a cameraman who had seen it all at the legislature in more than twenty years and who had a profane way of cutting through all the bullshit to get to the nub of an issue.

"You'll always regret it if you say no," he said, tellingly.

We asked Julia what she thought about moving to London for a year.

"NO," was her definitive answer. She did not want to leave her friends.

Slowly Isabella's resistance cracked, without ever crumbling. Finally she gave a qualified concession: "It's up to you. You do not have my permission, but you do what you want."

She did not want to go, but did not want to definitively veto.

She insisted I could only sign for a one-year contract, not the three on offer, and I had to have a break clause that would allow me to quit and come back to Toronto if it all crashed around our ears. And there had to be more money.

I made a counter-offer. They came back with a bit more cash and a fifteen-month contract.

We had little sleep. Yes. No. Yes. No….

Finally, the morning dawned on the day of my self-imposed deadline. A bleak sunny day. I was leaning toward a no. My stomach contracted into my spine.

Isabella was weary of the whole thing. There was nothing more to say. It was my decision and I had neither her veto nor her support.

As the day wore on, the yes side seemed to shift the balance. There was no good reason, other than perhaps Randy's words that kept resonating in my brain.

"You'll always regret it if you say no."

Nighttime. It was going to be a yes.

"Okay," said Isabella blankly. "It will be up to you to tell Julia."

I went into the basement to call the producer privately.

"That's great!" he said with what appeared to be genuine pleasure. Papers to be signed in the next few days. Somehow it felt right. My stomach released from my spine and a rush of blood went to my head. After all these years I was going to be a foreign correspondent. And I needed to move to London within a couple of weeks in order to cover the Royal Wedding.

Seconds after I hung up, Julia came downstairs with a quizzical smile on her face.

"Are we going?" she asked.

"Yes, sweetie, we're going to London."

Without a word she ran away upstairs to her room. I took a deep breath and followed. My little girl was weeping uncontrollably into her pillow.

"WHY … WHY?" she pleaded.

I really had no good answer other than it was something I had always wanted to do. I tried to assure her that I would make sure she had fun in London and that it was an experience she would always appreciate when she was older. Barren arguments to a six-year-old who could only see that she was leaving her friends, her beloved daycare, and her school.

I went downstairs and hugged my wife.

"Thank you," I said for no obvious reason.

"Don't thank me. It's not going to be easy." She was right, of course, but she did try to help make things work.

The plan was that they would stay in Toronto to finish the school year and to spend the summer at home so that Julia would have her friends for a few more months, Isabella could continue working as long as possible, and the kitchen renovation could carry through. They would hold down the fort while I embarked on my London adventure.

Suddenly there were a million things to do. In a flash my old job was set aside as I started to make preparations. The easy part was signing the contract.

The announcement was to be made on the afternoon of April Fool's Day. As it happened, I was to be taping my final *Focus Ontario* show at the same time — an opportunity for a bit of drama.

I wrote a one-minute script of goodbye to close the program, and waited to insert it in the lineup until the moment I walked into the studio, calculating that even the diligent production crew who worked hard to make me look good did not always necessarily read the content of my scripts in advance.

I tried to make it warm and wry, and not mawkish — thanking the guests, even the grumpy ones; the production staff; and the loyal audience.

Upon completion, the director, the always sunny and genial Amy, came into the studio and opened her arms to give me a hug. With typical grace, I tripped over a cable and nearly did a face plant as she approached.

Back at my desk, I saw that the email had gone out and the congratulations were pouring in ... many shocked, but all genuine and fine. A good day.

One hard part over. Now another hard part was set to begin. I just needed to rip up deep roots and shift my life to the other side of the Atlantic.

As I was about to learn, Britain was no longer so welcoming to immigrants as it had once been. I was not even going to be an immigrant, just a visiting journalist, of which there are hundreds if not thousands in London. No matter.

The website of the British High Commission office in Ottawa made it clear that they answered no questions about visas. All advice and processing services had been farmed out to a private outfit called WorldBridge. It was reached via a 1-900 number that charged a couple of dollars per minute for the call, so I phoned from my office desk. Someone with a heavy accent answered. They asked me to spell my name, which they then repeated back painfully slowly. A couple of bucks earned for WorldBridge just to identify myself.

"How can I help?" I think he said, given that he appeared to have only completed his first two weeks of English as a Second Language training. I recalled reading on the High Commission website that applicants for British visas required a working knowledge of the language, a prerequisite evidently not considered essential for those advising on how to obtain a visa.

"I need a visa for a visiting journalist."

"A what?"

"VISITING JOURNALIST VISA," I repeated slowly.

"You are a journalist?"

"Yes."

"And do you want to work in U.K.?"

"Yes. I'm an employee of a Canadian broadcaster and they are moving me to London."

"And you want a visa?"

"Yes."

"What kind?"

"A VISITING JOURNALIST VISA," I responded, raising my voice, as well as speaking slowly so that he could hear me in Venezuela or wherever he was stationed.

"Is your employer a British company?"

"NOOOO. Can-a-di-an."

"You are Canadian?"

"I'm Martian," is what I almost said.

As the minutes and dollars ticked away, he led me through the WorldBridge website, assisting me in filling out their application online — which is the only method allowed. There were several drop-down menus to navigate before reaching the correct visa choice.

Finally we were there.

"Okay, on this next menu you will see that the visa you need is ..."

Silence on the line.

"Hello?"

He was gone. As I just discovered, my company's phone policy stopped 1-900 calls after fifteen minutes.

I called back. Would not connect. The policy, it seemed, also did not allow two such calls on the same day.

A deep breath.

Call again, this time charging it to my company credit card.

"WorldBridge, how can I help?" said the woman who answered in what appeared to a Serbo-Croatian-Icelandic accent.

"I need a visiting journalist visa and I already know the drop-down menu to go to," I said speedily, trying to limit the cost.

"Could you please spell your name?"

"I've already done all that!"

"Could you please spell your name?"

About $30 later, having repeated exactly the same process excruciatingly slowly, we had worked our way through the online application.

"So, on this next menu you will find a selection for journalist," she said.

I saw a choice for sheepherder and one for fisherman. No journalist.

"It is not there," I advised.

"Yes it is," she responded with certainty.

"I'm looking right at it and it is not there."

"It must be."

"It's not."

"One moment please."

It seemed she had not been following along on her computer screen, so as the minutes and charges ticked by I waited for her to find the same spot on the application.

"It's not there," she finally concluded.

"Correct."

"It should be there."

"But it's not. So where do I go to find the right choice?"

"I don't know. I will send an email to the High Commissioner's office in Ottawa and ask."

This would be the same High Commissioner's office that refused to answer questions from applicants.

The phone bounced surprisingly high as I slammed it down.

Four expensive phone calls and a few billion destroyed brain cells later I finally succeeded in filling in the correct form. The next step was to print it out and for Julia, Isabella, and me to go to their centre in downtown Toronto to actually submit it, along with pictures, passports, birth certificates, fingerprints, a substantial fee, and my right testicle.

The office was in the centre of the city, a bleak place high in a tower populated by workers who appeared to have just graduated from high school, fresh from their first fast-food job.

Isabella was very concerned to confirm that her spousal visa would allow her to work in the U.K., so she asked the young woman who accepted our paperwork.

Her eyes widened and a frightened look passed over her face. Clearly she had only been briefed on how to put paperwork in a plastic envelope.

"I don't know," she said politely. "I'll have to call the High Commissioner's office." Of course.

WorldBridge offered a premium forty-eight-hour processing service. Given that it was a Tuesday and my flight to London was the following Tuesday, I decided to pay the extra and get it all done.

But of course the forty-eight hours did not start until the package arrived in Ottawa, the following day. Then there was another transit day back to Toronto. So it was actually a ninety-six-hour service. Starting to get a bit tight, given that I had to submit my passport. Would be most inconvenient to miss my flight if I did not get it back in time.

I took a deep breath and hoped that it would all work.

The next day an email arrived from an anonymous official in the High Commissioner's office. We needed to submit the long-form version of Julia's birth certificate, which of course we did not have. I sent back a pleading email to the faceless, nameless bureaucrat: Please process my visa so I can get it back in time while we search for the proper documentation for Julia.

While I sweated it out, waiting for a response, I called contacts in the provincial government to find out how to expedite a request for a long-form birth certificate. It turned out that there was one office in the city that was open late one day a week, which happened to be that day. I hopped in the car and screamed up to the north part of town, arriving fifteen minutes before closing to fill out the paperwork and get it done: another forty-eight-hour service that actually took ninety-six.

Coincident with the paper chase were the more stimulating preparations. I bought the biggest suitcase I could find. Knowing I was covering the Royal Wedding, I visited a bookstore to buy a lightweight bio of Will and Kate, along with several royalty magazines that had them on the cover.

I asked the sales clerk for a bag to conceal the purchases.

As I started to sort out which clothes and personal effects to bring, Isabella and Julia watched in a kind of daze, both frightened and angry.

We consulted with my cousin Suzie, my only relative living in London. She made some suggestions about possible neighbourhoods. We resolved to look for a home near the international school where she worked, thinking that it could be a good fit for Julia, thinking that at least she would be with other expatriates. It was also within easy reach of the bureau.

We told her roughly how much I would be making and asked whether it would be enough to live in London.

"Well, you might be able to go out to dinner occasionally," was her intriguing response.

Emails were sent to estate agents: Do you think we could find a two-bedroom apartment for maybe £500 a week?

London landlords calculate rent by the week, but charge by the month. The better to squeeze a few more pounds out of the tenants. And we would also have to pay something called a council tax. And utilities. And more.

I was about to learn that the two biggest headaches for those moving to the British capital are housing and schooling.

Invariably, agents wrote back to say that we would have no problem, that there were no end of *lovely* flats just waiting for our arrival. I was also about to learn that London estate agents almost uniformly lie.

But that was a lesson that I would learn in the future. I was about to embark on my grand adventure as a foreign correspondent in Europe. At the same time, Isabella would be left behind to be a working single mother, soon to have no kitchen as the renovation began. To add to the hilarity, Toronto Hydro announced it would soon be ripping up lawns up and down the street in order to move power lines.

Isabella's enthusiasm was restrained.

"I don't even know if we'll come to join you — I can't guarantee it. I'm worried that this may cause real damage to our marriage," she warned.

My euphoria was thus muted.

As the weekend progressed, so did a complex packing job. I laid out my new giant suitcase along with two older ones in the office and allocated clothes and sundry essentials in each. Occasionally I would catch Julia staring at the piles.

Monday: my passport was delivered, with visa. One hurdle cleared, just in time. Isabella's and Julia's would come later.

The flight would be early Tuesday morning. Monday night saw virtually no sleep.

Finally the time arrived. Isabella hugged me and handed me a present. A journal. "I've always told you that you're a great writer. So, if you're going to put us through this you may as well write your first book." Despite all I was putting her through, she'd given me a fine, fine gift.

Julia was inconsolable.

"DON'T GO!" she cried, eyes streaming, hanging on to me as I tried to walk out to the cab. The monster Daddy tried to reassure her that I would be seeing them in a few weeks when they came to London for a visit to help me pick out a flat.

And then I was out the door. Dawn was just breaking on a cool April morning as I hopped into a taxi, heading to the airport and a new life.

Hoping I had not wrecked my current life.

Chapter Two

Through a strange confluence of events, I somehow managed to get into business class for my landmark flight to London. I asked if there was a complimentary upgrade available, and for some reason, one was — the one and only time that has ever happened to me.

It meant that I had a nifty little cubbyhole all to myself while the rest of the crew headed over for the Royal Wedding were jammed together back in economy. I could actually put up my feet, relax, and enjoy a higher level of service. Did not help. I could not sleep a wink, even though I was exhausted.

It was a day flight, meaning we left in the morning Toronto time and arrived late in the evening London time. Under normal circumstances, this meant a quicker recovery from jet lag. In my case, it was not so much a case of disrupted sleep patterns as disrupted life patterns.

Our hotel was a posh place in Mayfair, just off Piccadilly. Paparazzi were stationed out front. Rumour had it that Jamie Lee Curtis was staying there. They made no effort to raise their cameras when I approached the door.

My room was sleek, austere, and modern. I noted that the toilet required several flushes to take away the paper. Seemed strange, considering this was an expensive joint. I was about to learn that all English toilets failed to take away what they were supposed to take away. It did not matter if they were in Buckingham Palace or a fleabag bed and breakfast. The British built an empire upon which the sun never set — gave us Shakespeare, Newton, and Crapper. But their toilets are not worth a shit. At 2:00 a.m. I was wide awake. What the hell was I doing?

In the morning I took five steps out of the hotel and Mayfair announced itself through an endless parade of stunning tall women in expensive short frocks — often emerging from the Bentley or Jaguar driven by their middle-aged, burned-bronzed hedge-fund boyfriend. It is one of the poshest parts of town: the home of Claridge's, the Ritz, and the U.S. Embassy, which dominates Grosvenor Square. In those days, the Canadian High Commissioner's residence was just opposite, occupying a more modest slice (it was sold in 2013).

Mayfair is the most expensive property in the English version of Monopoly.

It had been twenty years since I had last seen London and I did not remember the sky being so blue and the women so beautiful. The city was in the middle of an unusual April heat wave. The flowers were blooming and fragrant.

Exhausted, drained, and disoriented as I was, I still could not believe that I was there, doing what I was doing. Europe Bureau Chief. Sounded pretty good.

It was time for the Europe Bureau Chief to find the Europe Bureau. Global's office was in the centre of the Camden Market. Despite having visited London on several occasions, I had never heard of the market. I was about to discover, however, that it was one of the biggest tourist attractions.

I could have taken a taxi but was determined to start finding my way on the Tube. Not yet conversant with the map function on my new iPhone, I invested in a quaintly archaic navigational device: a pocket version of the *London A–Z* map book. Armed with an address on Oval Road, I entered the underground at Green Park, hopped on the Piccadilly line eastbound, changed to the Northern line at Leicester Square, and rode north to Camden Town. This was going to be a snap.

One step out of the Tube stop, though, and my head started to spin. I was at the confluence of six streets, which came together in a typically London fashion — that is to say in a series of crazy angles, none of which was ninety degrees. Across the street was a pub called The World's End. The wide sidewalk was jammed. A busker was hammering away at his guitar. A vacant-looking guy was holding a sign advertising Indian food nearby.

Staring down at my map book I could see Oval Road only a few blocks away, but looking up I could find no obvious means of getting there. I tentatively took ten steps in one direction and was immediately lost.

I turned in another direction, started to cross a side street. *HONK.* A driver was pulling out through a stop sign, uncaring of my obvious right of way, and jammed on the brakes millimetres away.

"Watch where yer goin', mate," he barked out the window.

"Mate" expressed thusly in London-ese does not mean "friend" — a closer translation is "fucking idiot." As a good Canadian, I said, "Sorry, sorry," even though the mate was utterly in the wrong and could have ended my foreign correspondent's job before I had even completed a full day. I was reminded that London drivers tend to speed up when they see a pedestrian step off the curb.

Retrace the steps back to the station and start again, this time in the correct direction, north on Camden High Street. A guy with a blue mohawk haircut was handing out coupons for a discount piercing. He did not bother with me.

On the upper floors of the shops, there were large sculptures of shoes attached to the wall. The voices in the crowd were Italian, French, German — even some English. The Camden Market was jammed with shops manned by South Asians selling millions of cheapo Union Jack T-shirts, phone booth piggy banks, and masks of the Royal Family.

With increasing confidence, I took a left at Inverness, then a right along some stately houses on Gloucester Crescent — *maybe a good place to find a flat*, I thought. At the end of the crescent, there was Oval Road. Success.

I took a right again and looked for number 32. Except there was no 32. There were other buildings in the 30s, but not the number I needed. Not an auspicious start for the Europe Bureau Chief when he is unable to find the office of the Europe Bureau, even though he is standing on the street where the Europe Bureau is located.

I gave up and called my colleague Stu who I knew was working in the office.

"Ah … well, you see our address on Oval Road is not actually *on* Oval Road," he explained, as though it made perfect sense.

"Walk right to the north end, past the Pirate Castle, and look to your right. You'll see a red brick building with satellite dishes. I'll come down to meet you."

This was the Interchange — the Associated Press building. My new home. Thirty-two Oval Road was actually a block off Oval Road, at the end of a dead-end street called Gilbeys Yard. It was formerly a shipping centre for the gin company of the same name, right beside the Regent's Canal and the Camden Lock that I was unable to find earlier in my ancient map book.

Global TV's Europe Bureau was on the second floor (third floor in North American terms) amidst a United Nations of broadcasters. Russia Today was next door, Japan's TV Asahi at the end of the hall. Around the corner was CCTV from China. The Mexicans were a few doors down. And just opposite the elevators was Brazil's Globo — much larger than Global Canada. We always got their mail and phone calls.

Globo had an elegant, illuminated sign on their door. We had a torn photocopy of the Global logo, leading to what appeared to be a former closet — a long, narrow room with packing cases for TV equipment piled high on either side.

There was a couch jammed up along one wall, salvaged from the hallway after one of our better-resourced neighbours put it out for garbage.

My new desk was right beside the window, looking east over the market. Food stalls were bustling below, with canal boats tied up alongside. The water on the canal was turning a fascinatingly bright shade of green, with some kind of alien fungus coating the surface of the water.

I loved it.

With the Royal Wedding still a week away, and all my bosses still asleep back home in Canada, I resolved to use my first few mornings to begin the apartment hunt. The company would pay for a short let for a month or two until I found a more permanent place. Isabella and Julia would be coming to London in a few weeks, so my challenge was to find an enticing *pied-à-terre* that would encourage them to want to stay.

Of London's eight million people, roughly seven million are estate agents. They are unfailingly friendly and helpful. They will all tell you: "Of course we can find an absolutely lovely flat that's well within your budget."

I suspect that as a condition of their licence they are all required to take a course in creative mendacity. London has no apartment that will be both lovely and within your budget.

Every neighbourhood has a clutch of estate agency offices, usually grouped together. They have names like Chestertons and Black Katz, Foxtons and You 'R' Fucked.

I trolled through the offices near the bureau, most of which did not do short lets. Posted in all their windows were pictures of flats that appeared perfectly fine, but which were not actually available once I entered inside.

The first agent was a smiling young blond woman in a tight tube dress and ten-inch heels.

"Wo's yoh bo-jut?" she asked.

My hearing was already not the best. I leaned in, turning my good ear toward her, and asked her to repeat.

Twenty-three times later I finally figured out she wanted to know my budget.

"Ow ... royut. 'Ere's a luvly playce," she said, calling up a listing on nearby Gloucester Crescent. I remembered the stately houses on the street from my failed search for the bureau. Sounded promising.

"Okay. Can I see it?"

"'Course, luv," she said. She promised to set up something for the following morning, but somehow it never happened. She claimed the landlord had decided to not rent it after all.

Instead, she brought me to another "luvly playce" on Fitzjohn's Avenue, not far from the international school that we thought might be a good fit for Julia. Fitzjohn's is a nice street in Belsize Park lined with many grand-looking houses. At around 3:00 p.m. every afternoon during the school year, it is plugged with traffic. This part of North London is densely packed with schools and it is always jammed during pickup time.

She led me into the front door of one of the imposing piles. Underneath the staircase was a door leading to the flat, very much like the entrance to a dungeon. The dinginess at least had the benefit of making the dirt in the corners less evident. The square footage was roughly similar to the average mid-sized sedan, with a strange walk-up to an inside balcony where a tiny bed was perched.

Nope.

The morning flat hunts took on a depressing similarity. There was the garden flat in Kentish Town. "Garden flat" is an elegant English term for basement apartment, although they are not quite so subterranean as back home. This one had tiny rooms, with a ceiling so low that even someone of my modest height risked concussions on the doorways. It did have a walkout access to the garden, but it seemed that the moss had actually migrated inside.

Nope.

Around the corner from Euston Station, and next door to one of London's few strip clubs, I looked at a place in an apartment building. It was clearly a bachelor pad, with a black leather sofa. In fact, lots of black in the decor.

"Nope," said Isabella when I described it over the phone.

Although spinning my wheels in the search for accommodation, I at least managed to start doing some TV stories, relishing the chance to say, "Sean Mallen, Global News, LONDON!!!"

Yeah, baby. That's me in London.

Euphoria was tempered by tense calls home at night.

"I'm not happy about this," Isabella would say regularly. "You've left us. I'll try, but remember, there's no guarantee about this."

My stomach would turn in knots and sleep came with difficulty. But work distracted me the rest of the time.

A week before the wedding, a clutch of true royal fanatics started camping out across the street from Westminster Abbey. A similar cast of characters always gathered for these kinds of events.

John Loughrey was the first. A lean, slightly wild-eyed Brit, he relished being the earliest arrival of the band of eccentrics. He bragged that he had attended most every major royal event since 1981.

By the time I arrived, approximately 436 reporters had already interviewed him, and so his lines were beyond well-rehearsed — they were automatic. I simply asked him why he was there and he went on a three-minute rant, explaining his background, how he is a Diana fanatic, and showing his sleeping bag, his Union Jack hat, Union Jack carrying bags, and Union Jack flag with the happy couple pictured in the centre.

"How are you going to last all that time, camping out here?" I asked.

"Well, I'm organic. I've got lots of energy."

No other questions were really necessary. I resisted asking him whether in fact he had a life.

Finding Canadians in the crowd was a snap. Bernadette Christie from Grande Prairie, Alberta, was close to the front, displaying a giant Maple Leaf flag to match her Maple Leaf top. I was to see her again the following year, camped out on The Mall for the final concert in the celebration of the Queen's Diamond Jubilee. She also somehow got herself a ticket on a special anniversary cruise marking the centenary of the *Titanic* sinking, where she also managed to get herself widely interviewed.

The circus was most certainly in town. As I was quickly learning, the worldwide appetite for royal stories is insatiable and none was more newsworthy than the marriage of Diana's son to the reed-thin, perfectly poised daughter of rich party planners. "Waitie Katie," as the tabloids liked to call her, had played all her cards right, been patient, and got her prince.

When William attended the University of St. Andrews a decade earlier, mothers far and wide scrambled to get their daughters enrolled at the same time, hoping to land the heir. Catherine Middleton outmanoeuvred them all and hit the jackpot. Now her picture was everywhere and every frock she wore immediately became a bestseller.

Opposite Buckingham Palace, at Canada Gate, huge scaffolding was being erected with banks of cubicles for the world's broadcasters — each paying six-figure fees for their little studios with a view of the palace. There had originally been a long list of members of the *Global National* team back in Canada who were coming to assist in covering it all — until the bills started arriving and the budget was trimmed.

Behind the mediaplex in Green Park, acres of grass were being killed to accommodate all the trailers, satellite trucks, and porta potties that had been brought in to support the broadcasts.

My new collaborator, the Europe Bureau's cameraman-editor Dan Hodgson, had already been fed up with the spectacle for months. "Every time William gets a new brand of toilet paper to wipe his ass, we have to do a story," he groused.

"Resistance is futile," I advised.

My preferred term for the Royals was the "overpaid, inbred, spoiled anachronisms." Not that I ever used it on camera. As a history buff, I actually had an avid interest in the story. And as a lover of the absurd, who could resist the utter silliness of it all? For a journalist in London, it did not matter whether you liked or loathed the Royals, you would be covering their every move.

In a nod to balance, I interviewed a representative of Britain's sadly outnumbered republican movement. He did his best. But the Windsors had bounced back since the dark days of Diana's death and were now ascendant, an unstoppable PR machine. Here was an attractive, personable, and media-savvy couple riding a wave of romance and fascination. Barring an unanticipated catastrophe, it would be a triumph for the royalists.

The Windsors and their various assorted homes are among Britain's greatest tourist attractions, and there was talk of a boost to the economy of £30 to £50 million.

Margaret Tyler was doing her bit to be a one-woman economic stimulus package. She had something on the order of ten thousand items of royal memorabilia in her modest home not far from Wembley

Stadium. I gave her a call and asked if she would mind if we came out to do a bit of filming.

"Oh, that would be fine, dear," she said. "I have the Australians coming in the morning and the Indonesians in the afternoon, but if you could arrive around noon I could fit you in."

Mrs. Tyler was well on her way to being interviewed by every single one of the thousands of reporters in town for the wedding. And making a killing. "I hope you don't mind, but I usually ask £50. Would that be all right?" she asked sweetly.

This was my introduction to the British form of cashbook journalism.

She began her collection with the wedding of Charles and Diana and the hobby grew into an obsession. The Tyler house was a teeming, cluttered, chaotic shrine to the Royals.

"Bulging at the seams, isn't it?" she observed.

She knew what the likes of me needed and had her dining-room table covered with the latest wedding souvenirs. "Nobody eats here now," she advised.

Nobody really sat anywhere in her house either because every single square centimetre was occupied by a Royal photo, spoon, teacup, or pillow. There was a large portrait of Diana, her favourite Royal, as a centrepiece in a room that she has devoted to the late Princess of Wales. Alongside her Kate-and-Will loving cup was a Kate-and-Harry mug.

"I think it was made in China," she said with a twinkle in her eye.

Mrs. Tyler turned up her nose at some of the more satiric choices: the condoms (called Royal Jewels) were not part of her collection and neither were the wedding barf bags, for those who could not stomach the spectacle.

Despite her prodigious buying, the wedding threatened to be an economic bust when one factored in the multimillion-pound cost of security and the multibillion-pound cost of giving the nation the day off work.

The Windsors and their subjects would have a blast of a party, but Britain's struggling economy would pick up the tab.

A giant grandstand was erected opposite Westminster Abbey, just behind where Bernadette, John, and the rest of the campers had taken up their positions. This is where I would be standing, along with a couple hundred of my good friends in the international media, for four hours or more on the day of the wedding. We had a rehearsal on the eve of the nuptials. Dan and I climbed up the stairs at the rear, past the several large contingents working for the major American broadcasters, past their legions of makeup artists, field producers, sound guys, and gofers.

We were renting a strip of space about a metre wide, and a few metres deep — just enough for Dan to set up his camera and shoot me with the abbey in view behind. At events like this, one always must be wary of blurting out "fuck" or "cocksucker," because likely there is a broadcaster from Argentina or Thailand with a hot microphone standing mere inches away.

Those lucky reporters on the scaffolding would be the first live witnesses to the most-anticipated event of the day — Kate's appearance in her wedding dress. This particular frock was a closely guarded secret. There were rumours of multiple dresses — a bogus one to throw the tabloids off the track, and a backup one that would be pressed into service if a picture of the genuine article leaked out.

The frenzy over the dress left me a little cold. Far more amusing were the contortions of the British prime minister, David Cameron, over what he would be wearing on the big day. Cameron was most sensitive about his image as a "posh boy." This was a new term I was learning.

Cameron came from a wealthy, connected family. He was descended, illegitimately, from King William IV, thanks to a regal liaison with a mistress. In his Oxford days he was a member of the notorious Bullingdon Club — a group of what could only be described as rich young shits who would regularly get hammered and trash property, with little regard for the consequences. The mayor of London, Boris Johnson, was a fellow Bullingdon boy.

Cameron, only prime minister for a year in a coalition government, ardently wished to distance himself from the image. As a result, he hesitated to commit to wearing something so prototypically posh boy as a morning suit — especially given that a photograph had been circulating of him and Johnson posing in just such an outfit from their Bullingdon days.

Never mind that it was the traditional choice for a royal wedding — the prime minister did not wish to come across as a "toff" (another new word I was learning: it is more or less synonymous with "posh boy").

Cameron was finally bailed out when the deputy prime minister, Liberal Democrat leader Nick Clegg, announced he would be wearing a morning suit — as would the lefty head of the Labour Party, Ed Miliband.

Given sufficient cover by Clegg and Miliband, Number 10 Downing Street announced that the prime minister would in fact be wearing a morning suit, claiming with little credibility that the matter had never been in question.

As for me, I would be wearing a shockingly pink tie for my four hours of live broadcasting. Julia had picked it out for me at our favourite men's shop in Toronto, Caruso Fine Tailoring, on the Danforth. She sweet-talked the garrulous Caruso brothers into throwing it into the bargain for my latest suit purchase.

It was not only pink, it was fairly electric pink. But what the hell — it would likely be one of the least ridiculous bits of attire on display.

With all the streets closed off, Dan and I hopped on the Tube early on the day of the wedding to make our way to the abbey. Climbing up the stairs to our perch, I noted that a surprising number of reporters were wearing shockingly bright ties ... even pink ones. My six-year-old must have known something.

The day was overcast, but the rain held off. I had covered political conventions, a papal funeral, and natural disasters, but this was a different kind of exercise: hours and hours of silliness, with dashes of escapist romance.

For my first live hit, I jumped in with both feet, noting the numbers of women arriving for the wedding with fascinators, exercises in surrealist architecture, atop their heads.

Princess Beatrice, daughter of Prince Andrew, was wearing one that became an internet sensation — described as a cross between a toilet seat and a weapon of interstellar warfare from *Star Trek*. "Fascinator on stun!" was one clever online posting, with Captain Kirk pointing the Beatrice toilet seat at some threatening aliens.

"It's a good thing there's not much wind today or the breeze would be catching those things and carrying many of London's finest ladies out over the Thames," I observed.

In my ear, I could only hear silence from the anchor desk.

Then: "Thanks for that, Sean."

These kinds of events are old home week for all the crowned heads of Europe and the world. Most of the Europeans are relatives anyway. They all automatically get invitations and show up in all their finery. With one exception: King Norodom Sihamoni of Cambodia regretfully declined, claiming he had a tight and full schedule back home. Which meant that it was likely the one and only time that King Norodom Sihamoni's name ever appeared in a British mass-market tabloid — the *Mail* snarkily describing him as a "shaven-headed former ballet dancer."

At just about the time Will and Harry's limousine left Clarence House for the church, the abbey's bells rang out and the crowd erupted in cheers. Here was an electric moment, even for a republican.

Ten massive bells, the largest weighing 1,500 kilograms, produced a deafening, spine-tingling din. Within a few minutes, the prince and his brother emerged in front of the abbey.

The rest of the Royals followed them in reverse order of seniority, with the Queen and Prince Philip last. Then, there was Kate. My view from across the street was far inferior to anything seen at home on television. But I could definitely see her dress.

It appeared to be white.

Some weeks later, while on a tour of Buckingham Palace, I saw it on display up close. Her waist seemed to be about twelve inches.

I wondered about the happy campers Bernadette and John below and whether someone stood up to block the view just as the big moment arrived after their days of sleeping on the street. Kate's moment of arrival and display of the dress lasted less than a minute.

Even as she was stepping out of the limousine, the iPhones and BlackBerrys of thousands of reporters simultaneously buzzed with the delivery of press releases from the palace, describing her frock in minute detail. The royal press team is a sophisticated operation, with elaborate protocols for disseminating endless reams of trivia about the Queen, her family, and all her relations.

Except in this case, nothing about that dress was considered trivial in the eyes of the world's media. With a couple of billion people watching around the world, broadcasters now had a boatload of facts to help fill their time.

As was widely predicted, it was designed by Sarah Burton of the Alexander McQueen house. The release noted that it was a British firm, but neglected to point out that it was owned by the Italian fashion giant Gucci.

Members of the Royal School of Needlework hand-made the lace. To maintain secrecy, they were reportedly told that it was being created for an expensive costume drama. Hands had to be washed every thirty minutes and needles changed every three hours to ensure there were no greasy fingerprints or shredded threads on this item of worn history.

All very fascinating and duly reported to the throngs of royalists watching, but the real sensation trailed just behind Kate: her sister, Pippa, holding the train and slightly stealing the show as she paraded up the aisle in a bridesmaid's dress that perfectly displayed an exquisitely contoured ass.

While Kate's dress was later to go on display at Buckingham Palace, where it raised money for charity, Pippa's backside launched a web page, Facebook group, and a new target for the paparazzi.

As for us up in the stands, the beginning of the ceremony meant that we could take a break, as no one would be interested in our fascinating commentary when they could listen to see if Kate managed to remember all of Will's names as she recited her vows, or watch the prince jamming a slightly too small ring onto his bride's finger.

At the end, as the future king and queen paraded down the aisle and out into their horse-drawn carriage, it was time to stand up and start talking again. It was a challenge, because the abbey bells once again started ringing out in deafening fashion — a noise that would continue for another three hours.

My contribution to the broadcast at this point was something on the order of "It sure is loud here, Dawna. People are excited."

There were no plans to submit it for any awards of excellence. The challenge was just to continue filling airtime for an hour or so until the happy couple emerged on the balcony of the palace to deliver the kiss.

Someone came in my ear asking if I could offer any commentary on the fashions. My heart ran cold. The fascinator wisecrack was the best and only thing I had. So instead I recited David Cameron's moral struggle over the morning suit.

"Thanks for that, Sean," said our anchor, Dawna. "I had no idea...."

I suspect she wanted to hear about the lace, the handwashing, and the needle changing.

Finally, the happy couple emerged on the balcony and gave the people what they wanted. William added a second kiss for good measure. Times had changed for the Royals. These two people actually knew each other, unlike Will's parents who had only met a handful of times by wedding day. As one astute commentator once said, Charles and the Windsor team had the impossible task of finding a British virgin with royal blood and no embarrassments in her past. The Chuck and Diana kiss was thus forced, chaste, and a harbinger of what was to come in a disastrous marriage.

Now that the money shot had happened, we could at last sign off from the live broadcast. After we made our way down from the bleachers, I spotted the Canadian camper Bernadette Christie packing up her belongings as she prepared to go to a hotel and her first shower in days.

"I just couldn't stop crying," she said. "It was just beautiful ... spectacular beauty. The culture, the history. I can't say enough. I don't know what to say."

My only task now was to write and narrate a highlight package for the evening news. As I was to discover, much of my work in the London bureau involved watching television, choosing the best video and clips, and preparing a story without leaving the office. The technical term for this exercise is "melting" or "doing a melt." It is loosely connected to what we sometimes refer to as "journalism."

The day after the wedding, the whole crew of collaborators headed home to Canada. I would still be at the Mayfair for another day or two before shifting to a cheaper hotel closer to the bureau.

I was suddenly alone, and a bit lonely. Now what?

The search for supper had me wandering through the streets around the hotel on a warm London night, poking my head into tiny restaurants and pubs that were both full and expensive. As I walked in circles vacillating, the phone rang.

"Hi, Daddy!" yelled an enthusiastic Julia. "Guess what Mommy did."

"I dunno. What did Mommy do?"

"I can't tell you!"

"Could you pass me to Mommy?"

Isabella got on the line.

"You know, it's a bit crazy and I can't really tell you about it," she said enigmatically, with ill-concealed excitement in her voice. They were clearly driving and talking on speakerphone.

"Can you give me a hint?" I asked.

"I can't yet. It's really wild, but I feel really good about it."

I was leaning against a wall with a slightly wacky smile on my face as we played the game. At least she sounded happy.

Julia piped up from the back seat.

"SHE BOUGHT A CAR!!"

"You bought a car?"

"Well ... yes. AND IT'S SO CUTE!"

"Okay. What kind of car?"

"It's a Fiat ... a little Fiat 500. A convertible with a red top. AND I LOVE IT!"

"So ... you bought an Italian 'fix-it-again-Tony' ragtop. In Canada. Where it snows. When you're about to move to London."

"Yes, I did. You went to London and I'm buying myself a car I love."

I thought the Mazda was perfectly fine; better, it was fully paid for. It was too big for Isabella, though; the Fiat on the other hand was a sweet compact and a fun ride for her and Julia to enjoy in my absence.

The next day I moved to more modest accommodations. The Holiday Inn in Camden Lock was not exactly the Mayfair, but it was good enough and just across the canal from the bureau. Guests got a complimentary pair of earplugs — a useful item due to the late-night din at that time of year. With the weather being mild, young patrons of the many nearby pubs tended to spill out into the street at night, loudly proclaiming their presence.

The dreary hunt for a short-let apartment dragged on, ruining my mornings with frustration. They were too expensive, required too long a stay, were too far away, or mainly were just too crappy.

The breakthrough finally came when I expanded my search slightly north. There was a cluster of estate agent offices surrounding the Hampstead Tube stop, with what appeared to be many possibilities posted in their windows. Of course, I had been fooled before by what seemed to be promising pictures.

I took a chance and went into one office. A Cockney lass named Jade was sure she had a place, picking up the phone and talking to an owner. It seemed that he had had a flat up for sale for months, with no sign of a buyer. She talked him into considering it as a short let, so that at least he could get some income.

"How's the market for sales?" I asked her as we walked to her car.

"Shite."

The banking crisis still lingered. Many first-time buyers could not get financing. The rental market, by contrast, was booming, with rents rising impossibly.

Jade's car was a white Fiat 500, pretty much the same toy vehicle Isabella had just bought back home.

After what seemed like a very short drive, we pulled up to a leafy cul-de-sac with a building surrounded by neat and blossoming gardens at the end.

The flat in question was a 2.5 bedroom on the ground floor — not good. But it was bright, clean, and evidently well-kept. A mere £850 per week, which would work out to almost $6,000 a month.

But the company would be paying for this one, although the pressure would be on to get a permanent place.

Sold.

Back at her office I filled out a rental agreement that ran roughly 250,000 pages, each of which had to be initialed at the bottom. I handed over my credit card to pay six weeks in advance. Naturally the amount required went way over my limit, and the card was refused, leading to an emergency long distance call to Canada to get the limit increased.

Head spinning at the many thousands of dollars flying onto my little piece of plastic, there was a coincident feeling of relief. A place had been found. Hallelujah.

Two days later, I loaded my giant suitcases into a taxi and hauled them up to my new, temporary home. The landlord had already rented a few pieces of furniture — a tacky glass table; a tackier, black fake-leather sofa; and a couple of cheapo beds. All very much like the decor of student apartments from decades ago. The place still echoed with the emptiness.

There were a couple of pots and pans and about three wire hangers in the closet, but no plates or cutlery, and, crucially, no TV or internet.

In order to start gathering provisions, the folks at the estate agent's office advised a visit to the Brent Cross Shopping Centre and the John Lewis department store. There was a Brent Cross stop on the Northern line just two stops away, so it seemed simple enough. Except the Brent Cross Tube stop is actually nowhere near the Brent Cross Shopping Centre. I emerged on a residential street, with no sign of the mall. But there were at least signs, which led me on a circuitous route through a bleak industrial streetscape — a place strewn with beer cans, the grey concrete walls marked with profane graffiti, traffic passing overhead on an expressway. This was not the tourist's London.

After a fifteen-minute walk through British dystopia, I arrived. Brent Cross was a mall like any other I would find in North America and John Lewis very much like the department stores back home.

The list of necessities was long and the pressure great due to the need to find things that would meet with Isabella's approval. So I called her to talk me through the process ... describing the bed linens, cutlery, and plates that I had picked out. She asked me to just get the basics so that she could take care of the larger portion when she came to visit in a few weeks.

At checkout I filled four huge plastic bags.

"Would you like us to deliver?" asked the helpful clerk.

"Nope. I'm good," I said, the bag handles cutting deeply into my hands as I hoisted them. I was determined to get the flat squared away as soon as possible and did not want to have to wait for a delivery, a decision I kept repeating to myself during the short walk over to the taxi stand, my shoulder muscles screaming, my fingers turning purple with the blood flow cut off, and sweat beading on my forehead.

The cab driver watched with some amusement as I plopped the bags inside and collapsed onto the seat.

"Yah know, they'll deliver that for you, mate?"

"Mate" had the full London meaning of "fucking idiot" in this case.

No matter. Now at least I had the means to eat something other than pizza and to sleep in a bed that had sheets, pillows, and a duvet. A quick trip out to a discount electronics store produced a TV. Then another trip to buy a tool kit when I discovered that a nail file was not up to the task of attaching said TV to the cable.

Pick up some microwave dinners, cereal, milk, and a six-pack of beer, and things were starting to fall into place. But as I sat alone at the glass table, watching TV and eating greasy chicken tikka masala out of a plastic tray, it still felt more like a rather expensive camping trip than a profound experience of one the world's great cities. I could have just as easily been sitting in an apartment in Timmins, Ontario, drinking cans of Sleeman instead of John Smith's.

The acquisition of the short let was only the preface to the tragicomedy to come: the search for a "permanent" place for my reluctant wife and daughter. But at least their introduction to London would be in an enticing neighbourhood.

Without actually knowing it, I had stumbled into one of the most expensive parts of the city, reputedly with the highest concentration of millionaires anywhere in the United Kingdom. Crossing Frognal, I always had to take care to not be run down by a Rolls or Bentley. Along Church Row, there was a plaque announcing that H.G. Wells once lived there. In the overgrown cemetery farther down the street, there was the mossy gravestone of Hugh Gaitskell, a former Labour Party leader. The painter John Constable is also planted there.

The MP was Glenda Jackson, once an Oscar-winning actress, by then a bit of a gadfly on the left wing of Labour. Although well-heeled, Hampstead has also been a centre of liberal thinkers.

The streets surrounding the Hampstead Tube stop are lined with tony shops, charming cafés, and restaurants. I took note of the art supplies store and the PizzaExpress joint — two possible selling points. A few doors down from the Tube stop there is even a McDonald's, but one that had to fight to wedge its way into the neighbourhood in the 1990s. Ronald and gang battled it out in court with the hostile residents of Hampstead, finally reaching a compromise that saw a subdued storefront for the golden arches.

It is all on the edge of Hampstead Heath: the massive and ancient expanse of greenery — home to bathing ponds, a million dog-walkers, and one of the best views of the city.

The flat, which seemed a mere stone's throw from the Tube stop when riding in Jade's car, was actually a good ten-minute walk, all uphill. On my first substantial grocery run, I felt every step hauling several jammed grocery bags, which did further damage to my hands. I resolved to add a shopping trolley to my list of things to buy.

Given the hilly terrain, Hampstead Tube stop is the deepest in the city, the platform more than fifty-eight metres below the surface. Rushing to work in my first week in the flat, I discovered a sign at the entrance advising that the lift was out of order, so I turned to the emergency stairs, beside which is an advisory that there are more than 320 steps. How bad could it be? I held the handrail as I jauntily made my way down the spiral staircase. Partway down my head started to spin and there was a burning in my knees. Why the hell did they not have a backup elevator? Out of breath, sweat gathering in the small of my back, I arrived at the bottom, just as the other lift (the one that was not out of order had I properly read the signs) arrived with a load of passengers. The palm that had gripped the rail on the way down was now black, having rubbed off about a century's worth of accumulated Londoners' hand grime.

Holding my hand at a distance to avoid further contamination, I hopped aboard the southbound train just as the doors were closing. As I congratulated myself on my gazelle-like grace, forward progress came to a sudden stop. The doors had clamped onto my backpack, and it was now thoroughly jammed.

Pull once. No movement. Pull harder. Nothing. Pull pull pull. Now it was a desperate tug of war to yank it through. London Tube train doors are remarkably powerful. The backpack would not budge. Inside were both my laptop and my passport, which I now pictured being shredded and scattered along the deepest stretch of the Underground.

A guy on the platform witnessed my flailing, stepped up to the door with a look of impatience and disdain and gave a brisk push, just as I put all my strength into one last yank. Abruptly freed from the deathly embrace of the doors, I stumbled across the car and grabbed a post to avoid doing a face plant.

Sweat was now pouring down my face, which I wiped with my grimy hand, smearing a substantial black mark across my forehead. The doors had left a grease stain on the backpack, which in the struggle transferred to my formerly white shirt.

The other passengers on the car watched my fumbling performance with bored indifference. The Underground won this round.

As I walked into the Interchange, all the TV screens were dominated by pictures of Osama bin Laden. American intelligence had tracked him down to a house in Pakistan, somehow missed by the Pakistani authorities, even though his so-called hideout was a short walk away from a prominent military academy. A squad of U.S. Navy SEALs staged a raid in the dark of night and gunned him down, finally exacting vengeance for 9/11.

It was in the middle of the night back home, but someone was awake because my iPhone buzzed with an email: "We want you to go to Pakistan" — puzzling because we had a correspondent who was based in New Delhi, several thousand kilometres closer to the action. But in this kind of job, the correct answer is always: "Okay."

Isabella generally worried about my safety, even if I was going to northern Ontario. I was fairly certain she would not be pleased to hear that I was flying halfway around the world to a nation where al Qaeda was active and where its leader had just been killed by Americans who had staged a military raid without permission on sovereign soil, especially given that she and Julia were to be arriving in London in about a week for their first, crucial visit.

Luckily, it never became an issue because it quickly became apparent that a Pakistani visa was going to be impossible. But this was the first taste of how the demands of being a foreign correspondent often collide with the demands of family.

The days were whirling by toward the arrival of Isabella and Julia. The flat hunt was intensifying, and thankfully it was becoming marginally less futile as I was at least able to put together a short list of possibles that I could show them.

Isabella had started searching online and was regularly sending me listings to check out, including an apartment on Buckland Crescent, which was pictured with what appeared to be a quaint little balcony overlooking the street.

"I think this could be the one," she said.

Chapter Three

Once upon a time there was a hamlet called Heathrow. It was a peaceful place off the main roads and rail lines southwest of London, surrounded by farms that had been there for centuries. The old village apparently sat roughly where Terminal One is now, long since swallowed up by one of the world's busiest airports.

When I landed for my first visit in 1979, toting a ridiculously small and rudimentary knapsack, I was encouraged to discover that you could ride the subway all the way to the centre of the city. Seemed like a great deal. Although groggy after the all-night flight, adrenaline kept me going on the endless journey along the Piccadilly line.

No one but backpackers would do it. My cousin Suzy told of the time she tried the Tube after the long flight from Canada, ending up in tears as the train gradually filled to bursting with rush hour commuters who had no patience for her ordeal with two giant suitcases.

On my debut trip, when I emerged wide-eyed at the top of the stairs at Piccadilly Circus, a Cockney jumped in front of me and started snapping pictures.

"Royt ... 'old that one. Bee-oo-tee-ful, mate!" he said, directing me in a series of poses. Stunned and sleep deprived, I complied until he pulled out a notebook to ostensibly write down my name and contact information. It dawned on me that it was almost certainly a scam to separate a young rube from some of his meagre money and I walked away.

"Owww ... don't ruin it!" I can still hear him complain.

Somehow I managed to find a fleabag bed and breakfast, where the toast was cold, the butter hard, and the bacon leathery. But it did not matter. I walked astonished through the streets until my feet screamed, drank warm beer in the pubs, and then fell asleep as I watched the world's greatest actors on stage.

London had me then and never let go.

Much older, if not wiser, I took the gleaming Heathrow Express out to the airport to meet my wife and daughter — a mere fifteen-minute ride from Paddington. A taxi was arranged to bring us all back to the flat. Sean was all grown up.

When Julia spotted me at arrivals, she dropped her bag at her mother's feet and ran the last few metres for a most satisfying jump into my arms. Isabella struggled over with the extra bag. Ballet left her with chronic back pain, meaning that long flights were exhausting and tough. She embraced me wearily.

"Okay. Let's see London," she said.

There is no fast way to drive from Heathrow to north London. Parts of the journey are on expressways, but most of it is a confusing zigzag through city streets.

Julia fell asleep in the taxi. Isabella made tentative observations.

"There do seem to be a lot of trees. That's good," she said. "Some nice buildings, too. But don't get happy."

Don't get happy. This was a phrase I would hear many times.

It was at least a sunny day and the well-maintained gardens in front of the short-let building were all in bloom.

"Nice," she offered with little enthusiasm.

"Oh ... a ground-floor apartment. Hmmm."

I did not expect her to be wowed by the sparse decor and indeed she was not. Nor did the high window in the living room do much for her, despite the evidence of greenery and flowers outside.

"We really need to sleep."

My girls did not fall in love with London at first sight. But this was only Day One.

After their nap, I took them out to the high street around the Hampstead Tube stop, hoping they would be wooed by its charm. Julia made a beeline for a cute little toy store. Just inside the door was a stuffed giraffe, taller than me.

"Daddy, if I come to London will you buy this for me?"

"Sure, sweetie," I offered as Isabella eyed me. "He'll be waiting for you when you come in the fall."

This was the beginning of an extensive campaign of extortion by my six-year-old, who had astutely observed that she had me over a barrel. Isabella was regularly reminding me that it was no sure thing that they would be coming to join me. They were here effectively under protest, on a skeptical fact-finding mission.

Two things had to be done: find an apartment and settle on a school.

First, though, we needed to have an argument. The reasons were murky, but it developed as I expressed concern about Julia needing to be careful to not put any marks on the wall at the short let, fearing that I was going to be stuck with any repair bills.

"Leave the kid alone!" said Isabella.

And it went downhill from there, revisiting all the stresses that led up to my accepting the London job. All three of us went to sleep with teeth gnashing.

Morning dawned misty and cool with tinges of frost in our voices. They were both still jet-lagged, and we were late getting out the door for our tour of a school.

It was a short walk down Frognal, but they were continually lagging behind … or I was quick-marching ahead, depending on one's perspective.

"Come on. This is for you!" I barked. Mistake.

Isabella stopped in her tracks and hissed, "No, this is for YOU!"

Point made, I took a deep breath and beseeched them to please try to walk faster.

Our appointment was at an international school in Hampstead, which I thought might be a good choice. All the kids would be expatriates, so I reasoned that my child would not be singled out so much as she might in a classroom where everyone spoke with a British accent. Checking their website, the tuition seemed substantially less than many of the alternatives, about £6,000.

As we walked up to the door for the tour that I had arranged, Julia was noticeably quieter than normal. It was a handsome brick building in the midst of a leafy street with similar looking homes. All good. But a European culture shock awaited: the classrooms, although neat, airy, and pleasant, were all tiny; the "playground" more of a cramped courtyard with an artificial surface. Space in London is at far more of a premium than in Toronto. Julia's school back home had a playground that was a vast, grassy expanse. She loved playing on the monkey bars. No monkey bars here.

As the affable young registrar explained the teaching philosophy, another glitch arose: in Britain children are placed in grades depending on where their birthdays fall in the school year ... unlike Canada, where it's based on the calendar year. Given that Julia was born in December, it meant she would basically have to repeat Grade 1. Not good. Isabella asked if there might be some flexibility, which revealed another lesson about the Brits: flexibility on the rules is a colonial concept. But the registrar offered as least some hope that the teacher could tailor the program so that our daughter could learn some Grade 2 material.

We were told that there were still some places available, but that they might go soon. To submit an application, we would need a letter of reference from a teacher, plus a report card — along with a non-refundable £200 fee for the privilege of asking them to consider our daughter.

Whew. So: Julia would not only have to move to London against her will, she would effectively have to repeat a grade in school. Things were going swimmingly.

While Isabella took a nap, Julia and I played in the backyard of the short let, kicking a ball around for a bit.

"Daddy, are there any monkey bars around?" she asked, bored. I took her up to the Heath, which was vast and verdant with wonderful walking paths. Much later I was to learn of a playground on the other side, at the base of Parliament Hill, but on this day, when I desperately needed to impress her, all I could find was greenery.

We walked back to the flat, with me feeling defeated. All the more so when we walked in and realized Julia did not have her little pink raincoat.

I went to the backyard to see if we had left it there. As I was poking around, a hatchet-faced older fellow emerged from the building and eyed me suspiciously.

"Can I ask what you're doing?"

I approached him with a big smile and introduced myself as the new tenant in the ground-floor flat, here on a short-let basis for a few weeks.

"Ah. Canadian then, is it?"

"Yup."

"I used to know a Canadian. Lived near Toronto, in a place with an Indian-sounding name. Can't recall it now."

"Mississauga?"

"Yes, that's it. But never mind, he's dead now anyway."

"May I ask your name?"

Given that he had designated himself as a higher life form, he deigned to reveal only his family name. In the interests of avoiding future litigation, I will not write it here, but let us just say that it sounded like a sneeze. Let's call him Sneezy. And, for reasons that will become clear, I will dub him BritFuck. And so, my first neighbour in London shall be forever recalled as Sneezy BritFuck, a name he earned with a series of actions that began only a few hours later.

It happened just after supper. To escape the boring flat, Isabella devised a game to play with Julia in the hallway. There was a spiral staircase, the top of which offered a fine opportunity for a little girl to drop a stuffed bear to see if it would make it all the way down to the mother at the bottom. There was much giggling, a hopeful sign. But I feared it would end badly.

Sure enough, Mr. Sneezy BritFuck emerged from his top-floor flat to confront my playful six-year-old.

"And what are you doing?" he demanded. Julia froze.

"Oh, it's okay. I'm her mother," Isabella chimed in sweetly from the ground floor. "We're just playing."

"Well. That's not permitted," intoned Mr. BritFuck.

Julia hightailed it back down the stairs.

"Glad he's not going to be our neighbour for long," I said.

Three flats were lined up for them to see. But it came down ultimately to two. A genial young Brit named Edward drove us to the Buckland Crescent place that Isabella had spotted online. I had already checked it out and found it passable, with the least objectionable price of all the choices: £550 per week.

As we walked up the dim staircase with the dirt-coloured carpet to the door of the flat, Isabella waggled a finger behind her back, signalling to me she did not think much of the dreary entranceway — a gesture that she would often remind me of in the months to come.

The balcony that looked so inviting online was actually a tiny thing with dead plants in the pots and a rickety metal table with some rust around the edges. The entrance was off the cramped, decrepit kitchen. The second bedroom was similarly miniscule, with a two-piece bathroom next door. Actually more like a 1.5-piece, because the ridiculously small sink could not properly wash any hands larger than a Barbie doll's.

But the reception room was airy, bright, and large, and the main bedroom an acceptable size. It also had some furniture in what I thought was a relatively inoffensive yellowish colour, but which Isabella described as closer to the hue of puke.

Candidate number two was pushed by Jade, the agent for my short let. It was the top floor of a red brick house on Frognal. The entranceway was at least clean, but the stairs upward never seemed to end. After a long winding climb we emerged, panting and exhausted, at a place that Isabella immediately loved. It was all newly renovated — new floors, new paint, new kitchen. But in the maddening way of London housing, it had three big bedrooms, but no closets, no proper place to put a dining-room table and a fridge large enough for perhaps one six-pack.

It was also £100 more *per week* than Buckland. I pictured Isabella fainting as she climbed the stairs, me having to put my beer out on the balcony to cool, a sacrifice that would still leave no room in the fridge, and all of us eating on laptop trays because there was no room for a table.

Jade pointed out that there was at least a mutual garden. The Brits call their backyards gardens, even if there is not a single flower. What it meant was that anyone in the building had access to the backyard — a compelling selling point for a family with a six-year-old.

Back at the short let, we were up late struggling with the pros and cons of our two choices. Isabella worked out a point system to help us decide, assigning scores for issues like cost, living space, and location. The two came up even. Finally, at midnight, drained and punchy, we decided to make a lowball offer for Buckland: £495 per week. Still a multiple of our Toronto mortgage. One thing I had learned about renting in London: the price is always negotiable. I wrote an email to the agent and turned out the light.

At 8:00 a.m. I was dragged out of a deep sleep by a ringing phone. It was the agent for Buckland.

"I can't make that offer. He would be most insulted and would likely seek another agent. For him even to consider it, there must be a '5' in the offer."

Very well then. Frognal it was. Jade had suggested the landlord would accept £600 per week, so we called her and made the pitch. Within an hour we had acceptance, so off we went to the agent's office. There was another book-sized tenancy agreement to sign, with another emergency call to Canada to up the credit limit on my card once again so that I could pay the deposit of six weeks rent plus a month in advance.

As I ploughed through the paperwork, Jade got a call from the owner of the short let.

"There's a bit of a problem," said Jade. "It seems there's been a complaint from another tenant. Your owner wasn't actually allowed to rent out his flat on a short-let basis. It's against the rules of the building."

It seemed that Sneezy BritFuck was also on the board of the building and had turned us in. I could feel my temperature rising and imagined the scene from *A Fish Called Wanda* where the slow-witted but dangerous American dangled a supercilious Englishman by his heels outside a third-floor window.

"So what does this mean?"

"You're being evicted."

"Oh. When?"

"Next week. But I'm sure we can work something out."

"I hope so because next week we're all going to be in Canada. Difficult to move out of a London flat when I'm in Toronto."

With homelessness looming before we had even found a proper home, Jade drove us down to the flat, where we took extensive measurements to assist in upcoming furniture purchases. Isabella planned to ask her designer friend Cameron to recommend the appropriate Ikea purchases to speed the matter along. The company provided some moving-expense money, which was supposed to cover most if not all of the furniture buys. My head whirled as I did the mental calculations about how much we were about to shell out in rent. But Julia had always preferred Frognal due to the availability of a backyard.

As we left, I noticed that the doorway to the backyard was locked.

"How do we access it?" I asked Jade.

"Hmm, not sure. Must be a key that comes with the flat key. I'll text the owner."

Back we went to Jade's office to finalize matters. Her phone buzzed with the owner's response.

"He says you would just need to make friends with the main-floor tenants in order to gain access," she said.

"Why is it we need to make friends with them if it's mutual access?"

"Uhhh." She started to look worried. "I'll phone him." She went out to the back of the office.

A few minutes later she returned, downcast.

"I'm so sorry. It is not actually a mutual garden."

I sat down heavily, dropped my head in my hands and concentrated on deep breathing.

"I think Sean is about to explode," observed Isabella with some concern.

"I wish you would explode and tell me off," said Jade remorsefully.

After a couple of minutes of head-pounding contemplation, I lifted my head.

"The agent's office for Buckland is right across the street," I murmured. "I'm going across and offering them £500 a week. If they take it, we're tearing up this agreement and getting our money back."

I crossed Heath Street in a daze, somehow managing to avoid being run down. The transaction was the fastest in the history of our time in London. The agent happened to be in the office, and when she called the owner he also happened to be at home and gave us an immediate acceptance.

Back across Heath Street where the stricken Jade was waiting with Isabella and Julia.

"Tear up the agreement and give me my money back please."

Jade complied with no complaint, but although the agency was able to extract many thousands of dollars from my credit card within a matter of seconds, it would take up to ten working days to get it back to me, minus the extra fee for paying via plastic.

As we waited to wrap up the sorry affair, the landlord of the short let called my cell and was most apologetic about our imminent eviction.

"I am so sorry about this and I don't wish to have your stay in my flat ruined by Mr. Sneezy BritFuck." He, of course, used BritFuck's real name.

He assured us that we would be able to stay as long as we liked, but I advised him that we had found a new place anyway and I would be moving as soon as I returned from Canada in two weeks. Presuming that my belongings were not out on the front lawn when I returned.

What a day: offer refused, offer accepted, offer falls apart due to miscommunication, eviction threatened from short let, original offer improved and accepted, offer number two dismantled, eviction put off. Yikes.

We walked over to PizzaExpress a few doors down and I ordered the largest bottle of beer they had available.

The remaining days of Isabella and Julia's London visit were mainly filled with sightseeing. Julia sat on my shoulders at the gates to Buckingham Palace and shot the changing of the guard on my iPhone. I took her to the Diana, Princess of Wales' Memorial Playground.

Uncertainty still hung over the future. We had not settled on a school, but the default choice seemed to be the international school, and although we now had arranged for a flat, Isabella regularly reminded me, "I'm still not saying that we're actually going to move here. Don't get happy."

We also visited my cousin Suzie.

She, her partner, James, and their dachshund, Archie, shared a former council flat a short walk south of Hampstead Heath. Strolling with them through the Heath gave us a glimpse of the British passion for pets and the subculture of dog owners. Having an animal on a leash meant that complete strangers would abandon their typical reserve, stop, talk, and smile at each other's pets. Surrounding the Heath are dog-friendly pubs, where you can bring your pooch inside to sit beside you while you have a pint and some lunch.

Archie strutted along the pathway as though he owned the joint, occasionally yapping at much larger dogs in what appeared to be a canine version of short guy syndrome. He also loved Julia, giving her a serious licking all up and down her legs, leaving her paralyzed with giggles.

Suzie nodded knowingly as we related our tale of woe about the flat hunt. She had endured a string of negligent landlords who cared little about the upkeep or safety of their properties. Fed up, she and James finally bit the bullet and bought their place, which, although modest, at least had a view of a church steeple out the back windows and was close to the Heath.

We gave her a rough idea of our economic realities — the pay versus the likely expenses.

"Oh well. The wonderful thing about London is that most of the permanent collections in the museums have free admission," she advised cheerfully.

It was a benefit that left Isabella and Julia cold, not being lovers of either museums or sightseeing.

Their first visit to London was stressful, frustrating, and guarded, with a few moments of laughter. In the end, it was generally inconclusive. Weary and drained, we got on a flight back to Canada, where I would spend a week wrapping up some unfinished logistics.

Toronto's skies were leaden, not unlike London's, as we rode a taxi home from the airport. Staring out the window at the industrial landscapes that surround the city, I decided to have another look at the brochure for the international school. We needed to finalize Julia's application shortly or all the available spots would be taken. I leafed through to check the deadlines and was struck by a sickening realization.

"Isabella, the tuition that I thought was for the entire year was actually for each *semester*."

"What does that mean?" she asked sleepily.

"There are three semesters. The tuition is actually three times what we thought it was. We're looking at close to $30,000! There's no way we can pay that."

"How could this have happened?"

"I goofed. Again."

Foolishly, we had not checked out any alternatives during Isabella and Julia's scouting trip. They would not be coming back until the fall, if they came. It would be all up to me to find a school for my daughter, without her ever seeing it in advance.

Jet-lagged and glassy-eyed, I leaned my head back against the seat and wondered what else could possibly go wrong.

Chapter Four

The week in Toronto flew by. With my new giant suitcase jammed with another load of clothes, I waited for the taxi to the airport. This time Julia had no tears, just a hug and a "Bye, Daddy." I was to be back in another month for my previously scheduled vacation.

"You're leaving us now," said Isabella flatly at the door. "I'm going to be here alone with Julia, living through a kitchen renovation and holding down a full-time job while you're a single guy in London being a foreign correspondent. Not exactly fair."

It was all true and I had no effective response.

"It's a huge sacrifice and I'm going to owe you," was the best I could muster.

"Oooh, yeah. For. The. Rest. Of. Your. Life."

It was my third time flying across the Atlantic in a month, so I had pretty much seen all the movies that interested me on Air Canada. The all-night flight was the usual ordeal of half-sleep and cramped neck. I had learned that it was useless to try to sleep upon arrival, so I showered and shaved at the short let and headed into the office, planning to just force myself to stay awake and get on London time as soon as possible.

There were four more days at the short let before moving down to Buckland. The night before the move I had a brainwave: to save a bit of money, I would just walk over, rolling two big suitcases, thus ensuring that I could fit all the remainder into one taxi.

It was at least downhill, but the wheels started to make alarming squealing sounds as they rattled over every bump in the sidewalk, raising the possibility that the cases might explode in the middle of the street, scattering my undies all over Fitzjohn's.

Somehow, they held together. Drenched in sweat and breathless, I hauled them up the dingy stairs to my new home. It was not a magical moment.

On departure from the short let the next morning, I somehow managed to avoid another encounter with Sneezy BritFuck. Had I been more creatively vengeful, I might have considered curling a steamer outside his door (a wonderful Canadian phrase for taking a shit). The image of Sneezy stalking out of his lair and stepping in a fragrant souvenir from the land of the Maple Leaf brings a smile to my face. But alas, I chose the high road. There were no wistful feelings as I closed the door behind me and loaded my meagre belongings into a taxi for the short trip down to Buckland.

Distributing everything around the flat took a matter of minutes. It was an empty place, but Isabella had asked that I leave most of the decorating to her so that she would have something to do upon arrival. Presuming she came of course.

Hearing footsteps upstairs, I thought it would be a good idea to introduce myself to the neighbours. Anetta answered the door, looking slightly fearful at first until I explained that I was the new tenant downstairs. And a Canadian. Everyone seems to relax a bit when they hear you are Canadian.

She was a slender woman in her thirties who appeared as if she could have been a model. She was the Bulgarian wife of an American banker who spent most of his time in Southeast Asia. Her daughter, Elena, crowded the door beside her, curious and ebullient. She was almost exactly Julia's age, a good sign — a neighbour who might be a playmate.

"How do you like living here?" I asked Anetta.

She shook her head with a rueful smile.

"They don't take care of this place very well."

Her son, who seemed about eleven, ran up to join the conversation.

"Did they tell you that the ceiling collapsed in your bathroom?" he asked gleefully.

"Uh ... no."

"Oh, yes," said Anetta. "It made a horrible crashing sound."

"How long ago was this?"

"Oh ... just a few months."

"We thought the whole house was coming down," chimed in the son with a huge smile. He clearly thought I was a rube for renting such a questionable dump.

"Well, I'm sure it's all fixed now," I said weakly.

Anetta and I agreed that our daughters would be sure to have a play date as soon as Julia arrived.

In an exchange of emails with my new landlord, he advised me to try to make friends with the woman who lived in the main-floor flat in the hopes that some kind of mutual cleaning agreement could be reached for the common areas in the hallway. According to him at least, she had always been opposed.

I could see a light on through the window above her door. But there was no answer to my repeated knocks. Her mail was piled up on a decrepit plastic chair in the hallway. As I turned away to head back upstairs, the door opened and a heavy-set woman in her seventies looked warily out.

"Hi. I'm your new neighbour. Just wanted to introduce myself," I said, beaming with the friendliest, most Canadian face I could offer.

"Oh ... how nice," she responded, offering a crooked-tooth smile, with a hint of yellow around the edges of her incisors. Her grey hair was unkempt, her sweatshirt stained and slightly fraying at the edges.

It turned out that she had inherited the flat from her late mother, that she was a musician, and that she was contemplating a legal war with the owner of the garden flat.

"You see, it is supposed to be a mutual garden in the back. But in order to reach it, we must walk across the front yard to reach the gate. The yard is officially his. And he refuses to allow us access."

The front yard was roughly ten square feet of toxic soil held together with weeds.

"I'm thinking of consulting with my solicitor about taking some kind of action. But it's a lot of money, you know. What do you think?"

I pleaded ignorance of British law, but commiserated that she certainly seemed to have a case. The garden flat was vacant, but undergoing renovations, and I had heard from the estate agent that the owner was hoping to sell it for the equivalent of close to a million dollars. A basement apartment in London was worth more than my home in Toronto. Clearly it was even more valuable if no one else could use the garden.

London real estate is replete with these kinds of ancient battles over tiny patches of valuable land, the combatants using archaic and loopy regulations as weaponry.

Gently I broached the touchy topic of the cleanliness of the common areas.

"Oh, it is horrid, isn't it?" she said, shaking her head as she looked down at the dust-caked carpet. "The property managers really don't keep it very tidy."

"My landlord suggested that I speak to you about the possibility of agreeing to some kind of regular cleaning, with the costs shared among the owners."

"Oh, well, I would certainly like to see it tidied more. It's all a matter of cost, you see. I don't have much money."

There was an awkward silence.

"Did you say you were a journalist?"

I nodded.

"Have you done any stories on the British National Party?"

"Uh … no."

The BNP is a far-right party that advocates for what it calls the "voluntary resettlement" of immigrants back in their homelands. Many prefer to call it by other names, such as "fascist."

"Well, you really should look into them," she said with concern. I expected her to say that the BNP represented a disturbing undercurrent of intolerance in British society.

She continued: "Many people say bad things about them, but you know much of what they have to say is really quite sensible."

I pressed my lips together, nodded thoughtfully, and took a step back.

"Well, I must be going now. I hope you'll give some thought to the cleaning issue."

"Oh yes. But really, I do insist: investigate the BNP," she said. "It's very, very interesting."

Far more urgent for me was to find a school for Julia. It was now June. Most good schools had locked up all their places months before.

Even though we could not really afford it, I decided I had better get an application into the international school. During the visit in Canada, we had obtained the necessary glowing letter from Julia's kindergarten teacher and a transcript of her Grade 1 report card. But when I contacted the school, the brisk registrar informed me that there were no longer any places. I was of course free to put in my application, along with the non-refundable £200 deposit, to have Julia placed on the waiting list. No guarantees.

I sought advice from one of my few contacts in London. Harshini is a Sri Lankan woman who was close to one of my cousins. She had married John, a Canadian lawyer, and they settled in London to be roughly halfway between their two homelands. We met over Sunday brunch, with their sweet three-year-old, Mimi.

They had, it seemed, been researching Mimi's school since roughly three minutes after conception, and Harshini had consequently become an expert on London schools.

There is of course a state school system in place so that, officially, all children have access to a free education. In practice, though, the best schools are difficult to access. You have to live in the proper catchment area and you have to apply.

As Harshini explained, it leaves parents in our situation with a choice: "pay or pray."

That is: get your kid into one of the better church schools (some of which also charge) or spend the money to send them to an "independent" school.

She promised to forward me a list of good choices in North London and advised me to go online and get a copy of the *Good Schools Guide*. Finding an education for your child in England is a challenge matched only by the search for reasonable accommodation.

My mornings before work were now consumed with online searches and calls to prospective schools. Most of them had long since filled all their places. Julia was baptized as a Catholic, so the pray option was available, just not quite so available as if she were Anglican.

There was what appeared to be a good Catholic school just up the street. The affable registrar gave me a tour, showing off classrooms that seemed to be full of smiling children in uniform, walls covered with their artwork, and what appeared to be overall an atmosphere of kindness and support. Even better: it was free. The only catch was that there were already three kids on the waiting list for her class. I put in an application anyway.

Another Catholic school in Belsize Park was housed in a gorgeous old mansion, built by a nineteenth-century magnate. The main lobby was framed in lush dark wood, with a grand staircase and a quaint chapel off to the side. The grounds were impeccably groomed. It had places available, but there was tuition. Application submitted.

Not counting on that, I continued my search online, where I found an alluring link to "the school with a heart in the heart of Hampstead." The Royal had a picture of the Heath rather than the school building, which gave me pause. But all the other descriptions and reviews sounded appealing.

For one thing, it had a history. It was founded in 1855 as a noble cause. In those days, there were several charities to assist the orphaned sons of soldiers who had been killed abroad, but precious little for the daughters. The school began its life with the mandate, "to nurse, board, clothe, and educate the female children, orphans or not, of soldiers in Her Majesty's Army killed in the Crimean War." It was born with the blessing of Queen Victoria and even now had a royal link: Prince Charles's wife, Camilla, was the patron.

London is a city of villages. As it grew over the centuries, it swallowed up smaller communities. It means that there is no downtown in the traditional sense. Instead, each neighbourhood has its own high street and commercial area, remnants of the independent village that each used to be. It is one of London's most attractive qualities.

It is also why, in part, the same street will change names inexplicably. Camden High Street ran beside our bureau, then turned into Chalk Farm Road, Haverstock Hill, Rosslyn Hill, and then Hampstead High Street. It was up that particular road that I walked to have my first look at the Royal. It was uphill, past the imposing old St. Stephen's Church, along a narrowing road lined by trees and increasingly trendy shops and cafés.

On the left, along the Rosslyn Hill stretch, was the entrance to a dead-end street called Vane Close. Now I could see why the Royal used a picture of the Heath on the website. The school building was a drab block of a thing — industrial, grey, and cold. Not very promising.

Inside, though, I was met by the sunny-faced head of the junior school. As she led me through the place, its charms quickly grew on me. The walls were covered with students' paintings and the girls in their cute, red-striped summer dresses all had smiles on their faces. She told me that they valued music and the arts and that they prided themselves on adapting to the needs of each girl. Out back there was a playground that actually included a bit of green space. I took pictures of everything.

In a vestige of its long history, it was still a boarding school for about 10 percent of the girls, who stayed in the top floor residence. It meant that there was always staff around, and if a parent happened to be delayed picking up a child after school, there would be someone who could care for her.

Most importantly, they had space in their upcoming Year Two class. The Royal seemed like the best candidate, but I feared what Julia and Isabella would say when they saw the grim exterior. On my way out to the high street I stopped to take a shot of it. A teacher walking out spotted me and I explained that I was thinking of enrolling my daughter in the fall and needed to send a picture to her and my wife.

"Oh, then please don't show them the picture of the building," she said with a laugh. "Then they'll never come. It's what inside that counts."

She was right.

As anticipated, my ladies were dubious about the look of the place from the outside, but the Royal seemed to offer more than the Catholic school with the lovely building, and we could not count on Julia ever getting off the wait list for the free school.

She had to go somewhere, so it was back up to the Royal to lay down a £1,000 cheque for the deposit, fill out the paperwork, and hope that I had not sentenced my daughter to a year of academic purgatory in England.

By this time I had managed get myself a British bank account so that I could actually write a cheque. It is not a simple matter. The regulations seemed to have been drafted by Monty Python, inspired by *Catch-22*, with a consult from the estate of Franz Kafka. To get an account, you need to present some kind of proof that you have paid bills in the U.K., something like a utility statement. Except you cannot pay a bill properly until you have an account.

Fortunately, I had some good advice from my predecessor in the bureau: open an HSBC account in Canada, show them your work visa, and then they can remotely open a British account for you. It still required several visits to the bank and a wait while they mailed my card from somewhere else in the country. And of course I immediately forgot my PIN.

The friendly people at the Royal invited me for a parental get-together, a preview of the year to come. Seemed like a good way to start to meet people, one of my great weaknesses. It was in the school's tiny gymnasium one morning, which was packed with well-dressed parents, uniformly younger and probably much more affluent than me, all chatting in little groupings as they sipped coffee. I strolled around, trying to look curious and engaged when in fact I was uncomfortable and tongue-tied. The head of the junior school rescued me by grabbing my arm and introducing me to the parents of one of the girls who would be in Julia's year.

Graham and Alanna glowed about the Royal. Their daughter had transferred a few months earlier from another school where she was struggling and now was doing much better.

"I'd have to say she was utterly transformed," said Graham.

I was starting to feel more confident about our choice.

Then, at my elbow was a comforting sound, a voice from home.

"I see from your Mountain Equipment Co-op backpack that you must be Canadian," she said.

Tara, as it turned out, was also from Toronto. Her husband was a banker who had been transferred to London just the previous summer. They had had only a matter of weeks to find a school for their two daughters, the younger of whom, Allison, would be in Julia's class in the fall.

Tara also spoke highly of the Royal and offered to arrange a play date when they were back in Toronto in August so that Julia could meet one of her classmates. She also set up a date for me to meet her husband, Malcolm, for a beer so that we could compare notes on expatriate fatherhood. Things were sounding better all the time.

A few nights later I walked over to their place, a mews house in the centre of Belsize Park. A mews (the same word is used for both singular and plural) is considered fashionable in London, even though they are converted stables. Tara and Malcolm's place was a small row house, but was gigantic in comparison to our flat on Buckland, and certainly much more expensive. As I was beginning to learn, expatriate employees in the financial industry get much more support in living expenses than us poor slobs in the media.

Malcolm was a lean, soft-spoken guy who was likely at least fifteen years younger than me. He was in the habit of jogging every morning down to his office in The City, an impressive six kilometres one way.

At the nearby Washington pub, he told me how Tara had had to get a leave from her teaching job in order to come. He was genuinely regretful at her sacrifice, calling her a terrific teacher. Another "trailing spouse." He shared the story of how his daughters struggled in their first days at the Royal.

Allison, the girl who would be in Julia's year, had not dealt well with having to choose her own food in the cafeteria. It seemed, in fact, that she was terrified, not eating at all and would come home in tears.

"Finally, she figured out what a jacket potato was, and that she liked it," said Malcolm.

For the Canadian girl, new to London, the potatoes were a godsend. Allison survived for weeks at a time on jacket potato lunches. But at least she was eating. Now, with the school year in its final weeks, both she and her sister were prospering. It was, I hoped, a reflection of how Julia would do.

Malcolm helpfully advised me of the brand of scooter that all the kids were riding to school, with a strong recommendation that I order one online. Scooters were not nearly so prevalent in Toronto, where they do not do very well in the snow. But they were the preferred form of child transportation in London, given that snow is a rare event and cycling is a hair-raising pursuit, a result of the narrow streets and aggressive drivers. Scooters did have their downside, though. Already I had experienced being smacked on the shin by one carried by a harried parent who was trying to herd her brood onto a jammed bus.

Chapter Five

School and flat sorted, my bachelor life workdays were starting to develop a routine. Typically, they started in a leisurely fashion because everyone back home was asleep until the early afternoon my time and the newscast was not on the air until 10:30 p.m. in London. No need to rush into the office.

I bought a membership at a gleaming new gym nearby, beside the Swiss Cottage Tube stop. I would stumble out of bed around 8:00 a.m., go for a workout, shower, shave, and eat — usually munching my cereal on the coffee table while I watched the BBC morning program. Then I'd catch the number 31 bus down to the market and the bureau. After a time, I realized that the bus ride was only about five minutes and the walk was about thirty. Here was a true luxury: being able to walk to work. It became my practice, often cutting through tony Primrose Hill and walking along the Regent's Canal before entering the market and stopping at a hole-in-the-wall coffee joint called Terra Nera to pick up my perfectly crafted morning cappuccino from the two genial Italian brothers who owned it.

Although we were filing almost every day, upward of 80 percent of the stories were invariably "melts" — sitting at my desk and writing scripts based on video from AP or Sky News or one of our other agencies. This is the fate of small bureaus in big media markets. The stories are almost always compelling, but you are not often an actual witness to the events you are covering, except via the TV. We would try whenever possible to add our own element by going out to shoot an interview with an analyst. There was always the bonus of a stand-up with the sign-off of "Global News, London," which carried a certain cachet — in fact, more than anything, the network was paying all the money for the bureau in order to have that sign-off and "presence."

At lunchtime there was a cornucopia of choices just outside the doors of the Interchange. I hurried past the ladies who were doing the hard sell on the Chinese food that looked suspiciously like it had been shrink-wrapped in plastic. My destination was the West Yard, in the heart of the market.

Dear reader, if visiting London you must go. The West Yard is a teeming mass of food stalls, directly beside Camden Lock on the Regent's Canal. It offered a dizzying variety of street food from around the world: Turkish sausage wraps, Lebanese falafels, Pakistani wraps, Indian curries, Argentinian steak sandwiches, Vietnamese stir-fries, British meat pies, Jamaican jerk chicken, Chinese dim sum, Polish kielbasa, Australian kangaroo burgers (these I never sampled), Peruvian, Ethiopian. If I walked another few metres over to the high street, there were Iranian, Greek, Moroccan, Mexican, Egyptian, and various vegan choices.

Here was lunch variety as I had never experienced before. At various times I sampled each and every one of the choices above and can only remember once having my intestines object. On warm days in peak tourist season the place is jammed with humanity feeding their faces. In contrast, during the bleak, grey days of winter there would sometimes be only one vendor braving the cold — typically the Jamaicans were the hardiest, despite their warm-weather heritage.

It was the world's greatest, coolest location for a workspace.

By early or midafternoon, we had usually settled on a story. Sometimes it was obvious, sometimes it was something we suggested, sometimes our colleagues in Vancouver would express a preference. I would pore through all the various agency offerings of video and interviews, choose the best, and prepare a script for a two-minute story that I would transmit to the mother ship for a vet around suppertime.

Once the script was approved, I would record my voice track and Dan would edit the story on his laptop. By 7:30 or 8:00 p.m. he would FTP the package to Vancouver and our day was done. While he would head home to his wife, I would generally linger for a while, in no great rush to get back to an empty apartment. I would deal with the myriad of logistical issues that still remained to set up our life in London, or scan European newspapers in search of a story to do. Every month I would get a notice from the accountants advising me of how much income taxes I owed Her Majesty and I would go online to remove a large chunk of poundage from my newly created bank account and hand it over.

At the end of my workdays, I would usually walk back to the flat. This was the time of year when the London daylight lasted deep into the evening and so it was a lovely and placid stroll through the leafy streets of Belsize Park, wondering about the lives of the people inside those stately homes.

We did not know when we moved into the neighbourhood that Belsize Park is London shorthand for posh. Celebrities such as Helena Bonham Carter were supposedly among its denizens, although we never saw her. It is replete with nineteenth-century mansions that were long since divided up into flats. Behind the stately exteriors are apartments that are lusciously decorated and impossibly expensive. Others are atrociously decrepit, but still impossibly expensive. That is London.

Inside the front door of my building, mail for past tenants piled up atop a rickety old table. The ground-floor neighbour never seemed to pick up hers either. For a time, I kept the letters for the guy who previously occupied my flat, some of which appeared to be demands for payment from various utilities. He had apparently moved to Spain, and had no interest in having his mail forwarded, so I started dumping them in recycling, keeping the *National Geographic*s.

The dim entranceway was charmingly decorated with a bare light bulb, peeling paint, and dirt-brown carpet. Thanks to the absence of any kind of regular cleaning, dust bunnies the size of basketballs and a pile of disused luggage lined the hallway.

The flat was quiet, sparse, and cheerless. Its most attractive feature, the spacious, even slightly grand reception room, which had a big south-facing window, was outweighed by its many failings. The room that would be Julia's was tiny, with visible, drafty gaps in the crappy window. The Brits famously shun the benefits of central heating. They also seem to consider the idea of windows that actually seal against the cold to be quaintly colonial — far better, dear fellow, to expel the expensively heated air into the brisk London night.

The main bathroom was both large and bleak, much like the communal cans you would expect to see in prison — the toilet permanently stained, the shower either freezing or scalding. The tiny kitchen had a door missing from one cupboard and it appeared that some kind of toxic waste had rotted away the finish on the cabinetry below the stove.

All this for a rent that was roughly double the monthly mortgage payments for my four-bedroom, fully renovated, newly landscaped Toronto home.

Not motivated to cook, I kept a supply of microwave dinners and cans of British beer in the fridge. My lonely supper was eaten sitting on the couch: a greasy tray of chicken tikka masala on the coffee table, washed down with a can or two of John Smith's Bitter.

Just before bed, I would call home, catching Julia and Isabella right around their suppertime.

"Hi, Daddy, bye, Daddy," was my daughter's usual greeting before running away from the phone. She was not really that interested in long-distance conversations, preferring to watch inane comedies with loud laugh tracks on TV.

Isabella would often sound tired and exasperated. I could scarcely blame her. We had agreed to share child rearing, with me overseeing more mundane tasks and her taking the lead in finding creative activities to give our only child a richer life. But now it was all on her. She would call Julia to the phone and gently insist she talk to her distant dad. Adding to her single mom experience was the renovation, now fully underway — our old kitchen had been ripped out in preparation for the installation of the new one, and she had had to jury-rig an alternative in the living room: a bar fridge, microwave, and hot plate.

My rather mundane existence was suddenly enlivened when a major news story broke. The nation was gripped by the phone hacking scandal. It emerged that the top-selling tabloid, *News of the World,* had weaseled its way into the cellphone records of a missing fourteen-year-old girl, Milly Dowler, who was later found dead. The story went that some of her voice mails were deleted, which gave her distraught parents a brief hope that she might still be alive.

British tabloids are infamous for their hardball tactics, and most of the time they get away with it because the targets are wealthy celebrities who might occasionally sue successfully but who generally enjoy marginal sympathy from the public. This was something different: it appeared that a grieving middle-class family was being victimized at the worst possible time. Revulsion was deep, broad, and devastating.

In an extraordinary move, Rupert Murdoch, the last of the great press barons, shut down *NOTW* in a vain attempt to defuse the anger. News cameras, even from his own Sky News, chased him on the street as he entered a hotel for a meeting with the Dowler family. Afterward, he was forced to step out into a raucous scrum to offer a public apology to follow the one he had delivered in private to the family.

The scandal exposed the cozy relationships among reporters, police, and politicians, and ended with daily arrests, revelations, and resignations. The head of Scotland Yard was forced to quit after it emerged that he had hired a former *NOTW* editor for media advice, a man who now had been taken into custody. It seems the cops had been feeding information to the tabloids for years, and that Murdoch, the king of the tabs (as well as the quality *Times* and *Sunday Times*), had been courted by fearful prime ministers of all political stripes and was a regular, unannounced visitor at 10 Downing Street.

It was all the standard way of doing business among British elites for years, but now the sharks were in the water smelling blood after the Dowler affair.

Murdoch himself was hauled before a Commons committee for a public thrashing at the hands of some of the MPs who had been regular targets of his hacks.

Murdoch was seated next to his smooth and well-briefed son James, who was to do most of the talking, but the old man clearly sensed the public mood and interrupted James early on to offer a penitent, but awkward, "This is the most humble day of my life." He had already shut down his bestselling newspaper, paid out millions in compensation, and suffered public denunciation on a broad scale. Murdoch was to remain rich and powerful, but he needed to do his penance — including suffering a glancing blow from a cream pie, delivered by a comedian later that morning. His young, third, and later divorced wife, Wendi Deng, achieved a moment of notoriety by whacking the erstwhile assailant.

In the early days of the scandal, BBC workers went on a one-day strike to protest against ongoing cutbacks. It turned out to be a happy event because it freed Caroline, my friend from Toronto, from her duties at BBC's *Panorama* so that she could host a barbecue at her home.

Over a delightful supper of chicken, shrimp, and Tuscan salad, her British media friends unanimously agreed that we had only seen the tip of the iceberg — many more journos were most likely hacking or otherwise flouting the law in search of a scoop, but had been lucky to not get caught, yet. There was no small delight among them in watching Murdoch's misery, given that his papers were harsh critics of the BBC.

All in all, it was a great show, an education in the ways of the British media and power elites. By comparison, Canada is tame — there are no press barons who put the squeeze on prime ministers, no tabloids who stalk celebrities and publish rancorous fiction about them, and no hardball battles among papers and broadcasters joyously seeking to destroy their opponents.

Back home, weekend mornings were usually spent dragging the little girl out of bed, getting her to swimming lessons, and catching up on house maintenance. Here, I would wake and stare at the ceiling for a bit before dragging myself out of bed. Although it was often painfully lonely, I was after all in London, so I determined to make the most of the chance to explore the city.

The National Theatre had a sold-out show called *London Road*, the most offbeat concept for a musical ever. It was the story of the citizens of Ipswich, who were coping with the rampages of a serial killer, and was told through their actual words as recorded in police reports. Not exactly *The Sound of Music*. But the reviews were ecstatic, so I showed up early at the theatre in search of returns. This is a tactic that almost always works if you arrive early enough, and given that there was only one woman ahead of me in line for the matinee, my hopes were high — but misplaced. She got the only single return and I was shut out.

Never mind, the Imperial War Museum was not far away so Plan B was to walk over and check it out. En route was the Old Vic Theatre, currently featuring Kevin Spacey as Richard III. The entire run had been sold out for weeks, but given I was walking past there was no harm in stopping to ask.

The matinee had already started and there was no one in line at the box office.

"Well, aren't you in luck," said the ticket guy. "A producer has just returned a ticket in the sixth row for tonight. Eighty-five pounds. Would you like it?"

A steep price, but this fell into the category of *things you should do while in London, no matter the cost.* Out came the credit card.

Spacey had been at the Old Vic since 2003, an American movie star coming to London to rejuvenate a venerable institution. Once the home of the National Theatre, the place had fallen on hard times in the earlier part of the century. A *Telegraph* article suggested that there had been talk for a while of turning it into a theme pub or a bingo hall.

Spacey told the paper that some snippy locals (relatives of Sneezy BritFuck, no doubt) had advised him in the early days that he should pack his bags and get the hell out of town. He gradually won them over with an honest respect for the theatre and a devotion to excellence. By the time I watched him limp out onto stage as Shakespeare's most delicious villain, he had the city at his feet. (This was years before men starting coming forward with allegations of sexual harassment.)

His Richard was both compelling and uncomfortable to watch. He twisted his body into what had to be a painful contortion that he maintained throughout. At the end, after having been killed by Henry Tudor, he was strung up by his heels, like Mussolini, and left hanging upside down for several minutes until the curtain call.

It was one of those performances that made all of us unhesitatingly jump to our feet when Spacey, drenched in sweat, took his bows. All of us were amazed that he could even stand up after three hours of what had to be agony. And it was his second show of the day!

The glow of a great night in the theatre faded into the dullness of an aimless Sunday morning. I thought about taking the train out to Hampton Court, or maybe trying the Tower of London. So many choices, such minimal decisiveness. After dawdling for several frustrating hours, I settled on an easier choice: the Victoria and Albert Museum.

The Tube is routinely packed on a Sunday afternoon, particularly on the Piccadilly line from Green Park down to South Kensington. The tunnel that joins the Tube stop to the series of museums nearby was similarly teeming, especially with parents hauling the kids out for some culture. I would get to know the walk very well with my daughter.

The V&A justifiably boasts that it is the world's largest and greatest museum of the decorative arts and design. It grew out of the Great Exhibition of 1851, as British imperialism was approaching its period of greatest glory.

Even now it holds that feeling of grandness. The entrance hall was dominated by a giant hanging sculpture in glass — a writhing mass of snakelike green and white tendrils created by American sculptor Dale Chihuly. You could not help but stand in awe. (It has since been transferred to a shopping centre in Singapore.)

Every corner of the V&A offered a new vision of beauty — my favourite was the hall of sculptures overlooking an elegant garden with a string quartet playing.

When I got home, I could not wait to share the news with Isabella — looking forward to showing it to her.

"The day started out kind of dull," I enthused. "I wasn't sure what to do and was getting a bit frustrated. But then I went to the Victoria and Albert and —"

"I DO NOT GIVE A FUCK ABOUT THE FUCKING MUSEUM YOU WENT TO AND FUCKING SAW TODAY!" was her response. "YOU FUCKING LEFT ME ALONE TO DO EVERYTHING — COOKING, CLEANING, PACKING, CARING FOR JULIA, EVERYTHING — ALL WHILE I'M HOLDING DOWN A

FULL-TIME JOB. SO KEEP YOUR FUCKING MUSEUM STORIES TO YOURSELF!"

You're sure you don't want to hear about the exquisite sculpture wing? I thought about asking but didn't.

The Buckland flat was starting to show its true colours. The water temperature for the morning shower and shave was becoming variable — scalding one moment, chilling the next. One night I returned from work to find a form letter from the National Grid: the gas had been cut off due to a leak. No word on when it would be restored. My expensive, dumpy flat now had no hot water and no stove. Great.

At least there was the option of using the change room at the gym. The next morning, after finishing my workout, I set up my shaving kit in front of a mirror where a sign advised: No SHAVING POLICY DUE TO HEALTH REASONS. Shaving certainly rates as one of the unhealthiest practices known to man.

Not wishing to incur the wrath of the club, I chose to shave in the privacy of the shower stall, learning how much one relies upon a mirror when scraping one's face. Somehow I managed to get the job done without slicing off a chunk of my nose.

Back at the flat, barriers went up in front of the building and warning signs were posted advising that smoking would be inadvisable. Other than that, I saw no sign of any workers. I called the number on the form letter and got through to the National Grid operative in charge of our file.

"It's a very odd case," he said. "The very same day that the owner of the garden flat complained about gas lines running through his place he reported a gas leak."

This was the flat being renovated by the guy who would not allow anyone else in the building to walk across his patch of weeds to access the supposedly communal backyard.

"Perhaps it's more than odd," I suggested. "Perhaps it's criminal."

Buddy seemed to have calculated that because he did not like the pipes he would just poke a hole in one so that they could be moved in order to beautify his flat and push up the exorbitant price a bit more. So sorry if that leaves the neighbours at risk of being blown sky high.

Given life in my expensive cold-water flat, this would have been the perfect time for a road trip. Since beginning as Europe Bureau Chief a couple of months earlier, I had not travelled outside of London. Now would be the easy time to go, because I would not be leaving Isabella and Julia alone in London, having already left them alone in Toronto.

Before I could make any plans, however, a sickening story unfolded in Norway. Someone set off a huge bomb in the government district of downtown Oslo, killing eight people. A short time later a gunman landed on a holiday island not far away and started murdering young people at a summer camp for the youth wing of the governing political party. Before he was done, sixty-nine more people were dead, mainly teenagers.

It turned out that the same sick individual was responsible for both atrocities, a neo-Nazi lunatic named Anders Behring Breivik. It was quickly apparent that we needed to go to Norway. But it would not be me, because I was already booked for a "hazardous environment" training course for Monday. Dan headed for Heathrow and Stu would meet him in Oslo.

I came into the bureau on the Saturday, partially to write and edit a little feature story on the hacking scandal that had been pushed aside by the Norway massacre, and partly to help coordinate daily news video that would be needed by Dan and Stu. Under the circumstances, not expecting to be on TV, I wore a casual shirt and did not bother to shave.

Given that I had some basic laptop editing skills, I had offered to be a good, cost-conscious soldier and edit my own stories when Dan was occasionally away. Even though I was slow and not confident, I would be starting early so it should have been an easy day.

After my day at the office, I had, most unusually, plans to go out. My cousin Suzie's dad, Tom, was in town, visiting from Ireland, and we were all set to go to a pub that night for dinner.

Just as I was finishing the feature story in late afternoon, however, a bulletin came across on Sky News: Amy Winehouse had just been found dead. Not only was she dead, but she was dead in her Camden home, only a ten-minute walk from where I was sitting. Shit.

Shit, not only because a sublimely talented artist had died tragically before her time, which was very sad indeed, but she died when I was solo in the bureau, without a cameraman-editor. Within seconds the phone rang, and naturally Vancouver needed me to file an obituary. Meanwhile, I was still trying to figure out how to FTP video on the Norway story to Dan and Stu. Beads of sweat started to pop out on my forehead.

Luckily, piles of Winehouse material started moving almost immediately. Various editors at various obit desks at various agencies had evidently deduced that Amy was a prime candidate for an early death and had banked video. Writing and editing the obituary was going to be relatively easy.

Vancouver suggested that perhaps I could send out the story early and then head for the Winehouse home for a live hit into the news program. I pleaded that I was a slow editor and could not be sure I could get it done in time. They persisted.

"Okay, well, I have to tell you that I also haven't shaved and am wearing a casual shirt. Didn't know I'd have to be on camera today," I finally admitted.

"Well … you might have told us that earlier," said the blunt-spoken resources guy.

By early evening, my story was ready to go. Time to FTP back to Canada. I followed the idiot sheet that I had prepared for myself under Dan's instruction. It had all gone fine in my practice runs. Now, of course, it was not working. The sweat on my forehead was now joined by moist rings under the armpits.

The resources guy tried to talk me through the procedures over the phone. Still did not work. He went off the line to make inquires. Dan called from Oslo, asking me to resend the video that I had forwarded earlier because there was a sound problem. Now thoroughly flustered, I could not find the video. Sensing the rising panic in my voice, he said reassuringly, "Okay. No worries." And hung up to deal with his own problems.

It was now ninety minutes to airtime. With the glacial speed of our bureau's broadband, it could take up to one hour to send a story and have it flip into the system in Vancouver. Finally the resources guy found a solution and the story was en route. I watched its slow progress out of my computer, cursing the concept of FTP and taking long, slow breaths in an effort to slow my heartbeat.

At last it arrived in Canada, apparently on time. Nothing more to do now, except call Suzie and ask her to order me some fish and chips before the kitchen closed at the pub and to get into a taxi.

Suzie's parents, Tom and Sheila, had lived for many years in London. Now retired, they had bought a cottage on the west coast of Ireland. Tom was Irish and I knew he was a voracious reader of the *Irish Times*, so I was looking forward to pumping him for story ideas from the old sod.

But as I stumbled, glassy-eyed, into The Vine on Highgate Road, my first priority was to get on the outside of a pint of Guinness. Tom, Suzie, and her partner, James, all listened politely as I breathlessly ranted about my day. As a measure of calm returned, Tom happily expounded on several Irish stories I could do.

Most compelling was the story of the Magdalene Laundries. Generations of so-called "fallen" women were sent, often against their will, into the kind embrace of nuns who then used them effectively as slave labourers, washing clothes for the upper classes in Ireland. Their plight had only recently come to light, but the attention paid them had been generally overshadowed by the series of scandals involving priests sexually abusing children. This was a story worth telling and I resolved to pitch it to the *16x9* current affairs show.

The night out at the pub was a nice break from the loneliness waiting for me back at the flat. Sunday brought one of the few sunny, truly summery days that I had seen in London. I thought about going to a museum, but it seemed wrong on such a rare day. Instead, I took a book and hiked down to Primrose Hill, partly to scout out playgrounds for Julia, partly just to enjoy one of the most spectacular views of the city. It was teeming with pale Londoners, soaking up rays from that rare visitor: the sun.

That glorious Sunday offered only a brief respite, however. Awaiting me on Monday was another rite of passage for the modern foreign correspondent: hazardous environment training.

Chapter Six

Mr. Wikipedia tells us that there are 366 railway stations in and around London. They vary from grotty little outposts to the glorious expression of British pride that is St. Pancras.

Paddington is among the most storied — the home of a famous teddy bear and the gateway to the Heathrow Express. It is also the starting point for journeys to the southwest. My destination on a bright July Monday was Castle Cary in the heart of Somerset, where, in one of the prettiest corners of England, I was to learn tips on how to keep myself and my colleagues alive when covering stories in danger zones.

I doubt that the brave reporters who splashed ashore with the troops on D-Day, or who trudged through the jungles of Vietnam had to take hazardous environment training programs. While many died or suffered grave injuries, it was usually the result of an accident — caught by a stray bullet or bomb when they were doing their jobs in the midst of battle.

Now, journalists are regularly targeted. Big news organizations have security consultants on staff. The BBC has a detailed protocol that must be followed before crews are deployed into danger zones.

Several security firms, often staffed by former British SAS officers, have popped up to train reporters both in first aid and how to handle themselves in hazardous environments. News organizations cannot get insurance for an employee unless they take the training.

Jonathan, the organizer of my course, was a former cop, soldier, and war crimes investigator in the former Yugoslavia and had spent some time as a security consultant in postwar Baghdad. He advised that my course would begin within moments of getting off the train. There would be fake blood along the way, all perfectly washable, but he recommended that it was best to wear old clothing.

Friends who had taken similar courses warned that I should expect to be kidnapped at some point — blindfolded and pushed into the back of a car. It's all part of the routine.

Castle Cary is just a tiny rail stop out in the country. Jonathan was waiting for me on the platform, along with Julie — a freelance English producer who would be taking the course with me. As it turned out, we would be the only two.

True to his word, Jonathan got us started immediately, handing over some fake money and directing us to our "fixer," Mick, who was waiting in the parking lot at the wheel of a battered Land Rover. The scenario was that we were in a troubled nation that sounded very much like Kosovo, with a rebel movement battling an authoritarian government — both sides ruthless.

Jonathan warned us to expect to run into a checkpoint somewhere along the road.

As we drove away, Julie told me that she had been born in Kenya but was brought up in England. Her work was usually with the BBC and Channel 4. Initially, I pegged her as a small-timer, with naive ambitions. How wrong I was. In fact, she had been everywhere — several times to Afghanistan, all through crazy spots in Africa. The reality was that she was the veteran and I the novice. She had already taken several of these courses, but insurance companies require a refresher every few years.

We tried to extract some information from fixer Mick, who had an indeterminate Eastern European accent that we later learned was Romanian. We tried to find out if the border guards would be trigger-happy, would they expect bribes. Mick shrugged and grunted. His role was as an incompetent fixer — one of the hazards of the game.

The "border post" turned out to be a shack beside a rugby field. The guards, speaking broken English, brought us inside and kept us waiting while they scrutinized our passports. I regretted that I had left my day pack in the vehicle.

One of the guards called me up and demanded payment through gesture and muttered gibberish. I pulled out my play money and peeled off a few bills. Later, Julie gave me a useful tip: spread out the cash through different pockets so that it is not obvious how much you are carrying. A lesson too late this time because, sure enough, the guard spotted my wad of cash and motioned to me to add a few more notes.

There was a crack of gunfire, one shot, and then sounds of moaning from outside the door. We ducked down. Julie called to Mick, asking what was happening. No answer.

I crouched below the window, figuring that I was being pretty bright by taking cover out of sight. After a few minutes of uncertainty, Jonathan strolled in and told us that the exercise was over.

In the review afterward Jonathan advised that a bullet from a high-powered rifle would likely pass right through the wall I had been hiding behind and that I really needed to be lying flat on the ground for maximum protection. The first of several occasions that week when I would make a choice that, if it were real life, would have gotten either myself or a colleague killed.

These gruesome scenarios were played out in the heart of a bucolic and storied corner of England. Jonathan, an astute businessman, had clearly reasoned that it would be so much more pleasurable learning how to bind bullet wounds and negotiate with fanatical kidnappers if we were also able to admire the rolling hills of Somerset. In the same vein, he booked us into a beautiful little bed and breakfast called The Yew Tree on the edge of the village of Compton Dundon. Co-owner Sarah, who also worked as a hairdresser in the movie industry, had bought the place three years earlier and had tastefully restored its old farmhouse and the outbuildings to provide accommodations that were both cozy and elegant.

It was in the shadow of an old church and a thousand-year-old yew tree, thus the name. She explained that yews were favoured by pagans as a place of worship, and when the Christians arrived they would often build churches nearby in hopes of attracting new converts. I walked up the hill to have a look, noting the tilted and ancient gravestones in the church cemetery, daydreaming about pagans and Christians comparing spiritual notes in the Middle Ages.

Julie and I agreed to meet a couple of the trainers for supper at the pub in the village, only to discover that the kitchen was closed on Mondays. We arranged to get a lift over to the next village where there was food. Several bottles of wine were consumed through the evening as we exchanged learned and increasingly lubricated opinions on which of the Royals was most and least attractive.

As closing time arrived, we realized that we were several miles away from our bed and breakfast with no car. Here was an unexpected challenge to the resourcefulness of a group who were supposed to be experts in navigating unknown territory. Somerset did not exactly qualify as a conflict zone, but none of us wished to hike for an hour along darkened English country roads.

After some discussion with the pub staff, we offered a young waiter a few quid to give us a lift.

Day Two began with more first aid instruction and then our next field exercise. We piled into the Land Rover and headed off to a nearby wood. The scenario was that we had gotten a tip that a local wanted to talk to us about some mass graves. Along a rutted pathway, we saw smoke ahead. Moving closer, we could see that it was coming from underneath an SUV. A guy spurting fake blood emerged from the brush and pounded on our window, pleading for help and leaving an impressive smear of red on the glass.

We paused for a moment to consider the risks, having been warned that this can often be a ruse for thieves or kidnappers. But then the bleeder told us he was a TV guy, so we decided to help a fellow journalist.

The more experienced Julie immediately donned the latex gloves that we had been issued before we approached him. He collapsed, in the process squeezing an unseen balloon that sent a geyser of blood gushing from his wound, bypassing Julie and splattering all down the front of my pants. I recalled Jonathan's assurance that it would be washable.

While she started to treat his wound, one of the trainers suggested that I check the smoking vehicle to see if there was anyone else in need of aid. Sure enough, I found another victim, this one lying on the ground moaning, bleeding from the arm and with a gruesomely broken leg — the bone sticking out from his shin. Unfortunately, our Day One first aid course dealt only with treating simple breaks, not compound fractures.

I improvised, binding his leg to a splint with a bandage wrapped directly over the spot where the bone broke the skin, thus producing a lusty scream of agony from my patient. At the end of the exercise, as he pulled off the fake bone fracture, he advised that it is easier on the victim if you cut a hole in the bandage above the wound so you do not add to the misery.

Having survived the morning's exercise without getting ourselves or anyone else killed, we lunched on the grass outside the meeting hall, munching on sandwiches, enjoying the view, and listening to the next scenario. It was to be another tip about mass graves. This time a local farmer wanted to meet us to talk about it.

Given the morning's bloodbath, we would have been unlikely to bite if it had been the real world, but, in the spirit of exercise, we decided that it was better to go and see what transpired. Julie reminded me of another helpful tip for this kind of situation: call head office and tell them what you are doing and that we will be in touch at a given time to advise that all is well. That way they know to send out a search party for your bodies if you are late. This was a scenario I rarely faced while covering the Ontario legislature.

Fixer Mick again played the role of incompetent, deliberately taking wrong turns and forcing us to navigate ourselves. After consulting the ordnance map we had been issued, we found our way to a bumpy path through the woods where we bounced along until a local waved us down and motioned us to drive through a gate, which he then closed and locked behind us. Duh.

"Julie, this does not look good," I astutely observed. Even with my minimal experience, it was clear that we were breaking multiple rules for surviving hostile environments and were on our way to an unhappy end.

After driving around the wood for a few minutes, we got a mysterious call from the farmer who said he still wanted to see us but hung up before giving directions.

"I think it is now time for us to depart," I said with the conviction of a hardened war correspondent.

Too late. Three men in balaclavas burst out of the woods and pointed their fake guns at us through the window. Time for that highlight of every hazardous environment training course: the kidnapping.

Bags were pulled over our heads, our wrists bound, and, in an interesting variation, our captors led us by the thumbs — evidently a kidnapper's tactic for asserting control, as if the large firearms were not enough.

We were bundled into the back of an SUV, dumped gently on our sides, and driven around a bumpy road for a while, the thoughtful kidnappers keeping a hand under our heads to keep us from bouncing our noggins.

Eventually they stopped, pulled us out, made us kneel, and wordlessly touched the barrel of the gun to our ribs. Then it was over. The bags were pulled off our heads, the kidnappers reverted to being the smiling trainers again, one of whom handed back my glasses, which he had prudently removed to avoid damage.

It was really only a taste of what to expect, and knowing it was all play-acting, we could easily laugh about it. But best to take it seriously, because it does happen to reporters, and the real-life result is at minimum traumatic and at worst fatal. In the debrief later, Jonathan discussed tactics for dealing with one's captors and none of the scenarios were good.

"If you're kidnapped in Iraq, however, you'd better try to escape," he advised gravely, based on his first-hand knowledge of the land of Saddam. "Because they're going to cut your head off. Although it might help to emphasize to them that you're Canadian, not American or British."

Charming.

Julie had to leave that night to return to a gig, and I would miss her company and experience for the remainder of the course when I would be solo and trying mightily to not kill, maim, or otherwise traumatize my trainers in the play-acting.

There was the industrial accident out back of the meeting hall: a teenager ran at me screaming that he had burned his arm. I got him to hold a hose running cold water on it, then realized I had neglected a more serious case a few metres away. The trainer named Marlon had evidently fallen off a ladder and was on the ground unconscious, blood seeping from his leg. Poor fellow had suffered yet another compound fracture. I left the moaning, complaining teenager behind and treated Marlon's break — correctly this time. My only mistake was not to go to him first. Here was the concept of triage.

Later that day, Marlon posed as the victim of a car accident, slumping over the wheel of his Land Rover. I managed to haul him out onto the ground, verified that he was breathing, and then did exactly the wrong thing: laying him on his back and giving him my backpack as a pillow for his head, effectively shutting off his airway. Fixer Mick pointed out that Marlon had stopped breathing and I belatedly remembered a key part of the training — the recovery position. I turned Marlon over on his side before he expired.

The first aid course covered a colourful range of calamities: sunstroke, frostbite, belly wounds. I learned that if your colleague's guts are spilling out, do not try to stuff them back inside — better to bind them with moist packing to just hold them in place and leave the intestinal repair job to a medical professional.

The mass grave theme kept recurring. In one scenario, I was led along what I was told was a safe path through a minefield into a copse where some insurgents were holding a soldier hostage. With a gun held to his head, he finally revealed the location of the graves. Here was an ethical dilemma: I asked the rebels to hand over the soldier to me. They refused, so with no other bargaining chips than my sparkling personality, we left. On our way out we heard the crack of a rifle, clearly an execution. It encouraged us to hustle back to the vehicle.

Navigating using the ordnance maps, I managed to only get lost once before we at last arrived at the graves. However, that mistake resulted in us being caught in a vicious round of crossfire between insurgents and the army. Fixer Mick suffered a gruesome belly wound, with Plasticine posing as his guts. Crawling around on the ground to minimize myself as a target, I manage to get him bound up more or less in the prescribed manner.

Thus ended the violent portion of my training. That night Sarah, the owner of the B&B, kindly gave me a lift into Glastonbury so I could meet Jonathan for supper. The movie-makeup business was evidently treating her well because she was driving a gleaming new Mercedes-Benz convertible. It was a perfect night to have the top down — warm and clear.

"If you're lucky you might see a Druid on the street," she said, the corners of her mouth rising ever so slightly.

Myth and legend, rock and roll, all collide in this ancient town. There is evidence of human habitation going back to the Neolithic period. For such a small place, it has had some celebrated visitors — at least, so the stories go.

Dominating the landscape is the mystic hill rising at the edge of the village: Glastonbury Tor, with the ancient ruin of St. Michael's Tower at its peak — an evocative landmark, visible for miles around.

It has been speculated as one of the homes of the Holy Grail, while some see it as the outline of the breast of a goddess and others as the entrance to the land of the fairies.

Arthurian scholars have suggested it could be the site of the Isle of Avalon, the place where Excalibur was forged and where the enchantress Morgan le Fay cast spells as the leader of nine naughty sisters.

In centuries past, it was a favoured place of execution. Unlucky wretches would be drawn and quartered while enjoying a fine view of the countryside.

A representation of the Tor was built for the opening ceremonies of the 2012 Olympics in London — a green hill where the flags of the participating countries were displayed, to the delight of the Brits who know the story, even if the image left the rest of the world bewildered.

About ten miles to the east, in the Vale of Avalon, a more contemporary form of British mysticism plays out most years. Since 1970 the Glastonbury Festival has attracted thousands to its peculiar celebration of music, mud, rain, and discomfort. And the Brits love it. The Glastonbury Festival had already happened a month or so earlier, with U2 and Beyoncé headlining.

I was not to hike to the top of the Tor on this night. Instead, Sarah dropped me in the centre of the village, where I strolled past the rows of New Age shops to meet Jonathan at a funky tapas bar for supper. He regaled me with tales of Baghdad in the wake of the war, and how he shook his head at the fumbling attempts of the new leaders to build a proper gallows upon which Saddam was to be executed.

I was among Jonathan's first clients (in hazardous environment training, not gallows construction). I told him it was all very enlightening, but considering how much time I spent sitting at my desk writing stories based on video shot by others, I wondered how much I would actually need it.

"Unless, of course, the Camden Market is invaded by terrorists," I joked.

It was a line I was to remember just a few weeks later.

The final day of the course was short and light. The subject was preparing for an urban demonstration that turned violent. Here was the one area in which I had a bit of experience. For the field training, Jonathan chose the picturesque city of Wells. Although only a village, it gets to be called a city because of the ancient (and still unfinished) cathedral. It also boasts a stately bishop's residence surrounded by a shallow moat. Why a bishop would need a moat remains unclear.

We strolled around the narrow old streets, talking about how to protect oneself when protesters start throwing rocks, cops start responding with tear gas, and reporters are caught in the middle.

I was in Toronto during the 2010 G20 meeting of world leaders when just such a scenario played out on the streets. But in that case I used my experience as a veteran journalist to avoid the nastiness, insisting that I be assigned to cover the actual conference, which generated little news, but which allowed me to relax inside the police barriers, sipping the complimentary Ontario wines, munching the complimentary canapés prepared by the city's top chefs, and watching with interest the live coverage of my colleagues on the streets being drenched in a driving rainstorm and tear-gassed by the cops.

The walking tour of Wells brought the hazardous environment training to a close. An afternoon train brought me back to London, where I met Stu and Dan at a restaurant near Oxford Circus. There was a going-away party for Tom, a Canadian radio reporter headed home after a three-year stint in the U.K.

Tom and I had exchanged emails weeks earlier, planning to meet and compare notes about moving a family to London. Now, after having had a few, he told me it was a wonderful experience, that his wife and two children had loved it, that it was the world's greatest city, the best kind of experience for a reporter, et cetera.

He was most insistent and enthusiastic.

"You don't need to convince me," I told him. "It's my wife and daughter."

Chapter Seven

The gas line had been repaired while I was away, so hot water had returned to the flat and the building had not blown up — a mixed blessing. It was now approximately one month until the arrival of Isabella and Julia.

I was fast asleep that first night back at Buckland when the phone rang. As I reached for it I could see on the clock radio that it was 1:15 a.m.

It was Isabella.

"Julia's got something for you," she said.

"Uhmg," was my erudite response.

"Skype us right now."

"Ah … okay," I said, the fog slowly lifting.

I made the video connection on the phone and there was Julia with a knowing smile.

"Daddy, Mommy took me to Build-a-Bear today … and look!"

She held up a teddy bear, a shocking pink teddy bear.

"Her name is Sherbet!"

"Oh … That's great, sweetie. But did you really need another bear?"

"No, Daddy, she's for you! Listen."

She squeezed the bear's paw and out came a recording of her six-year-old's voice: "I'm Julia Mallen from Global News National. Hi, Daddy! Me and Mommy are missing you. See you later. We love you!"

"Did you hear it? That's me!"

For a moment, I couldn't speak because of the lump in my throat.

"Sweetie, that's got to be the best bear ever. Thank you."

"You're welcome. Bye!"

Isabella came on the screen.

"We're going to mail it, but Julia wanted to show it to you right away."

I knew of course it was her idea, her way of trying to keep a connection.

"Thanks for that," I said, inadequately.

Sherbet arrived in the mail a week or so later and shared my bed every night.

Sunday was one of London's rare sunny summer days. I strolled down Belsize Avenue to the cute enclave of shops and cafés at Belsize Terrace, bought the *Sunday Times* and had breakfast outside, feeling only slightly guilty that my wife and daughter were on their own back in Toronto.

Afterward, my mission was to buy the giant stuffed giraffe that Julia had spotted in a toy store in Hampstead.

On a gorgeous day such as this, Hampstead Village is lovely — the cafés jammed with expensively dressed locals, many with their expensively dressed children in tow. It is a kind of never-never land for a middle-class Canadian. I walked in their presence, breathed their air, smelled their croissants, but was separated from their privileged lives by a thin, impregnable wall of economic disparity. They cruised by in Bentleys as I exited the Tube, hiking to a store where I was to buy a toy that I could not actually afford.

It was a short walk up Heath Street — a hole-in-the-wall shop with shelves crammed with enticements for children rich or not so rich.

The owner informed me that the stuffed giraffe was among her bestsellers — she was in the process of packing one up to ship to Northern Ireland. Out came my card to lay down the £75.

The day had now become positively hot, too warm to think about walking all the way down to Buckland with a large stuffie, so I waited for the 268 bus out front.

It is remarkable how much attention one can attract by standing at a Hampstead bus stop with a four-and-a-half-foot tall stuffed giraffe on a sunny Sunday. Londoners who would barely give me a look at normal times offered knowing smiles as they walked by. A Hampsteader pulled his Porsche to a stop directly in front of me.

"Would you and your giraffe like a lift?"

It was an offer that straddled the border between genial and snotty, leaning toward the latter.

"Sorry. You'd need a convertible."

The looks on the bus were kinder. I milked it a bit, holding the giraffe affectionately close. He was going to be my sole companion in the flat for the next month. I took him out on the balcony for a shared selfie, which I forwarded back home.

Isabella emailed back immediately: "I love it! Thanks so much for that. It made Julia laugh! And it made me horny … I want to have sex with you!"

Funny how the purchase of a stuffed giraffe can bring so much joy.

Another middle-of-the night phone call. This time it was 3:30 a.m. I knocked the phone to the ground as I was reaching for it. Isabella told me that Julia had been watching a movie that was tied into the American Girl doll that she owned. In it, the father of the lead girl was a doctor who had to go to London to prepare for duty in a war. Julia had somehow related it all to me and started to cry uncontrollably.

"We need to Skype so you can talk to her," said Isabella.

I stumbled out of bed and turned on my iPhone. When we made connection, I did my best to explain to Julia that I was a reporter not a doctor and I did not plan to be going to any wars. I would just be travelling from time to time to do stories, much as I had at home.

In the back of my mind I wondered whether I would be called to go to conflict zones, a prospect that I put aside, hoping that I did not have to face such a decision.

Although only six, Julia was wise to any prevarication. She accepted my story, but with a note of suspicion.

After Julia left the room, Isabella said, "We sure have a smart kid. Our little sweetie really misses you."

"Yeah. Well, it's just a few weeks to go before you guys come. Please try to hang in there," I said wearily.

"We're trying. But this is tough, very tough."

In all of my six-and-a-half years of fatherhood I could count on fewer than the fingers of one hand the number of times I had bought clothes for my daughter. Isabella had always taken the lead and I happily handed over the responsibility.

But with only a month until the first day of school, there was a pressing need to buy Julia's uniform. The Royal had provided a long and specific list, all of which had to be obtained beforehand because she would be expected to show up properly dressed, with a full kit, from Day One.

So, one morning before work, up I went on the bus to the far northern regions of Finchley Road to the recommended supplier. Isabella had emailed measurements to at least give me a guide. Happily, the Royal's colours were red and white, acceptable for my girl. Top of the list: a pinafore. Aside from the title of a Gilbert and Sullivan operetta, I had no idea what the hell a pinafore was. I handed over my list to the helpful clerks and they pulled out a couple and started a pile.

"These track pants seem a bit small for a six-year-old," said the clerk.

I shrugged helplessly. She smiled and added them to the collection.

"Does this blouse look right?" she asked. "Because once you open the package it cannot be returned."

Duh, I thought.

"Let's just give it a go," I said aloud, feebly.

There were blue tights, a summer dress of red-and-white stripes, shorts and a T-shirt for P.E., and a boater hat with a red ribbon, which I thought was adorable, but which Julia would surely detest. I added a Royal bookbag as an extra, along with several iron-on name tags.

Two large plastic bags were filled as they added up the total: £326! I had spent more than five hundred Canadian dollars for uniforms that my daughter was going to hate. As I waited for the bus, I silently thanked Aunt Sheila for her generosity that was subsidizing this whole harebrained project.

Having spent a couple of months working in the centre of the Camden Market, I thought that it was time to learn a bit more about the neighbourhood. A quick internet search yielded the London Walks company — you just show up outside the Camden Town Tube stop at a given hour on Saturday, hand over five quid to a woman named Judith, and she leads you around.

About a dozen of us gathered on the wide sidewalk on a typically grey, drizzly August day. Judith Clute was easy to pick out as she adjusted the headset and microphone for her portable amplifier. A trim woman in her sixties with short grey hair, the website had described her as a local artist. She won me over with the first few words out of her mouth, speaking slowly and methodically.

"I hope you can all understand me because I have a very heavy downtown Toronto accent," she said, as though we were all language students from Mongolia.

"No problem," I said. "Go Leafs."

She smiled, as did a couple of other Canadians in the group. The rest looked puzzled.

Judith had lived in the neighbourhood for decades, managing to retain her hometown accent, and her tour revealed a deep and affectionate knowledge of Camden. In the last century it had been a tatty home for Irish labourers on the northern outskirts of London. Around the corner from the Tube stop was a childhood home of Dickens. The public lavatories opposite in the crazy intersection were thanks to a campaign by George Bernard Shaw to provide public conveniences for ladies. Male Londoners then and now still take a leak pretty much where they please, particularly after downing a couple of extra pints after closing time. But the boys later got a loo as well.

A few steps north along the High Street was the Electric Ballroom. It started as a dance hall for Irish labourers before earning fame in the late twentieth century for hosting performances by Sid Vicious, The Clash, and the like. All of which explains the piercing and tattoo parlours up and down the street. Transport for London proposed to demolish the whole block to upgrade the Tube station, but local opposition managed to hold off the bulldozers, and it survives in its spiky, middle-finger-raised glory. The ballroom later got a makeover, which unfortunately turned its gritty facade into a just another bland exercise in neon.

A couple of blocks over, Judith pointed out a pub where Amy Winehouse had one of her legendary blow-ups. Having gotten thoroughly hammered while playing billiards, she threatened to club one of her playmates with a cue. A peacemaker stepped between them and was rewarded with a Winehouse head-butt that broke his nose.

Next up was the Regent's Canal. I looked out at it every day from my office window but really knew little about it. It was another one of those huge nineteenth-century British infrastructure projects, part of a plan to develop north-central London.

Judith told us that it would freeze over periodically during extra-cold winters, and an entrepreneurial hotelier would send his men to chip out chunks and bring them down to his swanky bar. He neglected to tell his well-heeled customers that the ice decorating their fancy drinks was drawn from a canal seasoned with all manner of horse droppings, human pee, and miscellaneous toxins washed in off the streets.

Her tour wrapped up in our section of the market, the Stables. In the nineteenth century it was a horse hospital — a treatment centre for those injured while hauling barges along the canal.

Every day that I walked to work I would duck off the high street and cut through the cobblestoned passageways for a more scenic route to work. On the days when it had not already rained, workers would be hosing down the passageways to clear off the cigarette butts and other garbage from the night before. The vendors were starting to open up and display their arrays of touristy kitsch, antique clothing, rude T-shirts, and various crafts that tourists would buy as souvenirs that they would later sell in subsequent garage sales back home.

My route would take me by my coffee stop, Terra Nera. Sadly, they were later forced out by a rent hike and I took my daily caffeine business to Café Crema on the West Yard, right beside the canal. They not only poured a beautiful cappuccino (with a discount for those who worked in the AP building) but too often tempted me with a warm croissant or *pain au chocolat*. The coffee and croissants remained just as fine after Café Crema was remade into a Mexican joint.

Does it sound like I miss it? Yes.

Along the way were giant bronzes of muscular horses in heroic poses, evocative of the neighbourhood's roots. The sign at the entrance said SINCE 1854.

"Actually the market has only been around since the eighties," said Judith. The nineteenth-century date referred to its previous incarnation.

I chatted a bit afterward with Judith, thinking I might like to turn her tour into a travel article. She was excited by the idea and asked if I might be able to get her into the Interchange building for a look around.

Sadly, neither happened. And a few days later the charm of the market was briefly overtaken by a night of menace.

London turned.

Chapter Eight

I awoke Sunday morning to news that Tottenham had exploded in anger overnight. On Thursday police had shot and killed a young black man named Mark Duggan. The troubles started with a peaceful protest march, but it was hijacked by those who wanted to do damage. Years of frustration boiled over into street violence and arson.

I called Dan in from his day off and we headed for Tottenham. A burned-out police cruiser stood by the side of the road where the taxi dropped us. Crowds of people were milling around on the street in front of a building gutted by fire, the smell of scorched wood still in the air.

We approached a few people in the crowd to get their take on it all. There was some regret about the damage, but little about the anger. The grievances against police were deep-seated and long-lasting.

"They need to learn a lesson," a scowling woman named Eileen Edwards told us.

I asked her to explain.

"They need to learn what time it is. We want justice, that's all it is."

As it turned out, Tottenham was only the beginning, only the ignition point for something broader, deeper, and more troubling.

The following evening, there was more disorder throughout the city. As we watched Sky News in the bureau, there were live reports of street violence, clashes with police, and fires. They grew minute by minute, peaking with a giant fire in a furniture building south of the Thames. London seemed to be spinning out of control.

A Sky reporter named Mark Stone walked out of his flat, armed with an iPhone, and started shooting video with play-by-play. Pointing it into an electronics shop, he captured scenes of young men attempting to rip a TV off a wall.

"Is that fun? Is that funny?" he asked, provocatively, fearlessly, and probably recklessly. The vandals initially just pushed past him but then the video stopped. We learned later that they had turned on him and he had to run for his life into a nearby bar. All over the city there were reports of TV news crews being assaulted, having their gear stolen. We were spared the danger, we thought, because of the need to stay in the bureau to collect video from the various sources and prepare a story for an imminent deadline.

Then it came to us.

Dan, the Twitter master, said, "A reporter just tweeted that there's trouble in Camden Town."

I looked out my window down into the West Yard, the home of my treasured food vendors. It was now dark, the food guys having all closed up hours ago. Peering around a corner was a cop in full riot gear, joined seconds later by a colleague. They took tentative steps into the yard, clearly looking for troublemakers.

I thought about my wisecrack at the hazardous environment training course — the one where I said I was all prepared in case of an attack on the Camden Market. Now it was here.

"Let's go check out what's happening on the High Street," I said. "See if we can shoot a bit of our own video and maybe a stand-up."

Dan grabbed his smaller, more compact camera, the better to be able to run if need be.

We walked out the back door of the Interchange, along a short street called Camden Lock Place, which during the day is normally bustling with market vendors. Sure enough, police had set up tape across Camden High Street, blocking it off. Farther north, just out of sight, vandals had trashed a bicycle shop.

Young people strolling out of the many pubs and clubs in the area seemed oblivious to what was going on. There were a few guys with hoodies pulled up over their heads, hands in pockets, watching non-chalantly. *The likely troublemakers*, I thought.

"YOUNG LADY!" a cop snapped at a woman lifting the tape to try to walk past. "That is there for your safety. Choose another route!"

Dan and I shot a quick stand-up in front of the police line, with me describing how the trouble had come to Camden. We walked back along Camden Lock Place toward our office. What was picturesque in daytime now was ominous: aged brick walls, a cobblestoned street, and no one in sight. Jack the Ripper stuff.

Out of the corner of my eye I noticed two guys following about twenty metres back. Earlier they had been barking at us — the usual kind of "Hey, it's an American TV crew" that can happen just about anywhere. In normal times, harmless idiocy that you can laugh off.

But not now that these two yobs were wordlessly in our wake. Not with what was going on throughout the city.

The back door to the Interchange compound was an old metal gate that slowly creaked open when you flashed your pass card. It was a charming quirk most of the time, but a nerve-wracking failing tonight. The second we could fit through, I said calmly to Dan, "Let's just pick up the pace up the stairs."

"Yup," he said, having also spotted our followers.

We dashed in, and from above we could see our friends turning around and heading back to the High Street. Odds are they were more curious than predatory, but I was just as happy to have a high fence between us.

Not long afterward, our CTV colleagues Tom and David also tried going down to the High Street, but the scene had further deteriorated and they beat a quick retreat for safety's sake.

Later, we heard stories of how news photographers were being mugged in the hotter areas of London. The bigger TV agencies, Sky and BBC, hired security guards to protect their live trucks and still suffered damage. Many stories that night were shot on iPhones with reporters dressing down to blend in with the crowd.

There were days of troubles, with the craziness spreading to other cities. Even nice neighbourhoods were hit — thugs pushing their way into restaurants, demanding that patrons hand over their wallets and purses. This was no longer solely a race issue, public order was breaking down. Hooligans used social media to organize meetups to cause trouble.

A sixty-eight-year-old man named Richard Bowes tried to stamp out a fire started by goons in his Ealing neighbourhood. The mob turned on him and beat him to death.

Parliament was recalled. Prime Minister David Cameron said it was evidence of a "broken society." Outraged Brits demanded that welfare recipients who took part in the riots have their benefits yanked.

As it turns out, there is a long history of this kind of thing in the British capital.

In Peter Ackroyd's masterly portrait of the city, *London: The Biography,* he observes that "it stretches back as far as the written records." Ackroyd reminds us that when King Richard I was crowned in 1189, Jews were slaughtered in the streets.

In 1780, in what he describes as the worst riot of the last thousand years, mobs protesting against laws that would further the rights of Roman Catholics ruled the streets for days, burning several prisons and killing at least two hundred people. Hundreds of rioters were locked up and twenty-five offenders were hanged on the spot of their offences.

More recently, there was the Broadwater Farm riot in 1985. Residents of a mainly black housing development rose in anger after a woman named Cynthia Jarrett suffered a fatal heart attack during a police raid on her home.

In those days, tensions with police had been building for months and this was the spark that set the neighbourhood ablaze. In the midst of the mayhem, Police Constable Keith Blakelock was surrounded by rioters who set upon him with knives and a machete and effectively hacked him to death.

Ackroyd makes the point that in both 1985 and 1780 the troublemakers were generally poor and desperate, observing: "In both cases, however, the riots burned themselves out fierily and quickly. They had no real leaders. They had no real purpose except that of destruction. Such is the sudden fury of London."

In 2011, the initial theories as to the cause of the latest riots focused on a generation of disenfranchised youth, with few prospects of employment or advancement. Here, too, there were no obvious leaders, just a loose network knitted together through social media.

Speaking of which: Twitter, Facebook, and the rest also showed the good angels of London's nature. As Tuesday dawned, law-abiding citizens were organizing cleanup campaigns.

I came upon one on Chalk Farm Road as I walked into work.

A group of women were there, sweeping up broken glass from the vandalized bike shop. I spoke with Sia Yama, who had walked down with her broom from her home in North Finchley. "I'm ashamed of what people have done, basically. So I'm doing my bit to help, to ease my shame a bit," she said.

"You feel ashamed?" I asked.

"I do, as a Londoner."

Ms. Yama pointed out that she had been unemployed for two years, but would never dream of inflicting the kind of outrage on her city that was perpetrated Monday night.

As I prepared to leave the scene, another woman, who had observed my foreign accent, came up to me and said simply, "I apologize."

London is both the metropolis of "sudden fury" as described by Peter Ackroyd and also the city of deep civic pride, as displayed by the people with the brooms.

At the end of the week, after the madness had subsided, we went back out to Tottenham to see how people were doing. Walking along the High Road, we met a genial cop named Sergeant Jim MacPherson. The police were steamed because Prime Minister David Cameron had implied that they were slow to react to the riots. Cameron had been on vacation in Italy when things exploded.

MacPherson had not had a day off since it started and was unlikely to have any break for weeks.

He would not respond directly to the PM but did point out: "Being a cop as long as I have, you could have fifty thousand cops out here and it seems like it's not enough. It's a big, big city."

I asked for suggestions of business owners who might want to speak and he pointed me to a storefront with the sign H. GLICKMAN LTD IRONMONGER.

It has stood on the spot since 1880. Derek Lewis was the owner, having taken over from the Glickmans decades earlier. On the first night of the trouble, rioters broke in and ransacked it.

"It does hurt," said Lewis. "It's very sad because I'm very involved in the community around here."

Things were still tense in the neighbourhood. The famed football club, Tottenham Hotspur, cancelled its scheduled game, fearing that it was still too early to allow crowds to gather.

Lewis, though, had no thoughts of shutting down or moving.

"They ain't gonna get me down. Been here too long, so I ain't gonna be beaten."

That weekend, I met Caroline for brunch and learned she was caught up in the nuttiness too — returning home to her quiet neighbourhood in North London to discover someone had spray-painted "ROIT" on the front of her house.

"Is that 'roit' as in the Cockney way of saying 'right'?" I asked.

"No, that's someone misspelling 'riot' — evidence of the short-comings of the British education system," she said.

As Caroline stood in front of her place, ruefully assessing the damage, she encountered another, less savoury side of London.

A neighbour walked by, stopped, and appeared to commiserate for a moment.

"When do you suppose you'll be cleaning it?" he asked. She had no immediate answer.

"Well, you see, I'm trying to sell my place and I have an open house next week, so I'd be most grateful if it could be gone by then," he said in an impeccably mercenary tone.

London is blessed with many wonderfully generous people, but is also infested with a healthy share of self-centred shits.

Walking out of a play the next weekend, I looked at my iPhone and there was an email from our reporter, Tom — the specialist in war coverage: "Are we thinking of going into Libya?"

After months of vicious fighting, Moammar Gadhafi's regime appeared to be close to the end. The rebels were closing in on the capital, their military victories assisted in no small part by a NATO bombing campaign designed to keep the colonel from slaughtering his own people.

We would likely be sending someone and it appeared I was about to be faced with the question I had hoped I would be able to dodge: Was I ready to go to a war zone? The answer from my wife and daughter would be a loud no.

Back at the flat, I stayed up late watching Sky News's coverage. British reporters are renowned for their fearless reporting from conflict. At the top of the heap was Sky's Alex Crawford. Many of us felt that her bravery veered toward recklessness. Earlier in the Libya conflict, she and her crew were trapped in a rebel outpost, surrounded by Gadhafi's forces. She said later that she thought they were dead, but they somehow managed to survive.

Now Alex was leading the international journalistic pack in the regime's final days. I would flip over to the BBC News Channel's coverage and their top-flight, courageous reporters were on the outskirts of Tripoli, ducking gunfire, doing their best to convey what they were hearing was happening inside the capital.

Flip back to Sky, and there was Alex reporting live from the back of a rebel truck as they rode right into the centre of Tripoli as Gadhafi's forces apparently melted away.

It was an astonishing, award-winning coup for Crawford and her team. The next day, as the BBC reporters were again caught outside Gadhafi's compound, dodging bullets, wondering what was unfolding within, Alex was live *inside*, interviewing a rebel who was wearing the colonel's cap, which he had looted from the strongman's abandoned bedroom.

The *Telegraph* and some tabloids delighted in reporting Alex's triumph and mocking the BBC for being beaten. All more than a bit unfair. As I learned from Caroline, the BBC has a rigorous protocol to be followed before deploying journalists into hazardous environments —

procedures born from hard and tragic lessons learned when they had people killed or grievously injured. It does not prevent their reporters from bravely following stories into manifestly dangerous places — it just ensures that they do so only with serious advance thought and planning.

Alex Crawford, by comparison, had fewer restraints. She also had a most understanding husband and two children. I met her a year or so later in South Africa, and found her to be a modest, pleasant, and approachable woman with not a hint of arrogance, despite her fame and courage.

These were all dilemmas I would not face. The choice was to send in Tom, along with our China crew, both of whom had been in war zones before. I was told that it was easier to spare the China team, who filed less frequently. I did not argue. Perhaps I should have been miffed, but I was not really — given that my wife and daughter would have been both furious and terrified had I gone.

As it turned out, it took them all a few days to get to Tripoli and things were much quieter by the time they arrived — with a nerve-rattling exception involving a trigger-happy security guard who panicked and fired wildly just outside the front doors of their hotel, forcing everyone in the lobby to hit the deck.

While my colleagues searched for trouble in North Africa, I prepared to go on my first travel writing junket of the U.K. adventure. The helpful folks at VisitBritain had arranged a lovely weekend in the Cotswolds. I was to grab a rental car at Heathrow (thus avoiding the trauma of making my left-side driving debut within London) and head to the charming countryside.

I was to meet a hiking enthusiast who would take me on a stroll through some of the most picturesque parts and enjoy a tasting of traditional English pudding at a hotel that has revived the passion for the old heart-stopping treat.

At the rental car place, the agent offered me an upgrade to an Audi or BMW. As I weighed the benefits of wheeling a cool car through the English countryside with the risks that I would dent it because of unfamiliarity with driving on the wrong side of the road, the decision was taken away from me.

"I'm afraid your driver's licence appears to have expired," the agent pointed out regretfully.

EXPIRED! And so it had. My birthday and expiry date being in July, the Government of Ontario had likely sent the renewal notice sometime in May, when I was in London. Isabella had no reason to flag the letter and send it to me. I was not only a man without a nation, but now a man without a driver's licence.

There would be no Audi or BMW for me, no Cotswolds hiking or pudding either. Merely humiliation as I trudged back to the airport to catch the train returning to London and spend the rest of the morning cleaning the tub and toilet in the flat.

Miraculously, though, when I stepped out onto the balcony, I could see there was a double rainbow over Belsize Park. The weekend had gone stupidly off track, but I was still in London. Take advantage, dummy.

I hopped on the Tube down to Westminster and bought a ticket to visit the Churchill War Rooms. It is a clever museum, playing on the vivid memories of Sir Winston and the brave Londoners enduring the dark days of the Blitz.

It was actually built before the war, in 1938, underneath what is now the Treasury building, in anticipation that the city would likely be bombed when the war came. It was never actually that secure, even after they installed a 1.5-metre layer of concrete, nicknamed "The Slab," in the ceiling. If there had ever been a direct hit, the whole place would have had to be renamed the Churchill Memorial Crater.

But for students of history, it is irresistible to peek into the bedroom where the great man occasionally slept, the map room from where the war was sometimes directed, and the space where the Cabinet occasionally met.

You also got to see his quirky taste in clothing: he had someone design a onesie that would allow him to quickly pull something over his jammies if he needed to get up in a rush.

Having checked that tourist stop off the list, I made my way over to Trafalgar Square and bought a ticket to a performance at St. Martin-in-the-Fields. There has been a church on that site since the thirteenth century. But for me, the name resonated from my young adulthood, when I would hear a CBC Radio host introducing recordings made by Sir Neville Marriner and the Academy of St. Martin-in-the-Fields.

Now here I was, sitting in a pew in that very church, listening to a mixed program of the *Four Seasons*, Mozart, and Bach. For no good reason I started to choke up, my eyes welling. For most of my adult life I had wanted to live in London and here I was.

One week to go before the arrival of Isabella and Julia.

On my final week of British bachelorhood, I was at last to get a road trip. The story was to be about Libya but the location far nicer. An international conference had been called in Paris to talk about what to do in the post-Gadhafi era. Prime Minister Stephen Harper was attending, so I was assigned to go. It would be solo, as Dan was away and a pool camera was shooting the PM.

My first visit to Paris was on my epic backpacking trip to Europe in 1984. In those days, it was an all-night train-ferry-train slog from London that ended just after dawn at Gare du Nord. I can still remember that first day: the smell of bread baking, the streets steaming with romance (even though I was alone), and how I walked and walked, enthralled, until my feet were screaming, not returning to my dumpy hotel until well after midnight, and had to wake the grumpy old lady who ran the place to let me in.

I came back later to take a French immersion course, and then again on our honeymoon.

Now it was as a *foreign correspondent*.

Travel between London and Paris is now easy — so elegant and civilized. It was a short cab ride from the flat to the gleaming St. Pancras station, a smooth run through security and then onto the comfortable Eurostar. Just over two hours later, you step off at Gare du Nord.

The smell of baking that I had noticed all those years before was no longer present, but as I rode in a taxi to the hotel my heart filled with joy: Paris was so beautiful and charming on an August day. We passed right by the famed Taillevent restaurant where Isabella and I dropped the equivalent of a month's rent on a memorable honeymoon meal. (She started out feeling guilty at the prices but before we left was asking if we could come back again the next day.)

I sagely timed my journey so that I would be arriving many hours before I actually had to do any work, leaving plenty of time to reacquaint myself with the city.

After dropping my bag at the hotel, I paid a visit to the Canadian embassy to meet with the friendly press secretary, Normand, ostensibly to get a briefing on the logistics of the PM's visit but more importantly to tap into his knowledge of Paris so that I could make the most of the visit and find an excuse to come back as often as possible.

He was a font of useful tips and insights. It seemed Canada had suddenly become cool in France, with Parisians clamouring to book trips to our side of the Atlantic. One of the most popular art exhibits was titled *My Winnipeg*! What a change from my month in Paris in 1989 studying French, when my teacher delighted in mocking the Quebecois accent, calling it *épouvantable*.

Continuing my preparation for the Libyan summit, I made my way over to the sublime Musée de l'Orangerie to drink in some Impressionists. Then it was back to the hotel for the short amount of work that actually had to be done that day: Preparing a brief "look-live" stand-up previewing the conference, which I taped in the early evening with a view of the Arc de Triomphe in the background — another memorable image for the old resumé.

The pesky distraction out of the way, it was back to the more important parts of the visit: eating and drinking. Normand had recommended several attractive restaurants close to the hotel. I settled on a place called Le Galvacher, where I opted for a traditional French choice: a barely cooked steak with some *frites* on the side and several glasses of red wine.

Travelling with the prime minister was no vacation. Stephen Harper's hostility toward reporters was deep and visceral. If they were to come with him to fascinating spots around the world, he would ensure they would be left little time to sleep and work, let alone actually enjoy themselves.

My colleagues who were on his jet from Ottawa flew overnight to the Trapani air base in Italy and were rewarded with three hours sleep before they were allowed to witness Harper saying hello to Canadian fighter pilots for a few minutes. Then it was on to Paris, where they arrived a mere couple of hours before his only event. They were then given a brief amount of time to file their stories before jumping back on the plane to Canada.

By contrast, the PM's timetable was a happy thing for me. After a leisurely breakfast, I made my way over to the Left Bank to search out a chocolate shop to buy gifts for my loved ones, leaving time for some shopping in the terrific men's clothing stores along the Boulevard St. Germain and an elegant lunch in a café. One of the clearest memories of my 1984 trip was a supper in a similar place, sitting in the open air, eating a simple but delicious chicken in cream sauce. I sigh wistfully at the thought of it. This time, I opted for *lapin à la moutarde* (I would never be permitted to eat rabbit in front of Julia and Isabella) and a glass of crisp chardonnay. Okay, two glasses.

It was now 1:30 p.m. and there was really no alternative than to go back to the hotel and actually prepare to work. More than sixty nations were coming to hear from the Libyan National Transitional Council on the future of their nation, post-Gadhafi. The colonel was still on the run, occasionally surfacing on radio to spout delusional defiance.

The French newspaper *Libération* had an explosive story that threatened to overshadow the conference: a report that Nicolas Sarkozy's government had cut a deal with the NTC in April, guaranteeing France 35 percent of Libya's oil once Gadhafi was gone. The high-minded NATO mission to protect rebellious Libyans from the murderous vengeance of their despot seemed to have strong commercial motivations.

My Ottawa colleagues pulled into the hotel in midafternoon, bleary-eyed after the long haul from Canada to Italy and then here. Shrugging off the fatigue, a couple of them buzzed out the door, determined to squeeze in an hour of walking on the Champs-Élysées in spite of the prime minister's grim scheduling.

Harper's single news conference was in a characterless meeting room at the embassy, a locale that could have easily been found in a hotel in suburban Toronto. It was noticeably lacking in news, and coincided with the closing news conference of the larger meeting, which was happening at the same time across town. It all made for a scramble in finding something to report and writing our stories. The PM added to the enjoyment by deciding to leave thirty minutes earlier than scheduled, which meant all of us TV reporters had to run out to the Champs-Élysées and quickly line up to await our turns in front of the pool camera to shoot our stand-ups before the Ottawa crowd had to run to the bus to the airport. Their delightful sojourn in the City of Light lasted about five hours.

While they jetted home to Ottawa, I had my own problem: the bistro that Normand had recommended for tonight was actually closed so I had to settle for a more ordinary meal in a touristy place.

As I awaited my order, I got an email from Isabella advising that the kitchen renovation that had turned our drab eating area into one worthy of a magazine cover was finally complete, and her crew from *House & Home* had been there to shoot a segment on it. The consensus was that it was stunning, giving our Scarborough kitchen the flavour of a French bistro, with new chrome appliances, marble countertops, and an antique lighting fixture as a tasteful contrast. All completed just in time for her to leave it behind in favour of the flophouse kitchenette at the Buckland flat.

The kitchen reno would be the subject of an article I wrote for the Homes section of the *National Post*, in which I talked about the five-month debt I owed my wife — incurred when I flew off to London to play at being a foreign correspondent while she stayed at home to be a single, working mother with no working kitchen. I concluded that I would be spending the rest of my life paying it off.

Isabella recounted a series of conversations she had had at a party in which mutual acquaintances kept telling her how conservative and straitlaced I was compared to her free-spirited nature. I ordered another quarter litre of wine.

Arriving back at the flat the next day, I found a letter from the Royal School. It seemed that after more than a century and a half the trustees had run into some financial troubles and so had cut a deal to sell out to a private educational conglomerate that ran several schools around the city. We were told that this would be the final year for the Royal under its current name but that everything would remain as it would have otherwise been — aside from some renovations to prepare it for its new role in the education empire.

It was only later that the true magnitude of the announcement came clear. The trustees and the new owners had waited until the very last minute to tell the parents, thus ensuring that it was would be too late for any of them to decamp and depopulate the Royal.

As of that moment, all I knew was that Julia had not even started at her new school and already it was being turned upside down.

Thus began my final weekend solo in London.

Chapter Nine

Sunday: arrival day minus one.

I scrambled off to Waitrose for the most pressurized grocery shopping trip of my life, trying to adapt the English offerings to what I thought my wife and daughter would accept. It seemed every single shopper was standing in my way as I navigated down the aisles of Duchy Originals and other exotic brands. Where were the damn Honey Nut Cheerios? Oh, the Brits call them Honey Cheerios. No nuts. Close enough.

My iPhone constantly buzzed with updates from home. To distract themselves from thoughts of their imminent departure for a new life, Isabella took Julia north for two days, indulging their newfound love for camping with close friends. She'd packed in advance, meaning they just left the camp early, parked the Fiat at home, picked up their bags, and headed to the airport.

My heart pounded as I searched in vain for the Goldfish crackers that were the only snack Julia would accept for school. I dropped almost £200 in groceries. The cart was jammed to overflowing and I had to haul two other bags across Finchley and back up the stairs to the Buckland flat, sweat now pouring down my face.

The fridge and cabinets filled, I collapsed on the sofa. I was ready, sort of.

With only a brief bit of time left to enjoy London solo, I decided to take in a last sight. In my four and a half months of bachelor life, I had never made it to the Tower of London. Now seemed as good a time as any, so I made the long Tube trek out to the east and got in for the final two hours before closing.

Amazingly, there was no lineup for the Crown Jewels viewing, and I was able to linger for an extended look at the Queen's stash, walking the wrong way on the treadmill that is designed to keep the tourists moving on crazy days. Although priceless, I do not think I would ever give them as a present to my wife. Garish, really.

Back at the flat, I chowed down on one of the microwave chicken tikka masala dinners, with a can of John Smith's — the combination that had been keeping me relatively nourished since April.

My iPhone buzzed again.

"We're in the taxi to the airport and I have to keep yelling at Julia to keep moving!"

Well, at least they were en route and likely to make the flight.

Sleep was deep and dreamless as the women in my life jetted across the Atlantic, headed to the world's greatest city for an adventure they never sought, never wanted, and would be enduring under protest.

Monday, September 5, 2011: my family was to be whole again. London's weather behaved for a change, delivering a mild, sunny day. On the train ride out to Gatwick, I stared out the window, wondering whether it was all really going to work.

At the arrivals gate, it seemed to take forever before they appeared. In brief moments of anxiety, I considered the possibility that they had changed their minds at the last minute and not gotten aboard. Then, there they were: Isabella struggling to push a luggage cart piled as high as her head, Julia pulling her little carry-on case, which she dropped when she saw me, shouting "DADDY!" and running into my arms.

Isabella's enthusiasm was more muted as I embraced her and whispered in her ear, "Thank you for coming."

"Okay, okay. It was a bit crazy, but we did it. There was absolutely no one there to help us with the luggage, though. We're exhausted."

She not only had a stack of large bags, but also had brought a folding table and seven pillows. I said nothing. Now was not the time for critical commentary. They were here.

With all the baggage, it was not practical to take the Gatwick Express train, so instead it was a ninety-minute taxi ride from the airport in to Buckland Crescent. Julia was a chatterbox, excitedly recounting their camping trip, the food on the flight, and anything else that came into her mind. Within fifteen minutes, she was silent and asleep on my shoulder.

I put my hand on Isabella's knee.

"You made it," I said, feeling honest and deep affection.

"Don't get happy ... yet," she warned.

At the flat she immediately headed for bed, having barely slept on the flight. Julia, by contrast, was now awake so I told her we should walk up to the Royal School so she can have a look while Isabella rested. I had already timed it as a seventeen-minute brisk walk from the flat, the last portion uphill. But that was seventeen minutes for a motivated adult. With a wary six-year-old in tow it was more like thirty-five minutes.

As we approached, I warned her again that the exterior was a bit industrial but that the inside was nice and the teachers seemed very friendly.

"Okay, Daddy," she said. The girl who was normally bursting with opinions was now noticeably quiet. School was to begin in two days and the signs were ominous.

When we returned to the flat, I dragged her reluctantly upstairs to introduce her to her neighbour Elena. The Bulgarian-American girl with the plummy British accent was keen to play, and her mother even more so, all but pushing her out the door.

Julia, not so much, but she tolerated a visit by Elena to our flat.

Elena demonstrated her flexibility after months of dance classes by lying on her back, and arching herself up into a bridge. Julia said little. I knew she could not do the same and felt a bit for her. The playtime was forced and one-sided, with Elena doing most of the talking. Julia was relieved when the neighbour was called upstairs for supper.

"Thank God she at least has her," said Isabella.

We were both desperate for her to make friends quickly.

On the eve of Julia's British school debut, I pulled out the uniforms for her to try on. Amazingly they fit. She at least joked about them ("These are great," she said, with eyes rolling), which I grasped on to as a sign of hope. The three of us made the walk up to the Royal, Isabella out of breath after the uphill stretch at the end.

"There's no way I can do that," she said. "We'll be taking the bus."

Wednesday, September 7, was the next big trial in the London venture: Julia's first day of school. The beginning was promising, as she got up, dressed in the uniform, and prepared herself without much wrangling. The 268 bus arrived in good time at the stop out front and deposited us all a block from the Royal.

As we approached the school, it all went awry.

"Where's Miley?" asked Julia.

Miley was her favourite stuffed bear, which we had promised she could bring to her first day of school to keep her company. We had managed to forget him at the flat, an omission that obliterated all our careful preparations and shattered Julia's tenuous hold on her emotions.

"Waaahh!" The tears flowed freely, her gait slowed to a near halt. "I don't want to go!"

"Please, sweetie…. Mom or I will go back and get Miley and bring her to you."

"I DON'T WANT TO GO!"

We were now in the schoolyard and the girls were lining up in their darling grey pinafores, white blouses, and black shoes — all clean and pressed for their first day of school, in a way they never would be again.

Other parents were staring, empathy in their eyes.

A lifeline reached out from home to save us from drowning in the first minutes of Julia's English school experiment. Alison, the girl from Toronto who Julia had met in the summer, walked over and said, simply, sympathetically, in her newly acquired plummy British accent, "Julia, I'll hold your hand while we walk to class."

Now I was ready to cry, or sing "O Canada," or at least reach out and hug the heroic Canadian girl who had come to the rescue.

"NO! I DON'T WANNA GO!" insisted Julia, but now there was a break. The teacher, Miss Eisele, briskly and calmly suggested that we should just quickly say our goodbyes and move away, reasoning that our daughter would stop crying when she could no longer see us.

So off she went in the line of girls walking off to class, shoulders heaving, hand in hand with the Canadian girl. I was ready to pass out from the tension, but at least we got her in the door.

Isabella and I stumbled around the corner to the Caffé Nero coffee shop, which would become a favourite meeting place for parents (mainly mothers) after the morning drop off. I tried, vainly, to convince her that once Julia was in class she would surely start to calm down and start to adapt.

"This is not going to be easy. I'm expecting more meltdowns," she said.

The rest of the day was a blur of errands. We decided that it was best that I go solo to pick up Julia as she was less likely to start to cry with me than with her mother. Somehow the time slipped away and I found myself running to the school, sweaty and out of breath, five minutes late to pick her up. On this of all days, when we did not want her to feel abandoned. Shit.

Bursting in the front door of the school, there she was, standing, arms crossed, looking sternly at me like I was the kid who had arrived late.

"Daddy!" she admonished, with a frown and just a hint of a twinkle in her eye, standing next to Miss Eisele.

"How was it, sweetie?" I asked, crouching down to look her in the eye.

"Fine," she said, as though nothing remarkable had happened at all.

"She did very well. The tears stopped right after you left," said her teacher.

I gave my daughter a long, grateful hug. In truth, Isabella was right, there were many dramas yet to come, but we had survived the first day. We walked hand in hand up Hampstead High Street to a crepe cart that is a local landmark, where we met Isabella and bought Julia what was to become a regular tradition, a Nutella crepe.

The next day, I returned to the office, but since my work schedule meant that my mornings tended to be free, I had the luxury of being able to walk with my wife and daughter up to the school and have a cappuccino with Isabella and some of the mothers before heading down to the bureau. Back home in Toronto, both of us would typically drive off immediately into rush hour traffic to fight our way to our respective offices.

En route to school, Julia gave us a warning sign of the next patch of trouble to come.

"I don't want to go to swimming class."

The Royal girls would go to the pool at the nearby Royal Free Hospital on Fridays. Julia had been taking swimming since she was small, but always with either her mother or father present. She did not want to go alone.

It blew up into another meltdown in the schoolyard on Friday morning.

"I DON'T WANNA GO TO SWIMMING," she wailed.

I advised Isabella to leave, once again reasoning that Julia might calm down if her mother was not in sight. But this time it did not work and her eyes continued to stream. She was determined. I resorted to bribery.

"Julia, how about this: you go to swimming and I take you for another ride on the London Eye?"

She had been campaigning for another expensive visit to the giant Ferris wheel and we had been resisting. But these were desperate times.

After making the offer several times in a row, her six-year-old anguish gradually abated. With Julia still sniffling, yet another Canadian girl rode to the rescue.

Zoë from Calgary appeared at her side.

"I'll hold your hand on the way to swimming, Julia."

The kindness of strangers from home was proving to be invaluable. Zoë was to become one of Julia's enduring friends in London.

We learned later that, once again, Julia's tears disappeared once we left and she adapted perfectly well on her first visit to a pool without her parents — with one glitch. We had forgotten to send along her goggles, which led to more quivering lips. But a classmate came through by lending her a pair. London may be a large and impersonal city, but we were to be constantly surprised by how supportive the teachers and classmates at the Royal would be for our daughter.

The first week of school was a mere three days, with two major crises — both solved.

Now for the weekend and new challenges.

I had signed Julia up for a swim course at the nearby Swiss Cottage club, the same place where I worked out. As we took her Saturday morning, she was visibly nervous. The teacher was a sympathetic but firm Russian named Anna.

"She will be fine," Anna declared.

Julia was immediately put to work doing laps and before completing a third of a length she was looking over to me sitting on the sidelines, where I gave her a smile and a thumbs-up. She responded with a thumbs-down and eyes that were turning red. Within minutes she was clearly in agony — not that she could not do it, but was simply intimidated by it all. We called it off.

"She's better than most kids," ventured Anna. She seemed to mean it. But Julia had had enough.

Off to Regent Street to spend some of our housing allowance money. The jaunt went awry in one of those puzzling ways that spouses find to argue. Isabella was asking something about sales taxes and how it would affect the price of everything in the U.K. Somehow, we managed to completely piss each other off and in a grand display of mutual petulance stalked away in different directions. Not such a great idea on one of the world's great shopping streets, teeming with people. Julia was beside me and asked: "Where's Mommy?" Isabella was nowhere to be seen among the throngs of shoppers.

Angry texts and phone calls were exchanged.

"Where the fuck are you?"

"I'M STANDING IN FRONT OF THE FUCKING ZARA STORE!"

"WELL SO AM I!"

Each of us was claiming to be at the Zara store that had been our destination. Problem was, there were two Zaras in the neighbourhood. Finally, we figured out that we had somehow ended up on opposite sides of Regent Street, sniping at each other via our cells. Zara turned out to be a very cool place with a huge assortment of fashionable items for the home. It was nice but our tour through it proceeded in grumpy silence.

Sunday was to bring Julia's promised next visit to the London Eye, but first we made a trek out to the giant IKEA store not far from Wembley Stadium. Our mission: to properly furnish our crappy flat with pieces recommended by Isabella's designer friend Cameron.

Working on a design show, Isabella grew to love decorating and believed improving your household environment makes you feel better about life. Our accommodations were mediocre but she was determined to make them better. Hours passed. Carts filled. The Eye visit was postponed.

At the checkout, we rang up an impressive £4,500 on the credit card, and only then did Isabella realize that we had spent most of our housing allowance. There was a short moment of panic before deciding to keep everything and make the best of it. Delivery and assembly (having had enough aggravation) were arranged and paid for. We returned, exhausted, to Buckland knowing that it would at least be furnished.

Our first weekend in London would not have been complete without another crisis. After supper Julia collapsed in tears, inconsolable.

"I can't do it!" she wailed.

The fears and frustrations of the move and her first days in school had built up and exploded. The catalyst was the cafeteria. A picky eater at the best of times, our six-year-old was intimidated by the concept of having to choose her foods from a series of choices that did not seem to include anything she liked. Frozen in fear, unwilling to speak up at school, it appeared she had been starving herself of any lunch.

"I WANNA GO BACK HOME!"

I was utterly flummoxed, but Isabella, dear Isabella who never wanted to come to London, managed to ride to the rescue by promising to talk to the cook and Miss Eisele and find a solution.

In the morning she took Julia by the hand, with me trailing, and marched into the kitchen, where she introduced herself to Christine, the cook — an ample Cockney lady who was soon to become one of my heroes of London.

"'Allo, sweet pea!" she greeted Julia.

Christine listened sympathetically to our dilemma as Isabella explored the possible options for sustenance that our daughter might actually eat. It was agreed on this day that Christine would set aside a couple of sausages that she had prepared for the breakfast of the boarding students and put some rice on the side.

At the classroom, Miss Eisele offered to make a special effort to help Julia make selections at lunch. Before the day was out, she had created a laminated chart for our daughter's lunchtime, complete with merit stars as a reward for trying something new or eating a healthy portion.

Wow. Teacher of the year. Did I mention that she also sent an email report to all the parents at the end of each week?

A visit to Christine became part of our daily routine upon arrival at school. Even now, with the passage of time and distance, I can clearly hear her hearty "'Allo, sweet pea" that she offered for Julia every morning and still see her face as she rubbed her chin and gave thoughtful consideration to what element of her menu she could adapt to fit the short list of Julia's acceptable food choices.

If I could, I would recommend that the Queen bestow an Order of the British Empire on the wonderful Christine for her kindness in helping a frightened little Canadian girl adapt to eating in a foreign land.

The Royal had a long list of extracurricular activities, all of which had to be promptly selected. Still unsure of herself, Julia was reluctant to sign up for any — but Isabella managed to talk her into taking gymnastics and art.

A couple of nights later, when I arrived back at the flat Julia greeted me with a demand: "Take off your glasses!"

When I complied, she grabbed the lapels of my jacket, stuck her leg behind my knee and attempted to throw me to the ground.

Seemed she had also signed up for judo — and was taking to it.

A couple of days later, after returning from a satisfying day of Foreign Correspondent™ journalism, another little girl crisis loomed at home. It was really the same crisis, just bubbling up in different manifestations.

"I want my life back!" was Julia's plaintive cry. There were no friends for her to play with, she said — no one to relate to. She missed her best friend, Ella, from home and her circle of pals from the daycare. She was a confident, self-assured girl, but the move to a new country where everyone spoke differently, acted differently, and already seemed to know the ropes was just too much for her.

I lay beside her in the lower bunk in her bedroom for a long time before she gradually calmed and fell asleep. Isabella knew her daughter well and had warned of eruptions. They had been in London barely a week and already there had been three major ones.

The second Saturday morning swim class brought more trauma. Julia asked for her nose plugs and I was unable to locate them. More tears. It was about more than just nose plugs. Once again, Anna had the kids immediately doing laps. Julia struggled with the front crawl. She caught my eye and made a cut-off gesture, to which I gamely replied with a smile and an encouragement to carry on. She did better with the backstroke, but this was not a happy girl.

The promised bribe visit to the London Eye distracted her for a time in the afternoon. It was pouring rain, which at least kept the line-ups down. The timeless attractions of London were proving to be of minimal value to my unhappy ladies.

Isabella had been to the Eye already and felt no need to visit again, so she stayed at the flat.

Not only was I a failure in my attempts to interest Isabella and Julia in the many attractions that London has to offer, so too was I fumbling the search for a suitable home for them to satisfy their spiritual needs. Finding a Catholic church to attend was part of my preparation work. I am not religious, but as Isabella is a follower, I would periodically attend Mass with her, and we had agreed that Julia would be exposed to Catholicism and go through all the rites. Her First Communion was looming for the coming year.

I found a church a mere five minutes' walk from the flat. It failed the test. The exterior seemed austere and unwelcoming, and the pews were half empty for the Sunday morning Mass we attended. This was not going to work, another London mishap.

I was flailing — every effort to bring joy into my family's London life was falling short in one way or another.

Chapter Ten

Through travel-writing connections, I arranged a weekend at a posh boutique hotel — a present that I hoped would inject some romance and adventure.

On a Friday evening in late September we splurged on a cab to make our way down to Belgravia. On my first backpacking trips to London, I remembered searching out cheapo B&Bs on the edge of the same neighbourhood, near Victoria Station. They were invariably dumps, with cockroaches, closet-sized rooms, dodgy toilets, and "English breakfasts" that I risked eating only because they came with the room.

Now I was to learn of the real Belgravia. It is one of the grandest parts of the city, one of the toniest, wealthiest in the world — and often depopulated because the rich property owners tend to spend only part of their time there. The streets were strangely devoid of crowds, with the exception of the Syrian embassy, where protestors were camped out front.

The Halkin hotel has an entrance so unobtrusive it would be easy to miss. A small brass plate was all that announced it. The lobby was minimalist, modern with sleek, straight lines. As were our rooms. Julia was thrilled that she got an adjoining room to herself and that there was a little stuffed bear waiting for her on the bed, which she nicknamed Halkie.

Otherwise, my ladies' enthusiasm for my little weekend treat was restrained. On the advice of the front desk, we walked over to a gastropub named Pantechnicon for supper. It was a chic *boîte*, with little food that was kid-friendly, let alone for a picky kid like ours. We attempted to order a burger for her, but of course it was a fancy one and she would not touch it. Tears filled her eyes. Isabella shook her head. My heart sank.

Saturday morning, Isabella opted to walk over to Knightsbridge to look at the swish shops while I took Julia to a chocolate-making session that the hotel arranged at the nearby Rococo chocolatier. Here was an activity that held her interest. A chocolate-maker in training taught us how to temper, which involved getting the mixture to exactly the correct temperature, then spreading it on a marble slab and scraping it back into the bowl. All very exact. We made little blobs of chocolate, dropping in sprinkles, salt, and other flavourings, and poured some of the sweet brown goo into molds to create bars, writing our names on them. Our instructor took us out back to a little patio for tea and tastings. Julia was enthralled. I shot some bits of video in hopes that it could someday be turned into some kind of travel segment. She was a willing performer for the camera and readily delivered a running commentary.

We were given darling little gift bags to wrap up and take away our creations. They stayed in the fridge for months, with me taking an occasional nibble before I finally threw the remainders out.

The next step in my wooing process was to bring Julia to one of the more famous kids attractions in the city. We hiked over to the far side of Hyde Park to Kensington Gardens to take a look at the Diana, Princess of Wales' Memorial Playground. A portentous name for sure. It was the first playground I had ever seen that had a lineup waiting to get in. It is often that way on nice days in high season.

It was one of the many tributes that sprang up in the orgy of grief that followed the death of the world's most photographed woman. But a playground is a playground, and my kid was glad for the opportunity to climb on stuff, particularly the pirate ship that was plopped in the centre of a big sandpit.

By the time she was done, our feet were sore, so I splurged on a cab to take us back to the hotel, en route shooting more video of my little girl taking in the sights from inside a London icon.

Back at the room, I discovered to my horror a note that had been slipped under the door from the Halkin's PR person. I had completely forgotten that I was supposed to be meeting with her. A big whoops, considering that this stay was complimentary.

After the previous night's debacle, we kept supper simple — opting for sandwiches in the hotel's bar, while we perused their displays of lush art books. No tears.

Our brief exposure to the chic life ended with an elegant breakfast Sunday morning in their swanky restaurant, where we were comforted by the sight of a couple struggling to satisfy their baby at the next table.

After the taxi deposited us back to the reality of our dump on Buckland, there was a crisis when we realized that Julia was missing Miley, her prime stuffie. I made a frantic call to the hotel where they were quickly able to determine that the cleaner had found the precious bear, meaning that our weekend would not be remembered primarily for the loss of our daughter's most cherished bedtime companion.

With the skies clear and the temperatures mild, I took advantage to haul her off to Hampstead Heath in the afternoon for some fresh air and, I hoped, a bit of work on her writing homework. The fine weather meant that the fields were utterly jammed with Londoners desperate to soak up the rare glimpse of October sunshine.

Not feeling like cooking, we chose to experiment with ordering a pizza for delivery. Our Dominos order cost us £18 — and they managed to get our choices wrong.

When the posh set seek to get out of town, many head north and west to the Cotswolds. We were manifestly not posh, but thanks to VisitBritain and a travel story commission from the *Toronto Star*, we could afford to go for the weekend, boarding the train at Paddington en route to a rural station called Kemble. This was a variant of the trip I was supposed to take in August, but which went off the rails due to my expired driver's licence.

Just to ensure the happy jaunt got off to a properly tense start, I attempted to assist Julia with her writing homework on the train. After thirty minutes of intensive negotiation, stubborn tears from the little girl, and head-exploding frustration from me, we managed to craft about three sentences.

A taxi met us at the station to bring us to Calcot Manor, an estate that dates back to the fourteenth century — now a swanky country retreat and spa in the heart of Gloucestershire. We were housed in a gorgeous, two-storey stone house, complete with a gigantic bathroom outside Julia's room on the upper level. Travel writing has its benefits, as we never could have afforded this joint on our own dime.

As we explored, I discovered to my dismay that the place had a pool. I, of course, failed to pack Julia's swimsuit. Never miss an opportunity to miss an opportunity.

The manor also had two hundred acres of meadowland attached, so we borrowed three bikes and went for a gentle twenty-minute ride along one of the pathways for a very short taste of the English countryside.

Lunch was at the Gumstool Inn pub on the estate. As I was discovering, British pubs were shattering their old reputations for crappy food. This place got a favourable mention in the Michelin guide and deserved it, judging from the twice-baked cauliflower and cheese soufflé I inhaled.

The tourism people thoughtfully provided us with a guide and driver for the weekend, useful given that I was still without a valid driver's licence. Anne Bartlett met us after lunch. She was a trim and proper middle-aged woman with the bearing of an earnest teacher, perhaps because she used to be one before reinventing as a "blue badge" guide — one of the guild certified by tourism authorities.

With Julia occupied with the iPad in the back seat so she would not be tortured with history lessons, we set out to explore the countryside. True to her background, Anne had done meticulous research to prepare the lessons for her clients. The Cotswolds, she explained, were once a huge wool-producing area. But the Industrial Revolution put an end to that in the nineteenth century. The local economy collapsed, many residents left and nothing much happened for decades.

"It allowed it to be frozen in time," she said, with many villages retaining their old English look and feel.

By the twentieth century, the Cotswolds attracted proponents of the Arts and Crafts movement, led by William Morris. He spent his summers at Kelmscott Manor, a Tudor farmhouse that he admired as blending in harmoniously with the countryside. He took out a joint lease with the flamboyant artist and poet Dante Gabriel Rossetti, who blended less harmoniously into the family. While Morris was away in Iceland, Rossetti developed what is delicately described as a complicated relationship with Morris's wife, Jane, who later became a subject of many of his paintings.

Now the same rustic charms have proven to be a magnet for the monied, titled, and famous. Prince Charles has his Highgrove Estate near Tetbury, which was our first stop. Once a centre of the wool trade, the town still proudly hosts the annual Tetbury Woolsack Races, where participants carry a sixty-pound wool sack up a hill. It is an event noted for serious consumption of beer and cider. Also, I'm guessing, for a thriving practice in chiropractic therapy to service all those drunks hauling heavy wool sacks.

England is full of these kinds of eccentric athletic competitions, celebrating both heritage and zaniness.

The woolen industry is long gone but the Royals, led by the Prince of Wales, are proving to be a boost for the local economy. His Highgrove shop in Tetbury does a steady trade in traditional English goods, the proceeds going to his charities. I invested in some Highgrove fudge.

Local tradesmen who service the heir apparent also get to display his three feathers logo, proof that their dry cleaning or plumbing business is patronized by the man who would be king.

Anne ferried us to the Westonbirt Arboretum, a home for English tree huggers for the better part of two hundred years. In the days of Empire and the Grand Tour, rich folks would bring back saplings from all corners of the earth to add to the collection. Now there are about eighteen thousand trees and shrubs, drawing flocks of English arborphiles to stroll around the groomed pathways and admire them. By the time we arrived, it was raining, so we did not have much of an opportunity to look around, settling for a visit to the gift shop.

As Anne drove us back to the manor, she related how a particular Gloucestershire rich guy became antsy at the thought of the nearby hoi polloi overlooking his grand estate. So he bought a whole village and moved everyone down the road, out of sight.

"It actually turned out well for the villagers," she explained. "They ended up with updated houses."

Dinner at the Calcot Manor provided one of the most memorable moments of our time in the U.K. When I eat out, I like to explore new food sensations, to try things I would never make at home. Generally to the disgust of my wife and daughter.

"Please don't order anything weird," said Isabella. "No pheasant, no rabbit."

Neither of these were on the menu, but it did, however, offer grouse.

"It's freshly shot on the owner's estate," the waiter advised proudly.

"I'll try it," I said, not noticing Isabella's glare until too late.

The grouse announced itself even before it was placed on the table. A strong, earthy odour suffused our sitting area as the waiter approached. Medieval, you might say.

It was a large lump, somewhat resembling a greyish turd. With a similar smell. The gnarly feet were still attached, with a few feathers visible. Truly freshly shot.

Isabella's eyes went wide. She frantically tried to hide it from Julia's view by shifting the salt and pepper shakers and a little flowerpot to build a concealing wall. It did not work.

Julia held her nose and started to cry.

"What's that smell?" she wailed.

"How could you order that?" scolded Isabella.

At that moment, the waiter returned.

"Would you like some of the sauce?" he asked.

"Uh … sure."

From a silver serving boat he poured a liquid that must have been drawn from the drippings: a deep crimson, covering everything, the carcass sitting atop some root vegetables which soaked up the fragrances and tastes of the bird.

Not wanting to be rude, I dug in. The flesh was slightly pink, barely cooked, the flavours rich, strong, and complex. It would likely make good compost. I imagined that it was the kind of fowl that Henry VIII devoured by the dozens in more rustic times.

"You need to get rid of that thing," warned my wife. My daughter was looking at me with an expression that was both wounded and outraged. Like I was chowing down on Granny's budgie.

After a half-dozen bites, I admitted defeat. While the vegetables were actually quite tasty, the grouse itself was strong. I now knew intimately the meaning of the word "gamey." When the waiter passed by to check on us, I regretfully asked him to take it away.

"It's just not for me. Sorry."

He looked stricken.

"Can I get you something else?"

"No. I'll just wait for dessert."

The rest of the meal passed in grim silence. The tale of Sean's grouse has become part of our family lore, with Isabella relishing her imitation of the bird's feathered feet crossed in its pathetic display on my ill-fated plate.

Anne picked us up early the following morning and we headed north for a whirlwind tour of Cotswolds villages.

There was Chipping Campden, home of the Cotswolds *Olimpicks* (yes, that's the way it is spelled) — another wacky English sporting event. It has been held on nearby Dover's Hill ever since 1612, meaning it celebrated its four-hundredth anniversary a couple of months before the arrival of those other Olympics in London.

It is a showcase for the eccentricities of English country life. There is Morris dancing, the inexplicably charming combination of bells, hankies, hops, and sticks — often performed by sweating, puffing, middle-aged men on the verge of cardiac arrest.

There are the traditional competitions, such as the tug of war, and the odd: shin kicking. In times past, shin kickers would toughen up by whacking themselves with wooden mallets. They needed to be tough, given that steel-toed boots were once allowed (they are now banned). The more delicate of the modern competitors sometimes stuff straw into their high-topped socks for a bit of padding.

No longer part of the Olimpicks is a sport that still persists elsewhere in England: dwile flonking. The rules are deliberately complex, and generally the most dim-witted citizen of the village is selected to act as referee to ensure no know knows what is going on. It seems to have been invented in the late twentieth century, but with medieval inspiration: a form of dodge ball, using a rag soaked in beer (the dwile) that you throw (flonk) at your opponents to try to tag them. Points are deducted for sobriety, and frequently no one can remember the score once it is over.

The Olimpicks traditionally end with a torchlight procession from Dover's Hill into the town — a fine, old-fashioned spectacle for a celebration. Also useful if you happen to be hunting for Frankenstein's monster.

Anne drove us through the picturesque villages of Lower Slaughter and Upper Slaughter (no sign of Wanton Slaughter) and lamented that it all had to be such a rush. The Cotswolds cry out for leisurely exploration.

She dropped us at our final spot: the Three Ways House Hotel in Mickleton, which is officially just outside the boundaries of the Cotswolds, but was close enough for the purposes of my story. It is the home of the Pudding Club.

Pudding touches something deep in the English psyche — a passion well-expressed by Sir Clement Freud, the writer, politician, and grandson of Sigmund: "There is something about the blandness of soggy bread, the crispiness of the golden outer crust, and the unadulterated pleasure of a lightly set custard that makes the world seem a better place to live."

But for a time in the late twentieth century, it went out of fashion, a corpulent dinosaur in the age of *nouvelle cuisine,* when huge plates contained microscopic bits of food sculpture.

The fact that it is now back on menus all over England is due in no small part to the efforts of the Three Ways House and their club.

After a traditional English Sunday lunch of roast beef, we bellied up to the pudding bar for a tasting. As I dribbled warm chocolate sauce over one of my selections, club manager Craig Matthews edged up beside me and whispered in my ear, "You're going to need a lot more than that, sir."

He took command of the ladle and drenched the already chocolate-rich pudding with an extra dose, then fairly drowned my spotted dick with warm custard sauce. The Pudding Club will never be featured on Weight Watchers, but it was undeniably a sweet, gooey treat.

Matthews, who described himself as the "pudding master," joined me at the table to explain the origins of the club.

"It was to celebrate the great traditional pudding."

The year was 1985 and the previous owners of the hotel were lamenting how the puddings of their youth could now scarcely be found, pushed off menus by foreign invaders like crème caramel and tiramisu.

They did a bit of research to find some traditional recipes and invited twelve friends for an evening of tasting.

It was the spark to the revival.

Soon the Pudding Club became a regular Saturday night occasion at the hotel. Up to seventy guests start with a light main course (essential, given the heaviness to come), then dig into seven different forms of English pudding, paired with appropriate wines. At the end of the evening, there is a vote to choose the favourite.

I asked Matthews the essential ingredients to a good English pudding.

"Stodginess and lots of custard," was his well-practised response.

He has faced interviewers from all over the country and the world. The Pudding Club is a canny marketing tactic to lure visitors seeking a taste of old-fashioned English cuisine.

Bellies full, we called a taxi to take us to the train. Our driver, Rob, told us that he used to run a hotel in the southeast. He sold it, intending to retire on the proceeds, but was overly generous to his children, and had a mishap investing in a Scottish golf resort. As a result, he now runs a one-man taxi service with occasional personalized tours of the Cotwolds.

"Oh, I've had many famous clients in my car," he bragged.

"Really? Who?" I asked as we all leaned forward.

"Can't name them," he said. "They don't wear badges identifying themselves."

Chapter Eleven

B arely a week back in London and we were on the road again. With Isabella's family only a short flight away in Italy, we had resolved to visit early and often. They reside in Treviso, an elegant city only a thirty-minute train ride from Venice.

Ryanair, the discount carrier, flies directly into the tiny Treviso airport, marketing it on their website as VENICE (Treviso). Convenient for us, as we could get cheap fares to go exactly where we needed to go. But the world of discount flying with Ryanair requires planning, patience, and a willingness to accept a certain amount of abuse.

I paid a bit extra to check a couple of bags and to get so-called Priority Boarding. These flights resemble nothing so much as flying buses, with a scramble for unreserved seats. Priority Boarding allows you to get ahead of the lineup of the unwashed who are ready to take their chances on the seat rush.

The flight was leaving at 6:25 a.m. from Stansted Airport, so we went out the night before to stay at an adjacent hotel. Lineups for check-in for Ryanair always feature frantic passengers off to the side, fumbling through their suitcases to shift belongings around in an attempt to meet the stringent guidelines for carry-on bags.

We joined in on the unhappy tradition with a last-minute scramble of underwear into Isabella's checked bag. We were warned that women only get to carry on one piece, which includes a purse. She grumbled as her passport, wallet, and basic essentials were jammed into a small backpack.

"Do they really enforce this?" she asked. Cowed by the airline's reputation for strictness, I did not want to risk it. Sure enough, there were several women pushing the envelope with both purse and carry-on bag who got away with it.

With Priority Boarding, there were only a couple of people ahead of us in line.

"Julia, it's your job to grab us three seats as soon as we get aboard," said Isabella.

Here was a task our six-year-old relished, readying herself to dash as soon as the door opened. In the end, a rush was not really necessary but Julia still threw herself across the first good row of three that she spotted.

For your discount fare, you get exquisitely uncomfortable vinyl seats that do not recline and have no pocket in front of you to store stuff. You can also enjoy a constant barrage of sales pitches throughout the flight for lottery tickets, e-cigarettes, and the delightful array of food choices that seem largely prepared from edible oil products.

But it is undoubtedly cheap, and with a flight of only about two hours, bearable.

As it happened, the Treviso Airport was temporarily closed for maintenance so the Venice (Treviso) flight actually landed at Venice's Marco Polo Airport, where Isabella's cousin Silvia was waiting for us.

Treviso is a small, prosperous city, one of the wealthiest in Italy, home to Benetton. It suffered terribly during the war, with much of the centre destroyed in an Allied bombing raid. I remember Isabella's father telling me that when word arrived that Franklin Roosevelt had died, people cheered — a shocker to those of us who admired FDR. But if your city had been levelled by American bombers, perhaps you might have cheered, too.

Isabella's late uncle joined the resistance that fought the Fascists and it is part of family lore that he was once arrested and tortured. Also part of the story is how Isabella's grandmother helped a young German soldier, starving and desperate at the war's end. She took him in for a few days, told the children to say nothing to anyone, and then advised him of the best time to flee. Forever grateful, he would return every summer to say thanks.

In the postwar years of privation, this part of Veneto lost many young men to the New World. Isabella's father considered Australia before settling on London, Ontario — joined a couple of years later (two weeks before I was born) by the young woman he had wooed in the post office run by her family.

While they built a new life in Canada, Treviso bounced back. The town itself was tastefully rebuilt, with new buildings melded with the fragments of the old. Canals run throughout in an echo of its celebrated neighbour, Venice. Entrepreneurs brought new wealth. In the picturesque hills surrounding the city, winemakers started marketing a sweet bubbly that had traditionally been only made for home use. Now Prosecco is a worldwide phenomenon. Sometime in the late fifties or early sixties, a creative chef (the originator is in dispute) came up with the idea for a dessert made of ladyfingers, mascarpone, coffee, and cocoa, and called it tiramisu.

We visited on our honeymoon, after which I decided to take some Italian lessons so that I could communicate on at least a basic level, and then we returned only the year before our move to London. Isabella's cousins Silvia and Maria Assunta each have boys who are of a similar age to Julia — Alberto, a year or so older; Gregorio, younger. On that 2010 visit, I wrote a travel story about Julia's meetings, her explorations of Venice guided by Maria Assunta, and how, in spite of herself, she ended up saying a few words in Italian, even learning how to play rock, paper, scissors with Alberto in the language of her grandparents (*sasso, carta, forbice*).

On this trip there was talk of taking us up to the family house in the mountains, where the family all retreat in the summer but instead we chose to stay in the city at the home of Isabella's Zia (Aunt) Valentina, mother to Silvia and Maria.

These visits are generally fun for me, as we are feted by all, and stressful for Isabella, as she feels the pressure to see as many family members as possible and to constantly speak in her imperfect Italian. Her cousins have passable English, which makes things easier for me, and I usually manage to score a few points by making the effort to say a few sentences in highly rudimentary Italian.

Although they could not converse, Julia immediately picked up again with her cousins — first goofing around in Valentina's front yard and then at a park that had a medieval theme where they could play-act as knights and lady. The boys were rambunctious — Alberto was a rugby player and little Gregorio was always on the move, but Julia held her own.

Silvia and her husband, Mario, a teacher, took us on a Sunday tour of a part of the Venetian lagoon rarely seen by outsiders. It was low, marshy country with the odd ancient and abandoned hamlet. All quiet and evocative — a suitable setting for an artsy black-and-white movie from the sixties.

The family had a condo by the beach at Jesolo. Only a couple of weeks earlier they had been swimming in the sea, but now it was a chilly fall day and we settled for a short walk on the sea shore.

Jesolo was a backwater for centuries, until Italians developed a taste for beach holidays in the 1950s. It was blessed with a sixteen-kilometre stretch of clean white sand, so entrepreneurs built resort facilities to take advantage. Isabella has a striking black-and-white picture of her Zia Valentina stretched out in a bathing suit on the Lido di Jesolo in its heyday fifty years ago. More recently the tourists have started going elsewhere and the city is starting to wear a bit around the edges.

But as we enjoyed Italy, work reached out to complicate matters. A big story broke in Israel with the release of Gilad Shalit, a soldier who had been held by Hamas for five years. As I was away, Stu was assigned to go. Another big trip missed, and to a place I longed to see again. I was starting to think I was snake-bitten.

Isabella was not impressed by my moping.

"Why are you complaining? You're in a beautiful Italian city. Enjoy it. There'll be other chances to go to places like that."

Travel was always going to be a problem in this job — trips taken and trips missed.

There was nothing to be done about it anyway, so I managed to set aside my disappointment as we carried on visiting, eating, and shopping in Treviso. For the latter, we paid a visit to Isabella's favourite clothing store just off the elegant Piazza dei Signori in the centre of the city. This was an expedition that would typically occupy several hours while she tried on many of the beautiful clothes on offer, consider how they looked, ask my opinion, and then ignore my milquetoast responses.

Julia and I would stay for short periods, leave to go get a gelato and explore the neighbourhood, then come back to find the pile of discarded frocks was growing as the patient, smiling saleslady kept bringing out more.

My daughter would regularly remind me of a mishap from the previous visit. I was walking along happily with her on my shoulders, looking into shop windows. A woman walking toward us opened her eyes wide with horror and reached out her arms in warning. Oblivious, I wondered why she was upset, until I heard a *clung* from above and realized that I had carried my daughter into a low-hanging bar that was exactly at the level of her forehead.

"Daddy, you can't carry me on your shoulders on this street anymore," she now advised.

In the end, several hundred euros were added to the credit card and my wife was well-stocked with new garments, all of which had to be carefully distributed among our baggage for the Ryanair flight home.

Having learned our luggage lessons on the outbound flight, we got everything properly distributed before heading to the airport. But the Ryanair experience held new surprises. Our Priority Boarding pass once again got us to the front of the line — but only to get on the bus that would take us over to the jet. When its doors opened on the tarmac, we were caught in the same seat rush as everyone else.

"It's not our fault," said a shrugging flight attendant. "Talk to the Italians."

The flight landed at Stansted after midnight and despite the hour, there was a huge lineup to get through passport control — neatly causing us to miss the final train. Instead it was a rush to the bus into the city, which naturally was caught in construction traffic. Our heads hit the pillows at 2:30 a.m.

"I'm never flying Ryanair again," said Isabella. She was wrong.

Chapter Twelve

One thing they do not tell you about the English school system is the astounding amount of time off they give the children. Julia had scarcely begun and already she had a week called "half-term." It coincided with another first for our London adventure — me playing single parent to Julia. Isabella had a backlog of work she needed to finish at home in Toronto, not to mention the need to check out our house, which had been sitting vacant, with a friend occasionally walking down the street to pick up our mail and ensure that it was still standing. And so, on a Friday she headed for the airport to catch a flight home. Julia and I would have ten sleeps together with no Mommy — the longest the two had ever been apart. I would have a week of vacation solo with my little girl in the world's greatest city. What could go wrong?

Isabella had advised that I needed to find something for Julia to do every day, as much as possible with other little girls.

Day One was a breeze. We went swimming at the Swiss Cottage leisure centre, and then I asked her which museum she most wanted to see. Having gone through so much to get my kid to London, I was determined that she was going to soak up as much as she could bear of what the city had to offer.

She humoured me, choosing the Natural History Museum. We had, in fact, been there already, but the first visit ended on a sour note when I gave a big buildup to the escalator ride through a giant sculpture of the Earth, only to have her in tears because we arrived too late, after it had already closed for the day. This time it all worked. She got her escalator ride, we edged our way through the mobs of kids on half-term break to stare at dinosaur bones and I took a video of her pretending to look scared in front of the T. Rex model that moved and growled.

Our Canadian friends once again were there to help us get through Day Two, with an invitation to join them for a Saturday morning movie at the nearby O2 Centre. Julia was content to scooter with the girls while I strolled watchfully with Tara and Malcolm alongside, wondering if they felt my unease bordering on desperation.

There was a minor crisis at the concessions counter as I bought Julia a different popcorn package from the other girls — my choice lacking the same decorative box. As her eyes filled and lip quivered, Malcolm rode to the rescue, ordering the same deal for her to add to those of his girls. My thanks to him for bailing me out was sincere.

The movie was *Mr. Popper's Penguins*, with Jim Carrey. The kids all sat together, but partway through Allison moved over to sit on her mother's lap. A few minutes later, Julia followed to climb onto mine. Here was a fine father-daughter moment — affectionate, natural physical closeness that I truly cherished — even if my legs went to sleep, rendering me unable to stand for a time after the closing credits.

Back at the flat, a revelation. Our daughter is smart, charming, funny, and beautiful. What she is not is willing to help much around the house. Any request to get her to pick up her clothes or bring her dishes to the sink requires browbeating, constant supervision, and a willingness to endure tearful cries of injustice.

Now, for reasons unknown other than perhaps the unprecedented absence of her mother, she wanted to assist with the preparation of dinner. She trimmed the ends of the green beans, with me watching carefully alongside her, and she even volunteered to set the table, complete with cutlery and elegant napkins (in reality ragged paper towels, but who cares).

Our daddy-daughter time seemed to be resulting in a sea change in behaviour — a sudden, heartening, and inexplicable desire to be responsible.

Perhaps I was not such an ineffectual father after all.

It was an ironic Sunday. Even though I was the agnostic in the house, I was charged with getting Julia to church. We had agreed before her birth that she would be baptized in the Catholic Church (as I was, even attending Catholic schools through Grade 8) and that she would be exposed to Christianity.

Now the non-believer was insisting that my baptized child get out of bed so that we could get to church on time for service. Having moved on from my earlier failure at finding an appropriate church, I discovered a lovely little parish up in Hampstead. St. Mary's was tucked away at Holly Place, at the top of a hill, in a quaint and elegant setting not far from my short-let flat and the memories of Mr. Sneezy BritFuck.

The lot of Catholics in England has improved greatly over the centuries. Executions more or less stopped in the 1600s. It may soon even be possible for an heir to the throne to marry a Catholic. But in a city replete with ancient churches, the papist houses of worship are relatively young.

St. Mary's was built in the early part of the nineteenth century and counts among its notable former parishioners Charles de Gaulle, who lived for a while in a house on nearby Frognal, now a home for an order of nuns associated with the church.

We arrived in time for the family Mass, which was jammed with squealing kids and patient parents, and was full of life and joy. It seemed that at least I had finally, belatedly discovered an acceptable church for my family. This was to be a big year in Julia's religious life: First Communion loomed in the spring, so it was important to find her a place where she could go to Sunday school to take the requisite preparatory courses. After Mass, the priest advised that I contact the nuns who lived in the former de Gaulle house, where they offered courses in what kids needed to know to qualify for the sacrament.

Religious duties fulfilled, we turned to secular matters.

It is to London's great credit that so many of its tremendous museums are so welcoming to children. With a little coaxing, I convinced Julia that there were plenty of things for her to discover at the

Victoria and Albert. They have an award-winning program in which they provide kids with backpacks that are filled with plans for exploring different areas of the museum.

Julia opted for the one that led her into an exposition of upper-class life in Georgian Britain and was drawn in by the search for figures in paintings on display. Julia is a kid unafraid to say when she is bored, but the exercise seemed to truly engage her. Each backpack journey took only about forty-five minutes, so when she finished the first she asked to do a second. She was less impressed by the exploration of medieval times, which involved a funny hat that she had to match with a figure in a tapestry.

But never mind. The V&A was a big hit. I was starting to think that I was successfully performing my fatherly duty in introducing my child to history and culture.

The best was still to come. On a perfect fall Monday, I had my finest day ever with Julia. From Waterloo station, we caught the train out to Slough — rhymes with "plough," if you were wondering (as I learned when I tried to buy a ticket to "Slew") — and made the quick change to Windsor, the station a conveniently short walk from the castle. This was to be full-on royal spectacle.

The Queen's weekend pad is the largest and oldest occupied palace in the world, built by her ancestor William the Conqueror roughly a millennium ago and regularly expanded, renovated, and laid siege to by a long list of notables. Now visited by more than a million people a year.

Julia lapped it up.

Compliments to the designers of the audio tours, who offer a version that is specially designed for kids. We were able to walk beside each other and get an age-appropriate commentary as we looked at basically the same sights. Both offer the same introduction from the Prince of Wales.

"Daddy, did you know why the Round Tower was built on a hill?" she asked, then provided the answer.

"Do you know why it has its own well?"

Kids were told to watch out for tiny toy soldiers, who were on guard throughout the displays — something else to engage their interest as they try to find as many as they can.

I credited her fondness for history to the CBBC show *Horrible Histories*. It's a true treasure for parents, and is full of quirky British humour about people dying in stupid ways and murdering others in creatively brutal techniques. I loved the song-and-dance number they did for the first four King Georges: "I was the sad one, I was the bad one, I was the mad one, and I was the fat one. We were born to rule over you...."

For all its solemnity and tradition, a scent of silliness wafts through British royalty. What can you say about an institution where the highest honour, the Most Noble Order of the Garter, is associated with a randy piece of women's undergarments?

The Garter Gang has been headquartered at Windsor for six hundred years. In St. George's Hall, rebuilt after the 1992 fire, heraldic shields representing the members cover the ceiling. As Julia pointed out, the handful of blank shields represent knights who have been "degraded" by the monarch — kicked out for disreputable behaviour. Kaiser Wilhelm II was given the bum's rush for waging war on Britain — his being a grandson of Queen Victoria was insufficient defence. Emperor Hirohito similarly got the big adios, but was rehabilitated after the Second World War and got his shield place back.

As we walked out, she giggled at the sight of a guard in a bearskin hat. She had seen them before when looking through the gates at Buckingham Palace, but here was one close enough to touch.

The bearskin hat stands proudly as one of the silliest of military anachronisms. Evidently when they were invented in the seventeenth century, the idea was to make soldiers look taller and more imposing on the battlefield. Even after the impracticality of the modified cone-head look became evident, they lived on for ceremonial uniforms. You feel for the poor grenadier who has to wear it even on the hottest day, occasionally rendered unconscious after hours of standing at attention with an 18-inch-tall, 1.5-pound remnant of a Canadian black bear perched on his noggin.

Animal rights activists periodically complain that bears are giving their lives for the sake of a goofy hat, but an artificial substitute has never been found. The Ministry of Defence says the skins are now provided by Canadian Inuit hunters, who shoot the bears as part of a cull to control numbers.

None of this really mattered to Julia. I urged her to pose next to him for a picture, which she did, holding a miniature crown that she had purchased minutes earlier during the inescapable visit to the gift shop.

This stereotypical tourist picture became one of her most prized possessions from London — a six-year-old girl holding a plastic crown, posing sassily next to an impassive grenadier. As is customary, the hat disguised his eyes but his chin did not yet seem to have felt the scrape of a razor blade.

We said little during the train ride back into the city, but as we sat next to each other, comfortable, content, and happy, my heart was full. She and I had never been so close, never enjoyed each other's company quite so much. All because of a few hours at a royal tourist trap.

The glow faded somewhat as Waterloo station approached and I started feeling a dull throb in my teeth. By the time we arrived back at the flat it had expanded into a sharp headache. Our medicine cabinet had not yet been stocked and we had been unable to find Tylenol in London. We still had some of Julia's baby medicine, Tempra, so I took a swig of it and tried to sleep. But in the middle of the night, I was awakened by the feeling that someone was power drilling into my left cheek. By morning I saw specks of blood in my phlegm.

I was to be taking Julia to a playground in Primrose Hill to meet some of her classmates, but instead we had to make our way to the clinic where I had had the foresight to sign us up earlier.

My iPhone more or less kept her busy as we waited ninety minutes to see the doctor. During this time Julia only asked about a dozen times, "Daddy, when will it be our turn?" Not so bad for a six-year-old. Allowing her to download several games managed to pass the time.

The pleasant doctor confirmed my suspicion that I had a sinus infection and prescribed antibiotics and painkillers. He made a bit of time for Julia as well, agreeing to take her temperature with a sensor in her ear.

Now late for the crucial play date, I held off getting my drugs and instead flagged down a cab to take us to Primrose Hill. I was the only father in attendance and knew none of the mothers. The girls had already gathered into groups and Julia's favoured playmate, the Swedish girl Nilla, was not there.

As I made awkward conversation with a couple of the mothers, I saw Julia standing equally awkwardly on the fringes of some of the games. Within minutes she ran over to me in tears.

"None of them are playing with me!"

I had no good solution, other than to urge her to keep trying, which she did with all the enthusiasm of a kid going to the dentist. My heart was breaking, watching her by herself, even as my head throbbed. After about thirty minutes, the girls and their mothers started to drift away to go to their other appointments and Julia and I gave up.

In a weak attempt to make her feel better, I took her to PizzaExpress for supper, but ate little myself as my exploding head gave me little appetite.

With the help of painkillers, the next day offered more promise. A play date was arranged with Nilla, and we headed off to a playground to meet her and her mother, Ulrika. But the skies were lowering and it had been raining on and off all day. En route to the park, Julia wiped out on her scooter, the wheels slipping out from under her on some wet leaves — a rare event as she was normally very adept.

"I need to go home to change, Daddy!" she wailed. She had scraped her thigh and her pants were wet and muddy. No choice. We turned around and headed back to the flat. What next?

After a quick change, once again late, I flagged a cab. When we arrived, Nilla was already busy playing with her older sister, Olivia, with mother, Ulrika, watching. To my relief, Julia readily and easily joined the two Swedish girls.

But within minutes the drizzle turned into a driving rain. It was pouring — no possible way to continue.

Ulrika suggested we adjourn to their house, which was close by, so that the girls could have more time together. It was a tall, skinny, plain house with four bedrooms — each floor with a tiny footprint, but collectively much larger than Buckland and about three times the rent.

While the girls played upstairs, she explained how both she and her husband worked for a pharmaceutical company, but he was on the managerial fast track so she took a leave in order for him to accept the London posting.

Another "trailing spouse." But it did not seem to bother her that her career was being set aside in order to further his. She said she appreciated the chance to spend more time with their daughters and to go to the gym and generally to make the best of it. Somehow, although complete strangers, we made a couple of hours pass pleasantly and in the process I succeeded in getting Julia some serious playtime with a girl who seemed sympatico.

Single parenting was hard work, as if I did not already know it, but we seemed to be coping.

As I checked off the list of things to do with a kid in London, there was a glaring omission: she had yet to go to the theatre, probably because she had shown zero interest. But I convinced her to give a puppet show a try.

I suggested to the Canadian mom, Roxane, to join us with her two girls: Zoë (Julia's classmate, the same girl who offered a helpful hand with our early swimming crisis) and Kayla. The plan was to take a canal boat ride from Camden Lock down to the theatre, grab some lunch, and see the puppet show. Naturally it rained, but at least the boat had a roof.

As we cruised along the picturesque canal, Julia spent most of her time on my iPhone and taking the occasional picture of herself. She particularly enjoyed the view as we went through a tunnel, taking pics that showed only her reflection in the darkened window.

Lunch was in a pub across the street from the theatre. As is the way with service in London, the guy took our order in lots of time but the food took forever to come. It finally arrived approximately ten minutes before showtime, meaning that we had to frantically force-feed the children and then run them out the door in order to not miss the beginning.

The Puppet Theatre Barge, inside a former canal boat now tied up at the dock, is a study in making the most of limited space. Somehow they managed to get several dozen seats into a tiny room in steerage below decks while also leaving sufficient space for a small stage for the puppets.

Puppetry can be pretty edgy. The first show was all about a character called Captain Grimey, an unwashed sea dog billed as the dirtiest mariner to ever sail the Seven Seas. No one can stand to be within whiffing distance until he meets a Golden Dolphin who teaches him to clean up his act. Second was a retelling of the Three Little Pigs, in which the wolf has a knowing smile that reminded adults of a certain breed of public relations guy. Despite the slickness, he still got his in the end, unlike in real life, where the PR guy ends up with the girl and the big salary.

Both shows were popular with all three girls. More importantly, I had managed to give Julia an outing with other kids, while also starting to build what turned out to be one of our most profound connections in London.

Halloween loomed the upcoming Monday, the same day as Isabella's return. My fatherly duty was to get Julia ready for that most important day for a kid.

Hampstead is replete with charming and expensive little shops up and down the high street, and on little pedestrian-only pathways like Flask Walk. Isabella had directed me to a fairy store, where I was charged with getting my daughter's costume. She had been reading a series of fairy books and decided that she wanted to dress up as Trixie the Halloween Fairy. We were on the hunt for a pair of wings. Several options were available in the store, some of which were expensive enough to make me think they would actually get the child airborne. I was able to convince Julia to pick a cheaper option. She in turn convinced me to shell out for a wand and some glitter dust to adorn her face.

Mission accomplished, we stopped in a coffee shop for a latte for me, a hot chocolate for her, and pastries for us both. She barely touched her drink, because I failed to notice that it was made with dark chocolate, not her preference.

Julia was regularly losing teeth during this period and I asked her about the status of her latest wiggler. She reached into her mouth to check and out it came, as she laughed uproariously and held it out for inspection while I admired the newest gap in her mouth. I snapped a picture and sent it off to Isabella. Having visited the fairy store, Daddy was now also charged with arranging a visit from the tooth fairy that night.

My brief feeling of accomplishment was deflated as soon as we returned to Buckland. Julia pulled her wings out of the bag, tried them on and decided immediately that it was all wrong.

"It's too much like a baby," she asserted tearfully.

"But ... but ... but," I responded with fatherly decisiveness.

"NO, DADDY!"

Okay, time for a quick readjustment.

"How about a witch?"

"A witch?" Sniffle, but tears slowing somewhat.

"Yeah, sure — a witch. Nothing babyish about a witch!"

After a few minutes of negotiation, she bought it. Luckily I knew we had something that approximated a witch's hat that I had bought earlier. Just needed a cape of some sort and we would be good.

Back on track. For the moment.

After she went to sleep that night, I did as my parents had always done for me: slipped a few coins (including a pound coin in this case) under her pillow as the gift from the tooth fairy.

Around midnight, the phone rang. Isabella. She asked about my tooth fairy strategy and was unimpressed.

"That's all? Just some coins under her pillow and nothing else?"

She believed in making it a special experience, with the fairy leaving decorations and notes and a larger amount of money.

"You just don't seem very interested," she said accusingly, which immediately set me off and we were into another one of those angry, transatlantic phone calls.

"We've asked Julia to move away from the little school she loves to another country. She deserves to have a lot more fun."

I had no argument because she was right.

The call ended with a frosty "*ciao*."

Bedraggled and sleep deprived, I at least knew that Julia had something to look forward to the next day because Roxane had come to the rescue with an invitation for Julia to attend a Halloween party at her flat. Her husband, Dave, was an engineer with an oil company and had a true expatriate deal — that is, they had enough money to sustain a lifestyle similar to home, unlike us. True Canadians, though, they were unfailingly thoughtful, helpful, and without airs.

Their place on Fitzjohn's was a spotless, airy, and newly refinished two-bedroom, with access to a garden out back. Likely almost double our rent.

She was perhaps the most organized mother I had ever met. A chef, she always had healthy food for the kids and had prepared a full afternoon of activities for a handful of girls from the Royal, including a trampoline out back.

To my surprise and relief, Julia agreed to stay by herself, freeing me for a couple of hours.

"Don't worry. Take a break," said Roxane. A good woman.

Our circle of friends was starting to grow, giving me hope that Julia could have a play date while her mother and father went out on an adult date. That is, if her mother and father did not divorce.

I hiked up to St. Dorothy's Convent on Frognal to get Julia registered for Sunday school. In the house where de Gaulle spent part of the war, I was met at the door by Sister Pauline — a heavy-set woman in her sixties who walked with difficulty, wheezing, ankles swollen.

In her tiny and cluttered office, I handed over a copy of Julia's baptismal certificate to prove she was a good Catholic (despite a spotty record of Mass attendance), bought the appropriate textbook for First Communion preparations and asked whether there would be time for my daughter to qualify for the sacrament.

"We shall see," said the sister. "She must learn the prayers."

Her accent sounded vaguely Germanic, but as it turned out she was born in Malta and had spent many years teaching in Italy, not far from Treviso. She seemed kindly, which was reassuring as I was about to hand over my daughter for her religious education.

The second Saturday of our daddy-daughter period arrived and I was flat out of ideas. Spent the morning cleaning up the flat, doing more organization, and generally feeling not very good about the world. By midafternoon, I hauled Julia out the door to another attraction: the Museum of London. Her interest was restrained, which is to say she had no interest whatsoever.

But at least she enjoyed riding the Tube. We were starting to learn the stops on the Jubilee line very well as we hopped aboard at Swiss Cottage heading south. She had quickly learned to mimic the announcement: "The next station is Baker Street. Change here for the Bakerloo, Hammersmith and City, Circle, and Metropolitan lines." Rendered in her little girl voice in a perfect accent: "The next station is Bakuh Street, change he-uh for the Bakuh-loo, Hammeruhsmith and City, Sih-cul, and Metropolitan lines." It became our party trick for years to have her show off her English accent for Canadian friends.

She swung around the poles, hopped up on the pads at the end of the cars where standers can lean, and generally just goofed around. Our Tube rides became one of our most effective bonding exercises.

The Museum of London is well organized, with plenty of kid-friendly displays, and Julia was utterly bored. Online they were promoting a sixties dance party for kids. We searched all over before finding it, only to discover that we were the only ones who showed up to the party. The facilitator was so desperately pleased to see participants that she ran over with a big smile, offering to dress us in sixties clothing. I opted for a leather jacket and a Beatles cap.

They played "The Twist" and I tried to get Julia dancing. When I was a small kid and the song was current, I provided endless amusement to adults by shaking my tiny butt in a rough facsimile of the dance. The attraction was lost on my daughter, however, and she stared at me quizzically as I tried vainly with stiff, middle-aged hips to reproduce those magic moments of half a century earlier.

As we were walking through the museum afterward, my cellphone rang. It was Isabella, so I handed the phone to Julia to talk. The signal was poor and the conversation was brief. I sent an email to Isabella, signing it as Julia, but she responded, writing that it did not sound like her at all.

Sunday was our final full day together before Mommy's return, presuming Mommy was returning. I managed to miss the news that the clocks were supposed to roll back an hour, but my new clock radio was smart enough to do it by itself, so we managed to get up at the appointed hour. It was another chapter in the book of religious irony: the agnostic father taking his daughter to Mass and then to instruction for First Communion.

St. Dorothy's Convent was a short walk from St. Mary's, down a steep walkway that led off Holly Walk to Frognal. The parents dropping off their kids were international, impeccably dressed in expensive jeans, and clearly affluent. Scooters lined the small courtyard by the entrance. A frazzled and frowning younger nun herded the kids to the correct classrooms. Julia's was a large, airy room with large windows that opened onto an internal garden where de Gaulle must have sat and seethed during his exile from France sixty years earlier.

Julia's classmates were uniformly grim, clearly indicating that they would much prefer to be somewhere else on a Sunday morning. When Sister Pauline limped in, I made a point of bringing Julia over to introduce her.

"Ah, you are the girl whose grandparents come from Treviso!" she said in her unidentifiably mid-European accent.

"Well, take a seat."

Julia whispered in my ear, "What is she saying? I can't understand."

"Just do your best," was my ineffectual advice.

There was a small lounge with a sofa just outside the classroom and I came equipped with a *Sunday Times*, which made the hour pass pleasantly.

When the door opened at the end and the other children ran for the exits, I asked Sister Pauline how Julia did.

"Very well! She was the only one to put up her hand when I asked what you get at Communion."

I raised my eyebrows and looked at my daughter with a mixture of pride and suspicion.

As we walked out of St. Dorothy's, Julia's eyes welled up.

"Daddy, I can't understand what she's saying! How can I learn?"

"If you can't understand her, why were you the only one to answer the question about communion?"

"That was the only thing."

"Okay, well maybe you will get used to her accent. Besides, this is the only place we have for you to take the course for First Communion."

Problem solved, we hiked back down the hill.

For some reason I was obsessed with getting the flat utterly spotless, so I frantically vacuumed (or "hoovered," as I was learning the Brits say) and dusted as though I was expecting a Royal to drop in. Perhaps it was a gesture of love or perhaps a passive-aggressive point about the need to keep our home clean. Either way, I knew it was a futile exercise because it would be a mess within minutes of Isabella's return. As we went to bed, we knew Mommy would be flying all night across the Atlantic.

Monday marked not only the return to school but also Halloween. I got Julia out the door to catch the 268 bus just in time. And there was Isabella getting out of a taxi. Julia enthusiastically ran into her arms. My wife and I awkwardly hugged, anger still lingering from the tooth fairy dispute.

I lugged her three large bags up to the flat and then, sweating and panting, got Julia on the bus to school, somehow avoiding a late arrival, while Isabella climbed into bed to start recovering from her journey. She hated the transatlantic flight and would take up to a week to get her sleep patterns back to normal.

I chose to walk all the way from Hampstead to the bureau, downhill all the way and a form of meditation that I knew I would always miss when this gig was done.

It was a historic day. The United Nations declared that the world's population had reached seven billion souls, symbolically designating a Filipina girl named Danica May Camacho, born that day in Manila, as the seven-billionth baby. Pulling a story together took all day. Dan was off and I had a freelancer filling in, which meant that I needed to stay in the office until I was assured that the story had been safely delivered via FTP to Vancouver.

By late afternoon, I noted that it was already getting dark. I had been warned about the shortness of the daylight hours in fall and wintertime. Hard to believe that London was actually farther north than my colder home in Canada. Isabella always hated the lack of sunlight back home and her anger about being forced to the U.K. would not be assuaged by an even earlier arrival of darkness in her new, unwanted home.

While I worked, Isabella supervised the all-important Halloween routine. Back home, it is known as one of the worst rush hours of the year as frantic parents desperately scramble back from work to get their kids out the door.

Somehow the tradition never took hold in London. We did some research, asking other North American parents how it worked in England, and were warned that there were only a few pockets of the city where homeowners would welcome costumed kids at the door demanding candy.

Isabella took Julia to hook up with an American mom named Adele, who advised that Flask Walk, the quaint lane off Hampstead High Street, was a good place to start. They learned that the London style of shelling out to trick-or-treaters seemed to have been inspired by Scrooge. Those few who would give out candies were invariably miserly, with one small treat per kid.

Fed up, Isabella advised Julia to grab a couple extra at the next house, reasoning that only someone with a heart of stone could deny a darling six-year-old girl dressed as the world's cutest witch.

She was wrong. The pissy Londoner demanded that our little girl put back the excess.

As Julia's eyes welled up, Isabella acted to save the occasion, popping into a corner store to buy six bags of her favourite crisps (potato chips for us North Americans) in order to fill her otherwise meagre loot bag. London might have a wealth of history, museums, and theatres, but, as Isabella reminded me, the British capital was a poor place for kids on Halloween.

We were now two months into our time together in London and few things were going right.

Top of the list of irritants was our apartment. Isabella had taken to calling our London *pied-à-terre* Fuckland Buckland. The bed we slept in was awful, squeaking with a cheap mattress — not a good thing for someone with a bad back. My assiduous cleaning of the flat did little to relieve its unrelenting grimness. And finances were already tight.

"I think you need to ask for more money," said Isabella. A request I knew was futile.

I had unsuccessfully settled my wife and daughter in a new country, taken them from our renovated, roomy home with a backyard and a lifestyle where we could pay the bills, save a bit, and take the occasional vacation in the south, and plopped them into a dumpy, expensive flat, where we were about to go into the hole and where we knew nobody.

Now, to add to the hilarity, I was about to go on my first road trip.

Chapter Thirteen

I first stepped onto Greek territory during my big backpacking trip in 1984. After an all-night ferry from Italy, I landed exhausted on the island of Corfu and promptly made the mistake of downing a gleaming carafe of tap water at a restaurant: so refreshing, so profoundly dumb.

Within hours my guts were grumbling. Fearing an explosion, I rushed to a pharmacy in search of anti-diarrhea medication. Too late. On the way back to the hostel, my ass cut loose a stream of sludge into my shorts. Corfu was where I learned the true meaning of incontinence and never again risked foreign tap water.

In all, I spent a month in Greece, where the messy-pants debut was followed up with many days of wonderment, joy, and inspiring sights: the Parthenon, and the crystal blue waters, the exquisite beaches, and the glorious breasts of the Swedish sunbathers. It all gladdened the heart of a young Canadian lad.

Aside from the Acropolis, Athens left me cold — it seemed dirty, loud, and unfriendly.

But twenty years later, it won me over when I returned to cover the Summer Olympics. The city had been made over, much of it at the last minute, and now was gorgeous, sophisticated, and welcoming. The Parthenon, illuminated against the cloudless night sky, was surely one of the finest, most timeless sights the world could offer.

The Olympics were such a point of cultural pride for the Greeks. On closing night, I was in a bar where volunteers were dancing, singing, and crying. I wrote that there could be no better place in the world to be on that night.

One day near the end of the games, I spotted the leader of the Greek opposition party, George Papandreou, walking through the press area. Knowing he'd studied for a time in Toronto, I approached him and asked for an interview, to which he readily agreed. Opposition leaders are so much easier to get in front of the camera.

Already there was talk that this small nation had overreached with the games, spent far too much on a party that it could not afford. I asked him whether it was a bad idea. No Greek politician with any ambition would ever admit in those heady days that it had all been a big mistake. And he did not: "I believe for Athens it has been a worthy investment. For Greece it has been a worthy investment, and we will be able to benefit not only psychologically, but financially also," he said with fervent and certain patriotism.

By the fall of 2011, Papandreou was prime minister, presiding over a country that could no longer pay its bills, where years of huge deficits had grown the national debt to an unsustainable level. Tax evasion by the rich was rampant.

Foreign lenders, led by the Germans, were bailing out Greece with multibillion euro loans, demanding huge cuts in government spending in return. The land of Plato, Pericles, and Melina Mercouri was being spanked for years of overspending and underbudgeting. Greek bonds were downgraded so many times they were valued at somewhere between gum wrappers and toilet paper.

Civil servants were being fired by the thousands, government services slashed. There were strikes, shortages, and riots in the centre of Athens. This ancient nation was now teetering and bankruptcy loomed, as did a withdrawal from the eurozone with consequences that could be calamitous for the world economy.

In late October, eurozone leaders agreed, teeth grinding, to put up another €130 billion in bailout money and to force lenders to agree to slash the debt. In return, Greece had to cut even deeper. They sent Papandreou home to pass it through Parliament, only to see him decide out of nowhere to call a national referendum on the package, which was sure to lose and blow up all their hard work and concessions.

This Greek drama was now drawing me back to Athens, even as I was struggling to keep my family life together in London.

As a trip to Greece loomed, the new Canadian High Commissioner to the U.K., former B.C. premier Gordon Campbell, invited the local Canadian press corps to join him for lunch at his official residence on Grosvenor Square. These kinds of invitations are one of the perks of a foreign correspondent gig. We were all Canadians far from home, stationed in one of the world's great cities, so it made sense for us all to gather for a convivial sharing of our good fortune.

In the pre-lunch conversations, a couple of the correspondents with far more experience in exotic locations shared stories from the road. The best was about flying with a rinky-dink airline in some desperately poor part of the world. It seemed that the pilot and co-pilot chose to leave the aircraft on auto so that they could both depart the cockpit at the same time to take a nap in first class — only to discover that they had locked themselves out. Almost certainly apocryphal, but a great yarn.

I had nothing to match that one, and chose not to share my story of filling my pants in Corfu.

Lunch was an elegant, three-course affair with formal service and fine Canadian wine. All very civilized — a taste of the higher levels of diplomatic life.

On the taxi ride back to the office shortly afterward, my phone buzzed with an email from Vancouver: Book a flight to Athens. Almost simultaneously there was a note from Isabella: "I'm really sad."

My stomach contracted. I called her on my cellphone from the hallway of the office.

"How long are you going for?" she asked in a flat voice.

"No idea. A few days, I guess."

"Great. We just got here and there's so much weighing on us and now you're leaving Julia and me alone."

It was true. She never wanted to come to London, never asked for the lifestyle of the spouse of a foreign correspondent.

Now utterly distracted, I stumbled into the office to write my story for the day and to prepare for departure the following morning.

It was a doubly weird week because the British clocks had gone back an hour, while in North America the switch to standard time was still a week away. It meant a disorienting four hours difference with Toronto instead of the usual five. I checked and double-checked *Global National's* airtime in Toronto — 6:30 p.m. Eastern. This was important because I would need to do a rare live hit into the show and had to hop a taxi down to a studio on the south bank of the Thames, about forty minutes away.

I left in time to get there at least forty-five minutes early for my 10:30 BST hit. At 9:25 p.m., in a taxi, my phone rang with Vancouver on the line.

"We can't see you in the chair," she said.

"Uh … I'm not on the air for more than an hour," I said with a touch of dread.

"Sean, our first show goes to the east coast at 6:30 Atlantic Time, *5:30 Eastern.*"

My breathing grew short and I felt the blood rushing to my head. If, sitting at her desk in Vancouver, she had a window into my cab rushing through the darkness of London she would see a sweating, blushing, and shamed dope.

Luckily for me, she laughed. Loudly.

"He's not going to make it," she shouted to someone.

"Ahhhhhhhh," I gurgled. "I am *so sorry.* That will never never never happen again."

I was in plenty of time for my hit for Toronto and did one more at 11:30 p.m. before heading back to the flat to pack, tiptoeing in after midnight.

Isabella was asleep on the lower bunk in Julia's room.

I went into the kitchen to discover that Isabella had actually taken the time to make a lovely supper, which I'd missed — my plate now sitting in the fridge. I washed the dishes, cleaned up the kitchen, and headed into bed where I found Isabella now awake, sitting up and looking at her computer.

She was grim and cold, angry and tearful.

"I never wanted this," she said wearily. "I'm doing my best — for Julia, and for you — but I'm so sad. I hope this will get easier."

She turned over on her side, back to me. The bed rocked and squeaked.

"This fucking bed."

"Please don't give up," I pleaded.

"I have nothing to do, no friends. Do not even try to touch me," she said, getting up and running weeping out of the room.

Exhausted, drained, and out of ideas, I fell asleep.

I woke up before the alarm, despite my fatigue and only sleeping a few hours. Isabella had returned to the bed in the night and was asleep beside me. As the alarm went off I gently suggested that she could go into the shower first because she needed to take Julia to school and my flight was not until noon.

After a sleepless and stressful night, she managed to drag herself out of bed and make her way into the bathroom. Equally fatigued, I went into Julia's room to wake her.

"I DON'T WANNA GO TO SCHOOL!" she wailed.

I was now being pounded from both sides, but I could not complain — my wife would just respond that I had asked for it. Getting them both out the door was like pushing a boulder up a hill, but finally they left, only a few minutes late.

I threw together my suitcase and headed for Heathrow. My first big trip in a trouble zone and I was facing full-on discontent and rebellion at home. My own little Eurocrisis.

Upon boarding the jet, an email arrived from Isabella, advising me that she had ordered a £1,200 bed.

"I have to have this for my back. Global is going to pay for it. If I have to live in London, at least we can have a comfortable bed."

Almost simultaneously an email arrived from Stu. (Dan was on holiday and Stu was flying to Athens from Prague to be my cameraman-editor.) The BBC was reporting that Prime Minister Papandreou was about to resign and call for a coalition government.

Both Greece and my family were in debt, angry, chaotic, and facing disaster.

I turned off my phone for takeoff.

It was dark in Athens when I landed. When my iPhone came to life, it buzzed with the latest news that Papandreou was now backing off the referendum but would be facing a confidence vote in Parliament the next day in which his government could fall and create a whole different kind of mess — elections would delay the delivery of the latest bailout money. Democracy in the nation that invented the word could force it into bankruptcy.

Anxious to do some reporting as soon as possible, I started quizzing the taxi driver en route downtown.

He had little English, but was able to say, "Little guys hurt ... rich get all."

Eager to demonstrate my mythical mastery of social media, I pulled out my phone to shoot a vlog — turning the camera on my face in an invariably unflattering framing to expound on all I had learned in my thirty minutes in Greece, travelling from the airport to the centre, panning from time to time outside the cab to capture blurry shots of lights passing by.

I reflected on my memories of the Olympics and of George Papandreou's wistfully optimistic comment from 2004. I also quoted from my six-word interview with my unilingual taxi driver. My insightful coverage of the Greek economic crisis was underway.

I only had to press send to fire it off to the online team back home. A miracle.

We were booked into the Hotel Grande Bretagne right on Syntagma Square, in the heart of everything — opposite the Parliament and right where all the riots had been happening. Hotel management told us we could shoot from our balcony — unless there was trouble, in which case everyone would be ordered inside with windows closed and blinds drawn. For some reason they believed that standing with a TV camera and a light above mobs of rioters might be problematic.

The centre was blocked off to traffic, so I got out and walked the last few blocks. There were cops in riot gear everywhere and the streets were teeming with activity, but no sign of trouble.

Stu had already arrived. We were close to deadline and had already decided we would just try to speak to a couple of people in the square to get a flavour of the feelings in play, shoot an ad-libbed stand-up describing what we were seeing, and quickly edit them together to send back in time for the first edition of *Global National*.

Back home, shooting "streeters" in Toronto was one of my least-favourite tasks. Panhandling for clips, I used to call it — an often-humiliating exercise where middle-aged guys in suits (i.e., me) approach wary pedestrians with a smile and a question and are often brushed off like a pest. A wise cameraman once told me that if your story cannot stand without streeters you do not have a story. But that does not stop us.

Typically, they are more of a production device than a journalistic exercise — clips and sound are inserted that help keep up the pace of your story and are a nod to the notion that you are taking the pulse of the average guy, rather than just putting up a bunch of talking heads. By "talking heads" I mean smart people who may have actually given some thought and research to the subject at hand and know what they are talking about. Far better, in the eyes of many news directors and consultants, to stick a microphone in the face of the first person who will stop and face the camera and deliver something that resembles a comment in ten seconds or less.

But that was Toronto. Now I was a Foreign Correspondent™. Now it was true journalism because I was taking the pulse of the Greek nation in the midst of a crisis.

At the east end of the square, opposite the Parliament buildings, we found a likely candidate. He was perhaps thirty, tall, lean, unshaven, with the remnants of a cigarette butt in his fingers — staring impassively at the commotion around him, exuding disdain. A Greek intellectual, I surmised.

"Do you speak English?" I asked earnestly.

He gave us a long look before nodding and agreeing to talk.

"What do you think of George Papandreou?"

"Ah. Our prime minister who speaks perfect English. A fine product of the international elite," he said, oozing contempt.

We spoke to a couple of other people, but his comment was the most telling.

Streeters gathered, stand-up shot, Stu edited our little report on his laptop, sent it out via the magic of FTP to Vancouver, and our job for the night was done.

The next day would see the confidence vote late in the evening, right around airtime back home. We would build the back half of the story in advance, searching for voices beyond the average guy in the street. Instead, it would be the average merchant on the street.

Stu and I hiked down Mitropoleos Street, off Syntagma, and came upon a tiny jeweller's shop owned by the Makriadis brothers, George and John. George was sitting on a high stool, unshaven, elbow on the display case, huge belly hanging over his belt. He was both weary and angry. Their shop had been frequently shut down because of the troubles on the square, and even when it was open, the tourists were not coming. Tear gas, riots, and political turmoil tended to mask the many charms of Athens for visitors.

What did he think of the people running his country?

"You can take them all and use them for dog food."

He was most upset about the damage to Greece's reputation.

"You must tell the people in Canada that Greeks are not lazy. We're hard-working," George said, wagging a finger. "Think of the Greeks you know in Canada — they all work hard."

Interview done, John brought out some of their hand-made jewellery. They were anxious to do a deal if they could and invited me to come back and pick up something for the wife. Under the circumstances, I was not sure a present from my Greek trip would go over very well.

Contacts from back home put me in touch with Constantine Katsigiannis, an elegant, honey-voiced lawyer who was president of the Hellenic-Canadian Chamber of Commerce. He welcomed us into his wood-panelled office, offering coffee and a high-level analysis.

Katsigiannis shared the jeweller's view that Greek work habits were being unfairly maligned, citing statistics that showed they were diligent. "The problem is a bloated civil service that we cannot afford," he said. "And to a lesser extent tax avoidance."

Not paying taxes was an unofficial national sport in Greece, with estimates of up to €30 *billion* uncollected every year. Avoidance had deep cultural roots in history. During the centuries of Ottoman occupation, denying the Turkish taxman his due was a statement of patriotic resistance.

The practice persisted after independence. The *Globe and Mail* reported a few months before my arrival that rich folks in the tonier parts of Athens feared the sight of helicopters overheard, wondering if they were investigators for the revenue department taking pictures of backyard pools at the homes of Greeks whose declared income was suspiciously low to afford such luxuries. Naturally, the ones most successful at dodging the taxman were the wealthiest and best connected.

I wondered about the extravagance of the 2004 Olympics and if they were the first step on the road to disaster. Katsigiannis's answer was nuanced.

"I don't think so. They showed off Greece at its best," he said. "But the facilities were wasted and mismanaged — never used properly."

Neither the jeweller nor the lawyer was optimistic, no matter what happened with the current government.

"We are doomed to continue in a very, very hard situation," said George Makriadis.

"It's a big question here, how long this will last — and how low the economy will go," added Katsigiannis.

Their interviews were to be the back half of my story that night. The top, to be delivered live, would be the result of the confidence motion. If Papandreou's government fell, Greece could be defaulting within days.

As the voting started after midnight, I stood on a balcony overlooking Syntagma Square, with the Parliament buildings off to the side. In the distance, the gloriously illuminated Parthenon sat shimmering and golden in the clear night sky. In front of me, behind the live camera, was a hotel room jammed with other reporters, watching the results on Greek TV, waiting for their turn to go live to Japan, Germany, or wherever.

The counting was still underway as I spoke live to Toronto at half-past midnight, looking past the camera at the TV, trying to discern what was happening as the commentary played out in a language I did not speak.

The result did not come until about 1:00 a.m., with Papandreou barely surviving, although he had suggested in his final speech to Parliament before the vote that he might step aside in favour of a new coalition government. It seemed he was likely finished, but Greece would not go bankrupt that night. Another live hit to Toronto with the news and then it was off to bed.

With the acute crisis having passed, the challenge for Saturday was to find an astute Greek analyst to explain what had happened and what was next. But most seemed to have the day off. We tried to reach an English-speaking journalist who I had been following on Twitter, but he was not available. We were bailed out by a fellow Canadian, *Globe and Mail* reporter Graeme Smith, who recommended a former finance minister, Stefanos Manos, and kindly passed along his cell number.

Manos answered his phone and readily invited us to his house to speak. It was a long taxi ride to the northern part of Athens, past the Olympic stadium from the 2004 games, up and up winding streets with the houses growing ever larger. The northern hills, where the air is cooler and cleaner, is where the Athenian elites call home.

Through the gates to Manos's house we spotted tennis courts and impeccably groomed landscapes. A tall, elegant man with a navy pullover sweater, Manos looked like a university president or a retired captain of industry who would have been at home at Harvard or a posh men's club in London.

By the time we met Manos, Papandreou's call for a new coalition government to implement the bailout package had already been rebuffed by the major opposition party. Manos, in near perfect English, told us that the prime minister was finished.

"He has to be replaced, number one. Number two, we need a good — whatever that means — prime minister who will lead us over the next year. That's what we need."

He suggested that it would have to be someone from outside politics — perhaps economist Lucas Papademos (who, in fact, got the job a few days later).

Whatever happened, had to happen quickly.

"Time is running out. The bomb is ticking," said Manos.

On the way back to central Athens, we had the taxi driver take us by the Olympic park. In 2004, there was a grand thoroughfare of white arches, beneath which thousands strolled between the venues. The arches were still there, but the place was almost deserted; the pavement was cracked, with weeds jutting through. A couple of guys were racing remote-controlled toy cars — their buzzing so loud you could scarcely hear yourself think. Some of the athletic venues, including the main stadium, were still being used, but a weightlifting facility and a softball stadium had been abandoned. Athens did get a new airport, subway line, and improved roads out of the games, but somehow the promise of it all seemed to have been squandered.

Our Greek adventure was at an end. On Sunday, Stu flew back to Prague and I headed for London, wondering what kind of reception I could expect.

Chapter Fourteen

To my relief, Isabella greeted me with great warmth and love, the anger of a few days earlier miraculously dissipated. I had no idea what had changed and did not ask. But I was fairly certain I was not in the clear.

She had taken the advice of another Canadian mom from the school and sought out the Hampstead Women's Club. One of the many community organizations that brings together some of the thousands of women yanked away from their homes and careers to follow a husband's ambitions, it's a place to make friends, support each other, and find new outlets for their talents. It was a lifeline. Isabella joined a singing group led by an Australian opera singer named Bernadette, a particularly gifted trailing spouse who came to London because of her husband's job in banking. Music had always been part of Isabella's life and lifting her voice in song was a boost to her spirit. And there was the lovely sewing school called Little Hands, where she started taking sewing lessons, a skill she'd always wanted to nurture. So enthusiastic was she that she encouraged other expatriate moms and daughters to join. She was rising to the challenge of living in London and searching for ways to make the best of things, while also building a social support network for us.

Meanwhile, my work kept opening new doors.

London has the world market cornered on grand and ornate halls, vestiges of past imperial glories. I had spent a career covering countless speeches in characterless hotels, but it seemed every time I attended a talk in the British capital I was rewarded with a room where the scenery far exceeded the quality of the speechifying.

The Drapers Hall oozes British grandeur: dark wood, lush drapery, giant paintings of past luminaries. We went to cover a speech by the governor of the Bank of Canada, Mark Carney, later to take over the Bank of England. The building was more interesting than his talk and we did not file a story.

But our day was not done. We were reassigned to report on an international pissing match among prominent leaders. It seemed that the president of France, Nicolas Sarkozy, had been overheard telling Barack Obama that he detested the prime minister of Israel, Benjamin Netanyahu. "Such a liar!" Sarkozy had reportedly carped.

In cases such as this, where there is a paucity of video, we would do a "look live" — a taped stand-up in which we would feign speaking live to the anchor and give our learned take on the unseemly name-calling among the world's elite, based on our extensive research of agency wire copy.

Having been away for several days the previous week, I was feeling the pressure to get home in time to have supper with Isabella and Julia. So once my contribution was taped, I rushed out to catch a bus back to the flat — a bit early for a change.

As I lifted the first forkload of spaghetti to my lips, my iPhone buzzed. It was Vancouver. It seemed that the Western world's most colourful leader, Silvio Berlusconi of Italy, was about to resign ... brought down not by scandal, not by "bunga bunga" parties, not by calling Obama "tanned" (*bronzato*), and not by calling his political opponents dickheads (*coglioni*). His demise was relatively prosaic, precipitated by Italy's teetering economy, which was only slightly better than Greece's.

I inhaled an extra mouthful of pasta, then put on a suit and tie, and headed back into the bureau to pound out a story, Sarkozy's insult of Netanyahu relegated to the sidelines by the comic opera in Rome.

Outside the presidential palace, Italians honked their car horns in celebration, sang the Hallelujah Chorus from *Messiah*, and shouted that Berlusconi was a "buffoon." It was the end of an era. I knew Isabella's cousins in Treviso were celebrating, too. They had even cancelled their cable TV, not wanting to patronize any of the prime minister's many media holdings.

Leaving Dan to finish off the editing of my third story of the day, it was off in a taxi to a studio overlooking the Thames to speak live to Vancouver. Once again, my daughter would be asleep by the time I finally returned to the flat.

The pressure was growing to get more involved in Julia's life at school. The next day there was to be a skating party and fireworks show, and Isabella said it was my duty to attend.

I was filing another euro economic crisis story, a mixed bag of ever-changing news centring on events in Greece and Italy. As the hour approached when I needed to run to the school, Vancouver asked for a rare script change — they wanted to insert an inflammatory clip from Christine Lagarde, the head of the IMF, where she warned of the dangers of a "lost decade."

I hammered out a quick rewrite, even as an email arrived from Isabella: "Tell me you are coming." She was desperate for me to relieve her with Julia. I recorded my voice track and left the elements with Dan to edit and send to Vancouver.

Naturally there were no taxis, so I began to power walk north on Chalk Farm Road. A couple of blocks along, sweat now pouring down my forehead, a cab appeared. Minutes later I ran into the schoolyard at the Royal. The fireworks were over, but the event was still unfolding, with the girls skating on a makeshift rink.

Isabella spotted me with weary relief. She appeared drained.

"Can I go?" she pleaded, as an enthusiastic Julia ran over and jumped up for a hug.

"Sure, sure. I'm on it now," I said. Isabella disappeared to head home.

"Come skating, Daddy," demanded Julia.

An outdoor rink in London requires ingenuity and technology.

Even in the depths of winter it rarely gets below freezing, and this was a mild November evening. What was unfolding at the Royal was a bizarrely artificial variant of skating. The surface resembled linoleum, the skates were dull and awkward. At the best of times I am a mediocre skater, never having properly learned as a kid, but I gamely gave it a try.

Within seconds, my knees were screaming, ready to explode. The skates had no edge and the ersatz surface of the "rink" did not seem to encourage gliding. Disaster loomed. After a few minutes of struggle, I begged off and encouraged Julia to continue while I watched.

As I stumbled over to the skate return spot, the phone buzzed. Vancouver was desperately trying to reach me. A producer had spotted a wire copy story indicating that the interim Greek government was about to collapse — a major development that would require me to redo my report. Teetering on the skates, I frantically searched for clarification on the phone.

Julia called over: "Daddy, you have to come back!"

Dan emailed: "So, what are we doing? Do I have to re-edit?"

"DADDY!" shouted my insistent daughter.

Here was a new level of stress.

Isabella was nowhere in sight, Julia was anxious to stay and play on one of the first nights when she had a real chance to socialize with schoolmates and I was faced with the prospect of another rush back to the office to rewrite a script with a pressing deadline. For good measure, my knees were aching as I struggled to stay upright on the nutty British skates.

After a few breathless moments, another email arrived from Dan with copy updating our story. Nothing had actually changed. No rewrite required. Whew.

With Julia still demanding attention, I wrote an email to Vancouver and then called to speak to the producer who had urgently been trying to reach me. He was now in a meeting and everyone had moved on, unaware of how the previous few minutes had caused me to shorten my life. Later in the evening, an email arrived: "Please advise when you leave the office in case we have questions."

Blood rushed to my head as I recalled how I had worked late through the previous weekend, away from my family, and how I merely wished to attend an event at my daughter's new school in a different country. Several wordings of responses came to mind, all containing the word "fuck." Wisely, I wrote none of them and just called it a night.

Another in the growing number of collisions between work and family in London.

While my beat was dominated by world politics, disasters, and Royals, every now and then I was able to do something about Canada. Not that we were any kind of major player in London. While the Brits are fascinated by Americans, Canadian culture is a blip on the British map, barely recognized and usually only mentioned in the context of bad jokes about how boring we are or in mocking stories about Justin Bieber. So it was a rare pleasure for us to make the long trip to south London and the gorgeous Dulwich Picture Gallery where Canadian masters were on display.

Snobby Brits might be inclined to say a show titled *Painting Canada* was an invitation to somnolence. But Dan and I had to elbow our way through the crowds filling the gallery to see works by Tom Thomson and the Group of Seven. I love my home country, but we lack the English passion for the arts. The Dulwich was jammed with what appeared to be mainly retired people, all of whom knew their art.

As we made our way into the showrooms with our bulky camera, a stern-faced Brit standing in front of Thomson's *The West Wind* gave me the evil eye, until I told him we were Canadian TV. The magic word: "Canadian." His face brightened into a smile without actually fracturing and he happily offered a comment for the camera: "It's lovely. Never even aware of Canadian painting previously! I'd love to hang one of these in my living room."

No wonder: there had not been a major show of the Group in London since the 1920s.

The curator of the show, Ian Dejardin, told us that he learned about Thomson and the Group when he stumbled across a book as an art student. "I was smitten instantly — the colour, the dynamism," he said.

It is a Canadian thing: getting approval somewhere other than Canada not only makes the country, its people, and its achievements more credible to Canadians, it is newsworthy.

It is also a Canadian thing to go more to art galleries abroad than at home. This tendency started to win Isabella over to London, as did the joys of simple pleasures.

After Sunday Mass at St. Mary's, we searched for a brunch place in the quirky and charming side streets around the Hampstead Tube stop. Down a pathway called Perrin's Court, we came across a hole-in-the-wall called Ginger & White and she fell in love with it. We sat elbow to elbow with other families around a large wooden table and ordered "soldiers" and eggs. Soldiers, we learned, were strips of toast, mated with artisanal peanut butter, preserves, and exquisite cappuccino.

London life was looking up. But the afternoon was without a plan, until my wife made my heart leap.

"Maybe we should go to the Royal Academy to see the exhibition of Degas dancers," she offered out of the blue.

"Great idea!"

"Don't get happy."

But I was and grabbed onto this tiny shred of progress. En route to the Tube, we bumped into Julia's Canadian school friend Zoë and her father, Dave. On the spur of the moment, we asked them if they wanted to come.

Thus was born a terrific and impromptu afternoon that we never could have had at home.

The Royal Academy of Arts is just another one of those venerable London institutions that you find pretty much on every block. Crazy King George III was responsible for starting it, in a no-so-crazy act in 1768. The sane and praiseworthy concept was to promote and teach art, and is traditionally led by artists, "academicians" they're called, with Joshua Reynolds as the first president.

The girls scarcely noticed the statue of Reynolds dominating the courtyard of the Academy, just off Piccadilly, around the corner from Fortnum and Mason. But I did. He was staring, open-mouthed, off into the distance, taking the measure, I supposed, of one of the many peers of the realm whose image he captured for posterity.

There was a lineup for tickets but miraculously it melted away and we were able to get in, revealing another miracle: the two six-year-old girls from Canada lapping up the show, *Degas and the Ballet: Picturing Movement*. Both Julia and Zoë loved dancing and there was something in the backstage scenes that Degas captured in 1870s Paris that seemed to strike a chord.

We got them the audio tours, and to our amazement they dutifully sat cross-legged in front of each picture, listening with interest to the commentary, ignoring the hordes of adults stepping over them.

Chapter Fifteen

Another foreign trip loomed. The Egyptian revolution was turning sour. Only nine months earlier, in the central moment of the Arab Spring, the popular uprising symbolized by the crowds in Tahrir Square brought down Hosni Mubarak.

The euphoria at the fall of the despot quickly dissipated. The army took over, promising elections, but the throngs in Tahrir were restless, suspicious that the generals had no intention of giving up power. Truth is, the army was always pretty much in charge. Mubarak was a general himself.

The protests in Tahrir were growing in intensity, as were the police crackdowns. People were dying in the streets. There were stories of poison tear gas.

It started to look very much like Dan and I would be getting on a plane to Cairo.

I initially said nothing to Isabella. But just before bedtime, an email arrived from Vancouver: Make preparations to go to Egypt.

I had only been back in London for two weeks since the Athens trip. Sleep was elusive as I pondered how to tell my wife and daughter that I was likely to be headed to a city where the authorities used poison tear gas on demonstrators.

The following morning, exhausted and stressed, I was glued to the TV, watching coverage of the events in Cairo as we started to pack up our gear, find an Egyptian fixer, and check out flights and hotels for our departure the next day. It was not only Isabella's potential reaction that was eating at my guts, there was an element of fear as well. We would be flying into a city on edge, where innocent people were already dying just by being in the wrong place at the wrong time.

At noon I could not delay any longer and called my wife to advise her of the possibility I would be going. She did not answer, but sent an email within minutes, asking if I was the one calling.

"Yes. There's talk of me going to Egypt," I wrote back.

"But, it's bad there," she responded. A calmer reaction than I expected.

I let on nothing to Vancouver and carried on with preparing an Egyptian story that we would file from London.

That evening the de facto ruler, Field Marshal Mohamed Tantawi, went on national television claiming that the military had no intention of clinging to power and promised to move up presidential elections to June 2012 — they had been expected in the fall.

I wrote a note to Vancouver: "Looks like the generals may have blinked. I'm cooling on the idea of going in the morning."

It was a conflicted note: I was torn by the journalistic instinct that pushed me into running to where the big story was unfolding, despite the risks, but did not want to terrify my family, or myself.

In any case, the producers concurred and we decided to hold off. I exhaled, but did not feel great. Stories like this came with the job. I sent a note to Isabella reassuring her that we were not going — yet.

Within minutes, though, it was clear that Tantawi's speech had had little effect. AP reported that protestors were saying it was not nearly good enough, that the generals needed to step aside. An articulate dissident did a live interview on Sky News: "They have no legitimacy. They need to go now!"

Back at the flat, Isabella was relatively calm, a better response than I expected. But Julia met me at the door and declared, "I don't want you to go to Egypt." She was a determined six-year-old.

"It is still a possibility," I told them. In fact, I knew it was almost certain.

As occasionally happened, Isabella fell asleep beside Julia and stayed there all night. I got up early to go to the gym, leaving my iPhone beside them with an alarm set so that they would wake up in time to start getting Julia ready for school.

When I returned, they were up. Isabella handed me my phone.

"I'm sorry. I didn't mean to look at your emails," she said. A note had arrived overnight advising that Egypt was likely a go.

By midmorning it was confirmed. We would be on a flight the next day.

"Oh boy," said Isabella's email when I informed her. "Tell them you have an event at Julia's school next Monday and I'll be really mad if you don't make it."

"Their elections start next Monday," I responded. "We'll certainly be staying."

Now the preparations got frantic. Through Stu's contacts, we found a fixer named Reem, a young woman who worked as an English teacher. I rushed out to the post office to get a wad of American cash and however many Egyptian pounds they had on hand, then stopped at the Marks and Spencer to buy a load of groceries for my family.

We would be leaving our big news camera in the bureau, instead taking a compact video recorder and a DSLR camera. We were told that customs officers had been seizing TV news gear at the airport, so we would be posing as tourists, buying visas when we arrived — a calculated risk.

Back at the flat, Julia once again met me at the door.

"I don't want you to go to Egypt!"

"She saw some video on TV of people lying down on the street in Cairo and it scared her," said Isabella. "You need to talk to her."

I took my daughter's hand and led her over to the sofa. She climbed into my lap, rested her head against my chest, and let out a tiny whimper. Despite the tension, it was a moment of closeness to be treasured, one of the finest, warmest feelings in the world.

"What if you get shot?" she asked.

"I'm not going anywhere close to where that kind of stuff is happening."

"But what is happening in Egypt?"

I was proud that she asked such perceptive questions. I explained that people were protesting because they wanted the generals who were running the country to step aside so that there could be proper elections.

Isabella sat opposite and asked calmly, but directly, "What do I do if you die?"

"I'm not going to die."

"But what if you do? I'm in England with a six-year-old. She'll cry and miss you. What do I do?"

Here were questions I probably should have anticipated when I took the job, but I never did, or if I did I pushed them aside. It was profoundly uncomfortable to discuss the plans for my death in front of our daughter. We went back and forth with the same question and same answer a couple of times, before I finally advised that she would need to call the *Global National* producers and they would help her. It was not a very satisfactory answer.

I took Julia to bed that night, reading her Roald Dahl's *Matilda*. We lay side by side in her lower bunk, warm and close. Usually I would demand that she try to read a bit as well, but on this night I let it go.

As I turned out the light, I told her that I would be leaving early, before she woke up.

"Daddy, I don't want you to go to Egypt."

"I know, sweetie. But I need to go. I'll be back before you know it."

A clichéd and forced answer that she was too sharp to buy.

"Will you say goodbye?"

"I don't want to wake you up."

"I want you to wake me up to say goodbye."

"Suppose I just whisper softly, 'I'm going now'?"

"Okay. Say it just like that."

I stayed beside her, as I usually did, until she fell asleep. It did not take long before she was in dreamland.

As I crept out of her bedroom, my phone vibrated. Vancouver, our assignment editor.

"You all set?" she asked

"Yup."

"This is the first time I'm deploying you to a place that might be dangerous," she said. "So ... be careful. Tell your wife she can call me anytime she wants."

"Thanks. I'll pass that along."

"I won't be calling her first. A cameraman once told me that if I called his wife while he was in a danger zone, she would assume that it was to tell her that he's dead."

"Understood."

I passed the message along to Isabella.

"Why would I want to talk to her?" she asked.

"It's just a courtesy," I said, avoiding the anecdote about the cameraman's wife.

I slept soundly, if only for four hours. Isabella woke only briefly to say goodbye. She had arranged a weekend of activities for her and Julia, including skating at Hyde Park — designed to distract our daughter from her father's assignment.

I crept into Julia's room, gently kissed her head, and whispered, "See you later, sweetie." She did not wake up.

Chapter Sixteen

Going to Egypt was both invigorating and unnerving. We were hearing that the tear gas used on protestors was causing victims to convulse and cough up blood. I sent several emails to our fixer, telling her that a top priority upon arrival was to buy gas masks. She replied that we need not worry; they were for sale everywhere around the square.

Upon arrival, Dan and I split up to go through customs separately — the better to carry off the tourist ruse. We worried that they might open up his huge backpack and ask pointed questions about his video camera — smaller than typical TV news gear, but still a large step up from that of the average tourist.

But we both sailed through with no questions. Our fixer, Reem, was holding up a sign with my name at arrivals. Still fearing we could be busted, we said little until we got outside the terminal and into her car.

Reem was impossibly young, only twenty-four — born two years after I started work at Global TV. She was a teacher of English and drama, the daughter of a prominent writer of books and newspaper columns.

As she pulled out into the creeping stream of traffic she told us that things had cooled while we were in the air. The army set up concrete barriers around the principal trouble spot: Mohammed Mahmoud Street, a principal artery leading from Tahrir Square to the Interior

Ministry building. Dozens of demonstrators had already died on the street that week as the army attempted to crush their protests against military rule. Walling off Mohammed Mahmoud put concrete between the uprising and the guys with guns and poison tear gas. The violence appeared to be ebbing.

Reem told us she had been going to the square every night.

"Do you feel safe?" I asked, knowing how many had died and how many women had been sexually assaulted.

"Oh yes. Very safe," she said with the confidence of youth.

"But you must stay away from the part of the square near Mohammed Mahmoud."

Pro-military provocateurs were rumoured to be blending in with the crowds, stirring up trouble. Reem was passionate about the revolution and disdainful of the military, known popularly as SCAF (Supreme Council of the Armed Forces).

The generals had posted notes of apology on Facebook for the deaths of protestors, a nod to the torrent of social media that fed the energy of Tahrir. But she was not buying SCAF's regrets.

"Nobody believes them or trusts them," she said.

The Cairene sky was greyish rouge in the early evening as she navigated her way downtown — coloured by all the pollution that seven million inhabitants can generate, seventeen million people if you count the broader metropolitan area. As it was November, we were spared the summer temperatures that regularly top forty degrees Celsius.

The buildings became taller as we approached the centre; most were tarnished by the soot of the smog. Broad boulevards met at chaotic intersections unencumbered by Western innovations such as traffic lights. Drivers edged their way through the stream, honking as they went in an improvised form of inter-auto communication.

"There are a few traffic lights in the city," Reem explained. "But if I stop at a red and there are no cars coming on the cross street, drivers behind me will honk and call me the worst possible names."

Finally, the fabled Nile came into sight as we pulled up at the Hilton. Earlier that year, Dan and Stu had been barricaded in the same hotel for a time at the height of the troubles that brought down Mubarak. But now all was calm and we were met with smiles in a lobby that could have been in Toronto or Tampa, except for the Arabic heard in the background.

We quickly checked in and, recognizing the new necessities of filing, checked the speed of our internet connection and updated ourselves on the latest. SCAF had just held another televised news conference, promising that the elections would begin on schedule the following Monday.

However, few believed that SCAF were much interested in abiding by the rules. In one of the more chilling episodes from earlier in the week, a prominent writer, tweeter, and profane critic of the regime, Mona Eltahawy, had been summarily arrested. The new, kinder, gentler SCAF allowed her to go free, but both her arms were in casts — she said she had been both beaten and sexually abused. Rape and all manner of groping were epidemic around the square.

After a woman reporting for a French television service was sexually assaulted, Reporters Without Borders issued an advisory for female journalists to stay away for their own safety, which in turn sparked a furious response from the many fearless women on the front lines. The advisory was quickly withdrawn.

Three American students had also been locked up, accused of throwing firebombs. They were now freed, however — a prudent move given that Washington was still pumping more than a billion dollars in aid to the Egyptians. The U.S. media naturally made the students key characters in their coverage. I wanted to ignore them in my story, reasoning that dozens of dead Egyptians were more important, but Vancouver insisted I give them a mention.

We started to hike over to Tahrir Square, just a couple of blocks away, to see what the protestors had to say. Walking to the rear of the Hilton brought us into a different world — from the elegance of a luxury international hotel to the grime of a big city in North Africa. We came to a multi-lane road passing beneath a greying, crumbling expressway cloverleaf. No traffic lights, naturally.

"Are you okay to go across?" asked Reem with a look of concern, likely fearful that her Western client would end up splattered on the windshield of a battered taxi.

"Oh sure," I answered, as my heart started beating rapidly.

With Cairene expertise, she spotted a minor break in the traffic and started navigating her way through what appeared to be somewhere between five or eight lanes, depending on the interpretation of the drivers. Dan and I stuck close as rusty, dented Toyotas whizzed past, millimetres away.

Without asking, Reem grabbed my hand.

"Okay, run," she advised, pulling me ahead past the final lanes, ensuring I survived the first life-or-death adventure of my first Middle East assignment as a foreign correspondent.

As we approached Tahrir Square, there was an unofficial security checkpoint, manned by young men bearing smartphones and self-appointed authority. Once we showed our passports and they determined we were North American journalists, they flashed broad smiles and said, "Welcome, brother."

Tahrir felt like a teeming carnival midway, with vendors selling popcorn, cigarettes, water, and gas masks (Reem had already acquired ours — flimsy things with goggles). My lungs started to feel clogged up, not from tear gas, because there had been none that day, but from the open-air roasters that were charring potatoes and any other edible that benefitted from smoke and heat.

A siren announced an ambulance that was edging its way through the crowd, but the medical emergencies had diminished with the violence. There was an open-air clinic where volunteer doctors had been feverishly treating the wounded at the height of the trouble. Now they sat resting, grateful for the lack of work.

I spotted a group of young men who appeared to have friendly faces and asked if any spoke English and would like to talk to Canadian television. They all did.

The one who stepped forward first told me of his outrage at how the police were gassing them, shooting at their eyes, he claimed. A crowd gathered as we spoke, hands tugging at my arms for attention, Arabic voices joining in a cacophony that made it hard to hear my interviewees.

A man who said he had been hit with some of the notoriously toxic tear gas suggested SCAF was guilty of war crimes.

What did they think of the parliamentary elections that were due to start Monday? Yes, they need to happen, said one man, a necessary step toward establishing a true democracy. Absolutely not, said another, impossible after so much bloodshed. The no side seemed to prevail in our conversations, with much talk of boycotting.

After thousands of years of autocrats, from pharaohs, through kings, and ending with Mubarak, Egypt was finally to get a chance to vote. And it did not know if it wanted to do it.

Even Reem told us she was uncertain, wondering whether it was right to proceed given the death and chaos.

A young man named Adam got my attention, claiming to be a "colleague" because he wrote scripts for Egyptian talk shows. SCAF's news conference promising early elections was weak, he said, and the Facebook posting expressing regret for the deaths avoided the real issue and took no responsibility.

"It was a contradiction — a paradox speech," he said. "They said they apologized, but still support the police that's doing all these things."

We had no shortage of Tahrir voices to build our story, so we headed back to the Hilton, stopping en route at the InterContinental Cairo Semiramis hotel, which was closer and had balconies with a clear view of the square. They had rooms available, so we decided to make a move in the morning, thus sparing us any more death-defying sprints through traffic and giving us the option of shooting spectacular stand-ups overlooking the drama unfolding in Tahrir.

The debut story from Egypt was straightforward: the violence had abated, SCAF had sort of apologized, the protestors were not molli-fied, and the elections were in doubt. With more potential fireworks tomorrow.

But as Dan and I ate in the hotel restaurant with a view of the Nile, there was a more compelling personal headline that blared in my brain: I WAS IN FUCKING EGYPT COVERING TAHRIR SQUARE!

In Muslim countries, the period after Friday prayers often sees pro-tests. In Cairo, on this Friday, the plan was to stage a "Last Chance Million-Man" rally in Tahrir. Last chance, I supposed, for SCAF to do the right thing and step aside in favour of a democratic, or at least non-military, government. Given the bloodshed of earlier in the week, trouble was a real possibility.

The generals delivered another nod to conciliation, hauling out another interim prime minister. But seventy-eight-year-old Kamal Ganzouri, who had been PM under Mubarak in the nineties, was not going to be the answer.

As we joined the throngs streaming into the square, I saw with alarm that there were many parents bringing young children.

I stopped one father to speak.

"It's basically solidarity with the cause," said Mohammed Omar.

I asked whether he feared for the safety of his children.

"It's okay. As long as you don't go over there," he responded, pointing in the direction of Mohammed Mahmoud Street.

The rally was staged in honour of the "martyrs," the victims of the clashes with soldiers and police earlier in the week. The wounded were given places of prominent honour.

Banners were paraded with pictures both of the dead and of some of the military leaders blamed for the violence. I shot a show-and-tell stand-up, pointing out the faces on display and the people who were holding up some grim souvenirs from the earlier clashes: expired shells from rubber bullets and tear gas canisters.

I noted one large photograph of a young man who looked at best twenty years old and figured he must have been among the dead. But when I asked Reem to translate the Arabic captions, she told me that he was a cop, reputedly a sniper who had been targeting the eyes of protestors. Now he was himself a marked man.

There was no single stage from which speeches were being delivered. Instead, there were mini rallies forming throughout the square: an impromptu festival of democracy in a nation where guys with guns and tanks still ran things. Pamphlets were being held out, polling people on who they would like to lead the country. The idealist goal was to have the square decide on the best candidates.

A huge picture was rolled out of Mohamed ElBaradei, the former director of the International Atomic Energy Agency — a moderate that the West would have certainly liked to see in charge. Everyone in Egypt knew he had little chance. The Muslim Brotherhood was best organized and most likely to win any election. It had played little role in the Tahrir rallies, having been suppressed by the military for decades, and it was cagily awaiting the chance to run candidates in an election.

The crowds grew throughout the day, reaching a peak of about one hundred thousand by nightfall, and despite the fears it all remained peaceful. A few kilometres away, there was a counter-demonstration by supporters of the military. It was dwarfed by the Tahrir rally.

Before we left to file our story, a couple of soldiers arrived on the square to support the democrats. They were treated as heroes, but I wondered what the reception would be like from their superiors.

As we walked out of Tahrir, the crowds chanted, "We're not tired … freedom isn't free."

Saturday saw the first clashes in days. Police fought it out with protestors who had been blockading the Cabinet offices and who were trying to stop the new interim prime minister from getting in. A young man was run down and killed by a security vehicle.

Despite those clashes, the crowds in the square had diminished, shrinking to a few scattered camps of hard-liners. We ventured in to gather some voices for an election preview story and found impromptu debates everywhere over whether or not to vote.

We also unexpectedly ran into our first dicey moments of our trip. It happened during an interview with a guy named Muhammad whose English was reasonably good. He told us that he thought he would vote if it appeared to be safe, but then diverted into a rant about losing his government job. One or two men stopped to listen, and then a few more gathered until it became a small crowd. The spectators started barking at him in Arabic, voices growing louder and angrier.

Reem tapped at my elbow and said calmly but decisively, "We should go."

I cut the interview short, thanked Muhammad, and motioned to Dan to move on, which we did briskly, smiling and nodding at the irate faces as the argument continued behind us.

"What were they saying to him?" I asked Reem.

"They said, 'What kind of poison are you telling? Are you telling our secrets?'"

I wondered if the hecklers were pro-regime operatives in the square to spy and stir up trouble. Or if Muhammad himself was a provocateur. So many layers to the Tahrir subculture and so hard for an outsider to understand.

It was time to venture out of the square anyway. Reem had arranged an interview with a spokesman for the Freedom and Justice Party, which was the chosen name of the Muslim Brotherhood faction. We piled into her compact sedan and headed out into the Cairo traffic fandango.

There were election posters everywhere. Dozens of new parties had sprung up, factions within factions. I shot a stand-up in front of one crowded wall where there was a picture of a woman running for a moderate party juxtaposed with a candidate for a group of conservative Islamists.

I could not get over the dirt everywhere on the buildings. Almost every single one was grimy. The biggest city in the Arab world — a vast, bustling, vibrant, and fascinating place — was impossible to keep clean.

So it was at the building where we were to meet the Muslim Brotherhood representative. The lobby was dim and ramshackle, with an old gentleman perched on a battered wooden chair — the doorman, I guessed. Reem asked him where to find our guy and he pointed us to a rickety, doorless elevator, barely visible on the other side of the lobby amid the gloom. On the way up, Reem casually reached over to Dan's huge backpack and tucked in a couple of straps that were hanging loose and at risk of snagging on the wall.

When Amr Darrag opened the door to his apartment, we stepped into an oasis. It was elegantly, if slightly gaudily, furnished — a metaphor for a city where the exterior view obscures an inner reality.

Darrag spoke perfect, almost unaccented English. He had studied engineering in the U.S. at Purdue University. Clearly the Brotherhood offered this genial smooth talker to Western media as a way of putting up a moderate face for a movement that caused much unease.

Freedom and Justice proposed that Egypt should be an Islamic state, ruled by Sharia law, but its interpretation of Sharia was unclear. It had female candidates, but ruled out having any run for president and advised the women that they would need to balance their public life with the traditional role in the home. It claimed it had reached out to Coptic Christians, an often-abused minority in Egypt, but none had agreed to run.

The Brotherhood had played little role in the Tahrir protests, a cynical tactic in the view of their critics, who accused them of not wanting to provoke the military into delaying an election that the Brotherhood seemed poised to win.

Darrag, himself a candidate for the Freedom and Justice Party, insisted their motives were pure. "This is the first step toward democracy, toward stability," he said. "The elections must happen on time."

The West need not worry about the prospect of Islamists dominating the new Egyptian Parliament he said. "There is nothing to fear," Darrag told me. "Egypt will not become Iran."

He was a charming man, though I wondered what the Freedom and Justice Party candidates were saying in Arabic to the voters in the countryside. These would be the candidates who did not go to an American university.

Reem brought us to a nearby restaurant for lunch, a labyrinthine place where dimly lit rooms led one into the other — a design, I surmised, to limit the effects of the blistering heat that enveloped Cairo for most of the year. We passed two young women sucking on hookahs, with a guy on a laptop sitting across the table.

Reem explained that our next interview would be in one of the nicer parts of town, and indeed it was. The building walls were more dusty than grimy. Said Sadek welcomed us into an apartment that could have easily been owned by an academic at the University of Toronto, the interior design several gradations more subdued than Darrag's. A political scientist at the American University, Sadek had been recommended by Stu as an astute analyst, having interviewed him earlier in the year during the anti-Mubarak uprisings.

Sadek was a reformer with a sense of humour. "The generals still believe in mummies," he said with a rueful smile. "They're old and out of touch with the young."

I asked him about the soothing words of Amr Darrag and he shook his head.

"Religious parties should never be trusted. We have seen the examples of political Islam in the area and it's disturbing. I don't want to replace the military dictatorship of Mubarak with a religious dictatorship."

Profundity is a challenge in a two-minute news story. But I hope that at least I sounded like I knew what I was talking about in the closer for my piece that night:

> Given all the blood that has been shed over the last few days, there is much doubt that this vote can happen peacefully, and cleanly.
>
> As imperfect and troubled as it is, Egypt desperately needs to get its first true election right.

We were done early enough to allow us to head to the famous Khan el-Khalili market in the heart of the city. The idea was to shoot elements for a Sunday feature on Egypt's suffering tourist trade. In the process, it allowed us to be tourists ourselves.

The market has been a centre for Cairene merchants for centuries and is normally a big draw for foreigners. There were plenty of people strolling the narrow streets on that Saturday night, but they seemed almost exclusively Egyptian.

Just inside the Bab al-Badistan gate we popped into a cramped shop with multicoloured scarves hanging from every square millimetre. The owner, Ahmed Abdel Sabbour, told us that not many foreigners were coming in to buy his wares and business was off 40 percent that year.

"In order to have tourists, you have to have security," he told me via Reem's translation. "And people don't feel safe."

Truth was that the troubles were almost entirely centred in the district around Tahrir Square, although the market and foreign tourists had been targeted in years past.

After our interview, I picked out a couple of scarves for Isabella and Julia with Arabic captions on them and wished Ahmed well.

He shrugged and smiled. "Egyptians know how to be patient."

Back at the hotel, a couple of emails had arrived from London.

"Julia has a stomach ache. You may have to come home early," was the first.

Isabella was taking Julia to a schoolmate's birthday party that was some distance away, not easily reached by transit. A few better-heeled parents had cars, but it seemed all were full, so Isabella had to spring for an expensive taxi coming and going.

"Fucking London snobs. Don't call us."

It did not take long for my absence to get to her. Every trip was an ordeal. Here I was on a journalistic adventure of a lifetime, and my family was miserable.

The real purpose of my pitching the tourism story was our Sunday trip to Giza — I could not go to Egypt without seeing the pyramids. I had no idea that it was actually just a suburb. On a clear day you get a good look at them as you land at the airport.

For about 4,500 years they had stood through all the travails of humanity, through empires rising and falling, to prevail as one of the great sights to see in the world. But few were seeing them these days.

As we arrived, guys kept waving us over and knocking on the window. They were not cops or any kind of officials — just desperate locals hoping to make a few bucks. The parking lot for the pyramids was almost empty, just one lonely tour bus. As we parked, a guy in a uniform bustled over to make further demands. Reem's voice rose as she engaged the guy. It was hard to tell exactly what was happening, but it seemed he had an issue with us parking in an empty parking lot.

After a couple of minutes of increasingly loud Arabic, he gave up.

Reem was beside herself. One Egyptian in six works in tourism and the industry was tanking, and here was an officious functionary complicating the lives of some of the few visitors.

To avoid further bureaucratic hassles, we had already decided to leave the video camera back at the hotel and shoot this part of the story with the DSLR — better to look more like tourists than reporters.

Every few steps we were accosted by the touts selling tours and camel rides, their normal persistence heightened to near ferocity by the scarcity of visitors. I had Dan point the camera at one of the first and most insistent, a guy named Walid, and I asked him the obvious: How was business?

"Things are really fucked up," he responded in a perfectly understandable and unusable clip. I thanked him and moved on, but he stuck to us, as did a teenage kid who had little English but plenty of opinions he wanted to share.

Ahmed Ramadan was the first camel ride guy we approached. He helped me mount his camel, named Oscar, as I asked him the same question. Ahmed's answer was far more nuanced.

"In Tahrir, people die. For me, it's just money. And money is nothing," he said.

Interview done, he carried on with his well-practised tourist shtick, leading Oscar to a prime spot for a photo of me riding him with the pyramids as a backdrop.

"Okay, now put this on," he said, handing me an Arab headdress.

I hesitated for a moment, then thought why not and asked Dan to take another picture.

"You sure?" he asked with eyebrows raised.

"Yup. Do it."

"Okay." Eyes rolled.

When I hopped down he showed me the shot and I groaned with embarrassment. Truly ridiculous. Hoser of Arabia.

Having remembered a key lesson from hazardous environment training, I had spread my wad of cash among several different pockets so as not to flash too much money at any one time.

No matter: as soon as it came out, I resembled a rump roast dropped into a school of piranha.

Ahmed has already agreed to $20 U.S., which I happily paid. Then, there was Walid, he of the "fucked up" clip. Twenty dollars for him. Then the kid. I proposed to just give him a couple of bucks.

Ahmed: "Small bills too hard to change." Another twenty flew out.

I told Walid that he could carry on with the tour for his twenty, figuring that he would keep the other touts at bay. And so he did. Occasionally an interloper would approach but Walid protected us with the ferocity of a lion standing over a freshly killed wildebeest.

He took us over to the Sphinx, where I spotted a rarity, a Western tourist. Jason was a Brit, although he was wearing a battered Australian hat. He was riding a horse being led by a tout. I asked him whether he was frightened to be in Cairo.

"No, because we had two weeks of rioting in London," he answered in a broad Cockney accent.

It was a telling comment, but I wondered whether the audience back home would find him credible, given that it looked like he had not had a bath since he was last in earshot of Bow Bells, and his scruffy beard was braided at the chin.

As we walked back to the car, my gaze wandered from the magnificent views above of the Great Pyramid of Cheops to the hazards of camel and horseshit on the pathway. Dan walked ahead with Walid bending his ear.

"Did you tell Dan that you already paid him?" asked Reem, anticipating what was about to happen.

"No. Don't worry about it," I said.

I was certain Walid would hit him up for more and sure enough Dan reached into his pocket and handed over another twenty. I did not care, reasoning that would be our minor contribution to a suffering local economy.

Walid, however, was shameless. As we shook hands to say goodbye, he asked if I also had some spare Egyptian pounds "for his children." Our generosity (that is to say Global's generosity) had limits, and I declined and thanked him for his assistance.

As we drove back into the centre of Cairo, Reem was still steamed about the bureaucratic barriers we had faced, as some of the very few visitors wanting to see the pyramids that day.

"We have huge assets and a fascinating country but no clue how to properly exploit them," she growled. She passionately loved Egypt but like many Egyptians was maddened by it.

It was only midday, hours before deadline, lots of time for lunch, so I asked Reem to bring us to a place where we could sample some fine traditional Egyptian food. Dan was tired (and he always admitted that his tastes ran more to Burger King anyway) so we dropped him at the hotel and headed onto the Nile island of Gezira, to the northern tip and the tony Zamalek district.

Sequoia was a restaurant that sounded like it should be in San Francisco, but looked like it belonged in a Lawrence Durrell novel. There were no walls, no roof — just low white sofas and a view of the Nile. It was also almost deserted, with a smattering of diners.

I told Reem to order and out came some delicious bread and dips, followed by molokheya, a kind of broth made from jute leaves, garlic, and coriander, served with chicken. It was exotic yet still accessible and tasty — but all overshadowed by the locale. Yes, that's *the Nile* I was dining beside. This Foreign Correspondent thing was feeling very Foreign Correspondenty.

Monday, the first round of voting, we drove to polling stations around the city, anticipating trouble but finding none. Lineups were long, often snaking around the block, but Egyptians appeared patient, willing to accept a wait to cast a ballot in what promised to be the first real election in their nation's long history.

An elegant, fiftyish woman named Magda Khalil told me, "Okay, it's crowded. But sometimes you have to stand up for yourselves and a new generation."

The debate over whether to boycott seemed to have been settled, with lots of people showing up to vote. In the sham elections under Mubarak, turnout was typically around 10 percent, but predictions were that it was to rise to well about 50 percent. We came across Sammy Ibrahim, who told us he carried dual Canadian-Egyptian citizenship. Was he afraid to vote, given the troubles of the previous week?

"No," he said. "I'm very happy. I feel a new life is coming to Egypt."

The rules specifically prohibited any campaigning outside polling areas, but it was widely ignored, with the Muslim Brotherhood the most efficient violators. We spotted a place where Freedom and Justice Party operatives had set up under a tent right beside the lineup to one voting area, tapping away at laptops as they interviewed voters.

"Nothing is perfect, but I think it will be fair enough," said a fashionably dressed young woman named Hanaa Benhaoussie, who was standing in line.

I wanted to get a shot of the Brotherhood operation, but the army was guarding the polling area and shooed Dan away, claiming we did not have proper permission.

We walked around the corner and I suggested to him and Reem that I would stroll back with my iPhone to surreptitiously get some video. They both looked worried, but a friend of Reem's offered to walk along with me and engage in conversation as a cover. It worked and the bored-looking soldiers never noticed. I made sure that Dan used the shaking, soft focus shot in my story, given that I had risked arrest to get it.

Reem drove us to meet her mother, Sahar Elmougy, a prominent columnist and lecturer at Cairo University. She was also a rare breed in the Arab world: a novelist who wrote from a feminist perspective.

In her spare, tasteful apartment she told us that she would be casting a ballot, mainly in the hope of heading off an Islamist sweep, but she considered the process little more than a rehearsal of a truly democratic process.

"In the long run, they're not credible elections because the people in charge of running them are murderers," she said.

Years later, when I sat down to write this book, I visited her website only to find that it had been hacked by someone with the nickname KkK. I wondered about her safety.

In a continuing effort to find a Canadian angle, I reached out to Sherif and Magda Ghobrial, dual citizens who spent about half their time in Toronto and half in Cairo. Their niece, a friend from my days covering the Ontario legislature, put me in touch and we headed out to their apartment.

The Ghobrials were Coptic Christians, a minority group that traditionally has been a favoured scapegoat during times of social unrest in Egypt. Only a few weeks earlier, dozens were massacred outside the state broadcaster's building in Cairo for daring to protest about their churches being burned.

Magda's English was better and she sounded more quotable, but she was camera shy so it was left to the genial Sherif to do the interview. They had already cast their ballots, but were justifiably nervous, given their religion and recent events.

"I'm almost sixty-five years old, but for the first time I think I have to put my vote, say my opinion," he said.

He feared the prospect of a Muslim Brotherhood victory.

"Maybe it'll be better than people expect, but, yes, I worry."

I wondered why they still spent so much time in Egypt, given the risks for Copts and their substantial roots in the much safer

Toronto. They never really explained it; it seemed that they just truly loved Cairo.

It was a good story, and our final one in Egypt. I had already suggested to Vancouver that this would be a good time to pull out, given that the elections would be carrying on for weeks and the street violence had ebbed.

There was also the impetus to go back home to London and my increasingly impatient wife. The reality of her professional sacrifice was hitting home, as her links to her previous, much-loved job were starting to wither. She wrote in an email that night: "I'll never make 80k again. You get a career upgrade and I lose mine."

I had no good answer. There was none. The trailing spouse typically gets the shit end of the deal.

We had reservations on a Tuesday morning EgyptAir flight. The hotel concierge booked us a car to the airport, assuring us that the fare would be 196 Egyptian pounds. But when the driver dropped us off, he insisted the actual charge was 350.

"One last shakedown," I muttered to Dan — but decided to pay up anyway.

When I asked for a receipt, the cabbie pulled a scrap of paper from the floor of his car and scribbled something in Arabic, with no number. I thought our numerical digits *were* Arabic. But never mind. I suspected that he wrote something like "Your father was a goat and go fuck yourself, sucker." I wrote 350 beside and stuffed it in my wallet. Good enough for our expense report.

Although I had already bought Julia a scarf in the market, I reasoned that a more traditional touristy gift might go over better. In an airport shop there was a small stuffed camel, likely made in China. Turned out that she loved it and the scarf went unused.

As we walked to the plane, wrapping up a personal career high point, Dan observed, "Well, I guess we really didn't need to come."

He reasoned that the worst of the violence was over by the time we arrived. But for me the sights, sounds, and memories of our few days in Cairo remain evergreen to this day. The Foreign Correspondent gig came to me late in life and would be relatively brief, but reporting from Cairo, riots or not, was a highlight.

Chapter Seventeen

Foreign Correspondentry, Tahrir Square, the pyramids, and the Nile gave way to middle-class parenthood upon return to London. Julia's Christmas show at the Royal School was *Born in a Barn*. I noted that, although she was retaining her Canadian accent, when she sang the title song it was "Bohn in a Bahn."

The performance was at the beginning of the school day, which allowed me and Isabella and dozens of other parents to jam into the Royal's tiny gymnasium, brandishing our smartphones to record the performance. We had a two-camera shoot, as Isabella also brought our fancy new Nikon.

When Julia auditioned she was desperate to play the wisecracking cockerel who had plenty of dialogue. Instead, she was left tearful after being handed the role of the dog, which only had two lines. But she was a trouper, with strong performance instincts, delivering both lines with gusto. Julia also did a bit of onstage directing, strong-willed as she is, whispering in the ear of the less-focused girl beside her with some reminders of where to go and when.

With Ms. Eisele playing the piano and the six-year-old voices raised in plummy received pronunciation accents, it was ineffably cute.

Performance over and congratulations heaped on the performers, I insisted that Isabella and I have a lunch date, our first grown-up time alone since she moved to London. I had taken the day off for the occasion. Off we went on the Tube south and east to the Tate Modern.

You have to love a city that envisions how a disused former power plant would make a wonderful home for modern art. Even in the bleakness of early December, the evenly planted grove of trees at the north of the building presented an elegant face to the river. I took her over to the west entrance, so that she could have a look at the giant turbine room — a massive open space that dramatically announces itself through its emptiness.

Lunch first at Tate's restaurant, which was terrific — Isabella lapped up the remaining celeriac sauce from my roast chicken wrapped in pancetta.

There was a Gerhard Richter exhibition. Philistine that I am, I had never heard of him, but his work was enthralling — some abstracts slashed by vertical and horizontal lines, and some realistic works, where he somehow managed to make them look like out-of-focus photos.

"How does he do that?" she kept asking.

Isabella loved it, and I loved that she loved it — we needed more London successes.

Having found some joy through singing and sewing, Isabella now proposed to call upon her cinematic skills for a video series starring our brilliant daughter. So, we packed up our new Nikon and tripod and headed for Southwark on a clear, chill Saturday morning. The idea was to create a video of Julia scootering in London. As I have mentioned, scooters were the favoured mode of transport among children of her age. We had no particular buyer for such a video, but it would be undoubtedly charming.

Outside London Bridge underground station we had her pose in front of the sign and scooter past it a couple of times. We were already in trouble, as I could not seem to manually adjust the iris. The camera manual had been read some months before, but little seemed to stick in my mind.

The ultimate goal was Southwark, which offers panoramic views of the Thames and Tower Bridge. We set up in front of London's City Hall, a building nicknamed the Onion that resembles a bicycle helmet and which former mayor Ken Livingstone called a glass testicle. We would have Julia zip around the open space to be as cute and picturesque as possible.

But then neither of us could figure out a way of properly mounting the camera on the expensive tripod that we had purchased. Finally, I managed to awkwardly jam the two together so I could shoot with a semblance of steadiness.

Julia was only marginally interested in the whole exercise.

"Sweetie, can you sing 'London Bridge Is Falling Down' as you scooter past?" I pleaded.

"Daddy, that's not London Bridge, that's TOWER Bridge," she responded, maddeningly, with the facts on her side.

After much cajoling, threatening, and negotiating, we managed to get her to do a few small laps around the courtyard in front of the Glass Testicle, neither of us confident that any of it had proper focus, exposure, or composition.

With Julia on the edge of tears, Isabella did not want to push any further.

"It's okay, sweetie," she said, hugging her. "We'll try another time."

But this moment of failure was succeeded by a triumph. Weeks earlier, she had reserved tickets for a Family Carol Sing at St. Martin-in-the-Fields. We hauled the mysterious camera and uncooperative tripod on the Tube up to Charing Cross station and then the short walk to the northeast corner of Trafalgar Square.

By the time we arrived, the pews were mainly full, with no reserved seats. Miraculously, there was room in the front row and we jammed in with a close-up view of the London Choir — passionate amateurs.

It was, dear reader, thrilling — for me at least.

Julia was bored and laid her head on Isabella's lap but for the sing-along portions I joined in lustily and tunelessly. My wife stared at me with open mouth and perplexed amusement. I never did this at home, but, hell, we were in London singing old English Christmas songs in a famed church that had been standing on that spot since medieval days. What could be better? The video debacle was forgotten and as we walked out of St. Martin, I could have flown back to Fuckland Buckland.

The first Christmas of my London posting was chocked full of logistical complications. Decembers were already busy for us, given Julia's birthday on the 15th. Now, given that we would be going home for the holidays, we were faced both with multiple birthday parties and multiple Santa visits.

Added to the fun: Isabella was now determined to hunt for a new flat. I said nothing about it because, much as I understood her dislike for Buckland, I knew that finding anything better in the same general area would likely involve spending considerably more money.

She found a place on Upper Park Road that she was convinced would be a big upgrade. It was a two-bedroom, south-facing flat, smaller than our current place but much better cared for with a superior layout. It was also about £140 more *per week*. She had already checked it out herself and now took Julia and me to see it.

I did my best to keep a straight face but inside my stomach was knotted as I contemplated moving a mere six months after getting into Buckland. I would have to take apart Julia's bed with the million pieces, pack everything up, and likely have to eat at least a couple of weeks of Buckland rent, even as our monthly payments jumped by close to a thousand dollars.

"I like it and I think we should take it," she said.

"Okay," I replied, uncertain if the quaver in my voice was noticeable.

I had noted the lack of storage space and how I would now face a much longer walk to the gym, but otherwise was as mute and neutral as I could manage.

"I'm going to make an offer," she said as we walked to the bus. "£600 per week."

"Okay. Well … I want you to be happy." Which was true.

Back at Buckland, she had a sleepless night and in the morning advised me that she had sent an email in the wee hours to the estate agent, declining to make an offer.

"You said there's not enough storage space and the owner probably would not want to wait two months for us to move in so that we could give the required notice to our Buckland landlord."

"Okay. But remember: I never said no to it" — a response given in the spirit of Pontius Pilate.

"You did say no," she said. "But now I've sent the email, so it's done."

But over the next few days she continued to regret her decision: "I'll never find another place as good. He was ready to accept us because I told him we were a nice couple from Canada who would take good care of it." The Canada card.

Having second thoughts, she wrote another email to the agent, who responded that there appeared to be an offer on the property. So that was that. But Upper Park Road would linger in our minds in the months ahead.

We had decided to do a partial Christmas celebration in London, which sent Julia and me on an expedition to Oxford Street to find a present for Isabella.

The holidays are a magical time in this part of town, with extravagant displays of Christmas lights hung over Regent Street. It is a magnet for shoppers year-round, but on the second Saturday in December it is a madhouse.

When we emerged from the Bond Street station, we found Oxford Street crammed. It is so busy at this time of year that they close the street to cars — but pedestrians still fill it from wall to wall.

"Hold my hand, sweetie," I said, clutching her tightly so that we would not become separated as we made our way into the mob.

At least we knew what we were in search of: Isabella had advised that she would appreciate earrings, so we fought our way into the John Lewis department store and headed for the jewellery department.

No salesperson could fail to be charmed by a six-year-old girl with her dad hunting for a Christmas present for Mom, so service was quick and friendly.

One of my wife's many salutary qualities is a dislike for gaudy, expensive jewellery, which meant that in short order we were able to find something both tasteful and not the equivalent of a month's rent.

Our main mission complete, my daughter the power shopper asked if we could go into Hamleys toy store around the corner. I was skeptical, but said we could at least look. As I expected, throngs of stressed parents with squalling kids were lined up outside, so I managed to dissuade her.

Still, despite the crowds, the fond memory lingers of taking my daughter Christmas shopping on Oxford Street. I recommend it for any sentimental parent.

Our mini-celebration in London came on the Sunday morning, when we gathered around the fake fireplace in Fuckland Buckland to open Christmas stockings. Isabella's earrings were only a partial success, as it seemed the metal irritated her earlobes. But she was careful to only tell Julia how much she liked them.

Drinking deeply of the English Christmas spirit, we then headed off on the Tube to the southern reaches of the great city, to Wimbledon, where we had tickets to that loud, brassy, and slapstick English tradition, the pantomime.

The show was *Dick Whittington and His Cat*, as London a tale as you could find. But really, all pantos have pretty much the same template: two pallid young lovers, overshadowed by a cast of overplayed stereotypes delivering broad, bawdy comedy, with old-time song and dance and endless smartassed asides to the audience. The headliner is typically the Dame — a guy in drag.

Whittington had none other than Dame Edna Everage topping the bill as the Fairy that Saved London. There was a subsidiary Dame: Sarah, the rotund cook who continually bragged, "My dumplings are the talk of the town."

Sarah's lover was played by a little person (it seems dwarves are also often part of the usual script), which made for a plethora of sight gags as he sidled up to his towering girlfriend.

Coincidentally, the dwarf issue led to some bad press for a Snow White panto playing elsewhere in London. The producers hired kids instead of adult little people (children being cheaper), and dubbed in their voices. Their innovation brought outrage from dwarf actors who naturally objected to being denied work.

Also part of the panto template is a touch of technological razzle-dazzle. *Whittington* had a 3-D film to portray an unlikely scene with the protagonists exploring an underwater shipwreck. Julia dropped her 3-D glasses at the crucial moment and chose to snatch Isabella's from her face, leading to a mother-daughter staredown.

At the end of the *Whittington* story, the panto carried on: one of the supporting characters, a comedian named Kev Orkian, took over the stage to read out some birthday wishes. This was a Daddy fail on my part to not know about it, given that Julia's was only a couple of days away. He called three kids up to act as foils for a wisecracking improv routine: "Who did you like best?" et cetera.

As I turned to Julia to apologize for not submitting her name, she clutched my shoulder, stuck her face in mine, and with wide, desperate eyes whispered, "I've got to pee!"

As we were in the middle of the audience, unable to get out, it made for an excruciating last few minutes of the panto. Just as Kev appeared ready to wrap up, he came up with another routine — even as my daughter's fingers dug ever deeper into my bicep.

When finally he said good night, she jumped over several people and edged past others to make a frantic and thankfully successful run for the can.

Although London does get chilly, it is not at all winter in the Canadian frame of reference. The average temperature in December is a relatively mild seven degrees Celsius. But the Brits find ways to synthesize the experience of the season, much as they might savour the flavours of Greece or Egypt by hauling in archeological artifacts to put on display in museums.

Witness the skating rinks that pop up in spectacular and historic locales throughout the city, even if no ice cube would last long in the mild English weather without artificial support. You could skate in the moat of the Tower of London, at Hampton Court, and in front of the Natural History Museum. It all happens in the month leading up to Christmas and ends early in the new year — so popular that one must book a specific time of arrival for an hour's worth of skating.

We opted for the stately strip of ice set up in the courtyard of Somerset House. Having grown up with backyard rinks or battered old barns of arenas in small-town Ontario, it was a grand experience to lace up the blades in the quadrangle of an eighteenth-century neo-classical public building overlooking the north bank of the Thames, previously home to the Royal Society, the Society of Antiquaries, and HM Revenue and Customs.

As mentioned earlier, my skating skills are at best rudimentary. But as I saw Londoners spasmodically propelling themselves around the ice, ankles turned in, arms waving, faces contorted in fearful concentration, I felt confident that I would be the Wayne Gretzky of Somerset House.

So it was with brio that I stepped onto the ice in my rented blades, ready to show the English what a true Canadian boy can do. I pushed off with equal parts bravado and incompetence, launching immediately into a double-windmill impression as my feet threatened to split off in anatomically impossible directions. But the moment of panic was brief. I caught my balance, and gently, tentatively started to glide around the rink, rising to my usual level of mediocrity but avoiding mishap.

As my confidence grew, it was clear that I was in fact one of the more able practitioners. Faint praise. A Londoner in his forties caught our eye. For some reason, he was wearing a trench coat, a choice more appropriate for a stroll through Regent's Park on a misty day. It was already covered in water stains and bits of snow — remnants from what must have been several spills. We glided by as he was preparing to step back out onto the rink for another go.

"He's going to hurt himself," said Isabella as she observed his precarious form.

Sure enough, after one or two tentative steps, both feet flew upward in front, his arms clutched for a handhold but found only air, his damp trench coat fluttered up into his face and his ass slammed to the artificially frozen surface, his head stopping only a millimetre away from what would have been a grievous concussion.

"Urgahhh!" he groaned impressively.

Although thoroughly battered, he was not conceding. After about an eight count, he crawled over to the boards, dragged himself back to his feet, face contorted like a stroke victim, and doggedly pulled himself around the rink, wisely holding onto the boards the whole way.

As he did so, my respect grew. It appeared that he was there with his wife and daughter, who was of a similar age to my little girl. They made their way over to him to ensure he had not suffered any permanent damage and they continued as a family to stumble around the rink, determined to not be defeated by the hazards of this unfamiliar and unnatural activity.

This was the spirit that made Britain great.

The Brits have their own variant on the skating assist devices for kids. Whereas back home we have workmanlike triangular frames made out of PVC pipes, here they had plastic penguins that the little ones could hold onto as they worked their way around the ice. Julia, of course, insisted that I haul one over to her.

I do not love skating. My skills are too limited, the risks of injury too present. I go only to have a family activity with my wife and daughter. Canada most certainly has rinks and places to skate that are more natural and in settings that are in their own way glorious. The Rideau Canal in Ottawa comes to mind, or Lake Louise.

But for me, gliding around the artificial rink in the centre of a grand old public building in the heart of London is one of the finest ways to go.

Besides, after our hour on the ice and an overpriced hot chocolate, we were able to spend an inspirational hour looking at the Impressionist collection in the Courtauld Institute in the north wing of Somerset House.

This was our last full day in London before Isabella and Julia jetted home for Christmas. They would be going earlier and staying longer than me, who had to linger due to the demands of work. The packing job had to be carried out with military precision and secrecy, given the need to hide away a selection of birthday and Christmas presents for Julia that had to be transported to Canada for delivery.

We all rose well before dawn the next day so that they could get in a taxi to the airport. I was once again to be a bachelor for a few days. As in the summer months when I was solo in London, I dawdled in the bureau for a time after filing, not having anyone to go home to.

It was almost nine when I jiggled the key in the lock to the front door at Buckland and opened up to a hallway littered with bits of paper, old newspapers it seemed. The trail led up the stairs, all the way to the second-floor flat. Anetta, her kids, and the absent banker husband had moved out a couple of weekends before, the place having been sold and about to be redecorated.

Now I was thoroughly fed up. Already there was no cleaning, due apparently to the reluctance of the eccentric owner on the first floor and now there was this casual littering, no doubt a harbinger of what was to come with the renovation about to be carried out above our heads.

With more anger than hope, I fired off another email to the property managers, demanding they make another attempt at arranging a regular cleanup of the hallway or at least to replace the threadbare rug in the front lobby.

The answer was typical: nothing to be done because they were unable to force the landlords to do anything. Oh, and by the way, we should expect the renovations to begin sooner than expected. To add additional colour to the London renter's experience: after months of scaffolding and banging outside as the finest of English craftsmen attempted to fix a dampness problem in the building, it seems the problem was not fixed at all. Which meant that the long-promised redecoration of the common area would have to be delayed again. It seemed the workmen were unable to trace the source due to the refusal of the ground-floor owner to let them into her flat to investigate.

"But we do wish you and your family a Happy Christmas," the email ended.

I was copying the landlord on all the communications, with zero response from him. So now I wrote an email directly to our landlord advising that in view of all the many and varied quirks, mishaps, and madness at Fuckland Buckland, we might well need to move in the new year and could he please be prepared to offer a margin of flexibility on the required two months' notice?

At length he responded: "I might not be able to be as flexible as I would like, given that it is hard to re-let a place at this time of year." English for fuck off, you have a contract, but Happy Christmas.

In truth, he would have a challenge finding new suckers — uh, tenants — given the colourful character on the main floor (who had now taken to playing the same song directly below our bedroom at eleven every night), the pigsty in the common area, and the major renovation happening above.

As a result, I now resumed the soul-destroying enterprise of searching online for another flat. There in plain sight was the storied Upper Park Road apartment, now apparently listed with several estate agents. I wrote to the agent who had told us there was an offer on the property. Her answer: "There was still an offer 'in progress,' but the owner might be prepared to consider us if we offered something closer to his asking price of £640 per week."

Did I mention that London estate agents are liars?

Julia and Isabella, meanwhile, were back in our spacious, renovated Toronto house. A few weeks earlier her friend Cameron (who designed our kitchen) moved in with his boyfriend, Jason — paying less than market rent, but at least caring for the place and giving us the option of staying there while we were in town. They would be there for a few months while they looked for a new house.

Isabella emailed that they were keeping the place spotless, but Julia, with all the creative energy a seven-year-old could muster, was rapidly making huge messes all over the house.

Having now lived for a few months in a London flat, she realized how little stuff we actually needed to live, and how much excess stuff we were jamming into our Toronto home. We were way overdue for a deep cleansing and downsizing.

With that, I left behind the greatest city on earth and my crappy little corner of it and flew home for Christmas. I had been away from Canada for six months, the longest period out of the country in my life.

Chapter Eighteen

Christmas was a disorienting whirl. I saw our new and spectacular kitchen for the first time. Cameron had created something like a French bistro feel, with a long, tall marble table that could double as a preparation space. The new appliances were stainless steel, elegant, and far beyond our modest cookery skills. We had fewer cabinets, but puzzlingly more storage space, including one ingenious drawer that contained garbage, recycling, and compost all in one.

I could find nothing, but felt strangely warm and comfortable there, even though we could no more afford it than we could our life in London.

Julia treated my jet lag as a great game. My usual coping tactic was to try to force myself as quickly as possible into the Eastern Time hours — the result was that at a certain point in the evening I would become both heavy-lidded and incomprehensible. She would ask if I wanted to play a game and I would answer from dreamland that I wore a size eight shoe. As my eyes slowly closed, she would creep up beside me and scream in my ear: "DADDY!"

My first urgent task was to head to a government office to renew my expired driver's licence so that I would be able to legally drive Isabella's toy car. She and Julia both loved it, loved to roll down the top in summertime and play music at top volume. The Fiat was still one of the few on the road in Toronto and my wife revelled in all the admiring looks and questions. As for me, I felt that when I stopped at the beer store I was in danger of getting beaten up for driving such a girly car.

Once I was able to drive, I set out looking for a Christmas tree. I wondered how the hell we would be able to fit one in the car. Julia shared Isabella's great solution. "Daddy, you just put down the top!"

And so it was that she and I drove home in sub-zero weather with the red top of the Fiat folded back and a seven-foot Christmas tree sticking out above, an Italian joke played on a Canadian hoser.

Julia got one birthday party with her friends at Chuck E. Cheese's and another with her grandparents in London, Ontario. We somehow managed to squeeze all our presents and clothes into the tiny car for the two-hour drive — a real feat, given the need to hide certain gifts from our daughter.

But somehow it all worked. Santa satisfied Julia, family members were visited, and the holiday season played out more or less normally, even in this year of mass disruption of our lives. Our friends Jen and Gregor hosted us for New Year's Eve at their house up the street. Their kids and ours had a ball staying up until after midnight, and Gregor, to my endless gratitude, encouraged Isabella to "embrace London." It was a nice try.

On the day after New Year's I had to head to the airport for an evening flight. Julia and Isabella would be coming a few days later, arriving in London when I would be in Ireland on a shoot. Not good. The stresses, never far away, bubbled up again as I packed.

"Why did you do this to us?" asked my wife.

Once again I had no answer. At least none that would satisfy her.

The once-exotic adventure of the Toronto–London flight was starting to get routine. When flying solo, I would always try for an aisle seat farther back in the plane. We were already so packed in that at least it gave a modicum of breathing room on one side and there was no need to wake up the seatmate when nature called.

The plan this time was to land, scoot into the flat to unpack the larger suitcase, load up the carry-on, and head right back to Heathrow for a short hop to Dublin, where I was to begin a shoot for Global's current affairs program *16x9* the following day.

I loved this kind of whirlwind of travel — Toronto, London, Dublin, all in a day.

The romance was blunted by travel hell on this journey, even though Paris was added to the list of destinations. High winds over Heathrow were delaying landings. It runs close to capacity almost all the time, so it takes little to cause a traffic jam. Having already flown over the Atlantic, our jet did not have enough fuel to circle for long, so the pilot informed us that we were being diverted to Charles de Gaulle Airport.

Our view of Paris was from a tarmac far from the terminal, where we sat for an hour, refuelling and awaiting clearance to take off again for London.

My idea for a run into the flat was blown away. Instead, I shifted a few things around from the carry-on to the big suitcase, dropped the monster bag in a luggage storage place, and with a brisk walk across the terminal managed to make my Dublin flight.

At the Dublin Airport I met Kirk, the lead cameraman for *16x9*, whose journey had been even more roundabout that mine. For cost-saving reasons, he had to fly via Frankfurt. We had last worked together in minus thirty-seven degree weather in the far northwest of Ontario for a memorable story on drug abuse in isolated Indigenous communities. He is both an award-winner, with astonishing creativity, and a blast to work with.

The Ireland journey was the fruit of a suggestion from Tom, my cousin Sheila's Irish husband. The story of the Magdalene Laundries was the latest chapter in a depressing and outrageous run of revelations that have turned the Irish away from the Catholic Church.

For decades, thousands of young women, unjustly and often cruelly labelled as "fallen," or prostitutes, were handed over to an order of nuns for rehabilitation. Their so-called crime might have been having a baby out of wedlock or perhaps resisting the advances of a stepfather or maybe just being unwanted.

Their punishment was hard labour in laundries run by the nuns, where the gentle ladies of God would often impart the wisdom of the Lord through daily humiliations. The women were effectively slaves and many spent large chunks of their lifetimes trapped in these shameful institutions.

The last of the laundries only closed in the nineties, right around the time when people started asking questions about what really went on. When the nuns sold off some Dublin property at a place called High Park, a mass grave was discovered — the last, undignified resting place for some of the women who had toiled in the laundries. When the grave was investigated, it was discovered that the nuns were about as negligent with tabulation as they were with human relations — there were twenty-two more bodies buried in the mass grave than they had recorded.

Those long lost "fallen" women now spoke from beyond the grave, forcing Irish society to probe old wounds. Former residents of the laundries, shamed into silence for so long, now started talking. I would be meeting two of them, with the luxury of all the extra time and higher production values of a current affairs program. Instead of two minutes to tell their story, I would get sixteen or eighteen.

It had been almost twenty years since my previous visit to Dublin. The last time I was there, it was still a dumpy, grey place, the Celtic Tiger only just awakening. The boom of the nineties and early twenty-first century transformed it. It had now gone bust again, but the years when the money flowed left behind a Dublin that was now a much handsomer city, with elegant buildings and tony restaurants and bars — not to mention some fine residences lining the Liffey, owned by Dubliners who were deep in debt, stuck with places not worth anywhere near the price paid for them.

Kirk and I were both severely jet-lagged, but thankfully we had time to go to the hotel and rest before starting the shoot the next day. In the morning we met Steve O'Riordan, a young director of a documentary called *The Forgotten Maggies*, in which he convinced many of the laundry survivors to tell their stories for the first time.

He had already graciously put us in touch with our two subjects and over coffee at the hotel gave us directions to places to shoot around Dublin.

It was Kirk's first time driving on the wrong side of the road, but he seemed confident, so we agreed that he would take the wheel most of the time. With the help of a handy GPS, we managed to avoid getting lost.

Donnybrook is the only place I can think of that is known better as a synonym for a drunken brawl. The rowdy, boozy fairs that gave rise to the nickname are long gone and now it is just another part of southeast Dublin. There, Steve pointed us to a convent that was the site of a former laundry and a graveyard where both nuns and the deceased penitents were sent to their final rest.

It was a simple, neatly tended cemetery, with rows of stark, black crosses. On an overcast day, the greyness of the scene matched the subject matter. Kirk, always a perfectionist, searched for the unexpected framing that would give the story more visual eloquence. We lingered for an hour as he shot every possible angle. Then a groundskeeper noticed us.

I spotted him before Kirk, who was engrossed in a shot. I grabbed one of Kirk's cameras, which was on a tripod next to me and hustled over to the car, muttering to him as I passed that it appeared we were busted and should get ready to leave.

Kirk seemed unconcerned and finished his shot before walking over to join me. As he approached, his eyes suddenly opened wide and he warned me, "Watch out!"

In the rush, I had not properly opened the legs of the tripod and now it gently tipped over as I vainly tried to grab it. His lovely Nikon smashed face first into the pavement, his expensive lens shattering.

"Oh, buddy, buddy," Kirk moaned as he surveyed the damage.

As it turned out, the groundskeeper did not even come close to us, but did warn from twenty metres away, in a manner that managed to be both blandly casual and threatening, that if we did not have permission, we would be asked to leave. We carried on, figuring we would get as much as we could before being kicked out — all while I apologized profusely to Kirk for destroying his lens.

Within minutes of our meeting with the groundskeeper, a trim and tiny woman in her sixties approached us. Although not wearing a habit, her conservative dress marked her as a nun. Suddenly I was transported back to Grade 5, with boyhood fears of sisterly disciplinary action.

She asked what we were doing and I explained with a cordial smile that we were a Canadian television crew preparing a story on the Magdalene Laundries.

There was what seemed to be a long pause as she fixed me with an icy stare and a thin smile.

"Well, I'll be taking your tape then," she said.

"I'm afraid I can't do that, Sister," I responded, with a veneer of bravery that barely concealed the memories of being traumatized as a nine-year-old by a mean, cruel so-called woman of God.

Another long, cold glare. "What is your name?"

I handed over a business card.

"I'll be informing the Mother's office of this. And we will be watching." Such menace from such a tiny person. No wonder the girls in the laundries were intimidated and fearful.

As we drove away, Kirk and I were able to laugh a bit about it. But this was a heartbreaking story.

We interviewed Patsy McGarry, the long-time Religious Affairs correspondent for the *Irish Times*, who had been covering this and other Church scandals for years and who was generous in sharing his encyclopedic knowledge.

As a kid who grew up proud to call myself Irish, even though it was my great-great-grandfather who was actually born there, one phrase of Pasty's cut through all the rose-coloured views of the old country.

"Ireland was a very poor and cruel country."

It had to be, to tolerate such abuses. And now the nation was turning against the Church. Only twenty years earlier, upward of 90 percent of Catholics attended Mass on Sundays. Now, after so many cases of priestly misdeeds, attendance had plummeted into the teens. And the full story of the Magdalene Laundries was only now being probed.

"It's well known that these women were just effectively in prison for life, for uncertain offences," said Patsy.

"There's a widespread sense that [they] were badly treated, that they have real grounds for grievance and whatever should be done for them ought to be done."

But by that time, there had been nothing. As Patsy pointed out, the Irish government had already paid out huge settlements to victims of abuse by priests. With a collapsing economy, there was little more money available.

Maureen Taylor was the first of the laundry survivors we met. A round-faced woman with neatly styled auburn hair and thin glasses, Taylor, now in her sixties, told us that she had not spoken about her experience for decades. "I was ashamed. I'd never told anybody I was in the Magdalene Laundries because I felt that you were a bad person," she told us in an interview we taped at our hotel.

But now she was proud to have survived the experience.

Taylor shared with us her story of the abuse she had endured from an unnamed family member while living in England before her mother shipped her back to Ireland at age sixteen, supposedly to a school. But it turned out to be a laundry — the High Park place where the mass grave was later discovered. The nuns decreed that she would from that point be called Monica — all the young women had their own names removed upon arrival.

She tried to run away several times but was always returned to the life of hard labour and abuse.

"It's a disgrace. Absolutely ... the Church, a disgrace."

She agreed to drive out with us to Glasnevin Cemetery, the most famous in Ireland, the final resting place of many of the heroes of the struggle for independence. In 1993, the women exhumed from the mass grave at a Dublin laundry were reburied in Glasnevin with a measure of dignity that was denied them in life.

The cemetery doubles as a tourist attraction, with a museum and tours that offer insight into the lives of some of the men and women who were key players in modern Irish history. The women of the laundries had now joined them; another heartbreaking chapter for a people who had seen much tragedy and injustice.

Maureen Taylor had known of this place ever since the reburial, but until now had never visited.

A cemetery worker at the front gate directed us to the gravesite. A simple, grey stone topped with a Celtic cross marked the spot, with a long list of names engraved — Margaret Corcoran, Rose Ann

Maguire, Christina Butler, Mary Mulhall. Real names were engraved on the stones, which meant Taylor did not recognize any of them, even though the dates of their deaths indicated they likely worked shoulder to shoulder at the High Park laundry.

"I don't because they were all given religious names — you were never known as your own name, your birth name," she said, voice cracking, eyes filling.

"It breaks my heart to see that, to be quite honest with you."

She was generous with her time, allowing us to shoot her in all the many and varied angles required for our story. She made the sign of the cross as she stared at the gravestone of the lost girls, retaining enough belief in the Catholic faith to make a religious gesture, something our next survivor would never do.

After dropping Taylor back in the centre of the city, Kirk and I loaded up the rental and drove just over an hour to the southwest of Dublin to the small town of Carlow. The next morning we rang at the door of Maureen Sullivan's house. It took a few minutes for her to answer. We had awakened her.

Sullivan told us that she often slept poorly, plagued by nightmares of the nuns.

"Well, you wake up, maybe, sort of, three o'clock in the morning, screaming because the nuns used to come in and check on you at that time, always vision them around your bed, you know, in their dark clothes and not knowing what they're going to do to you," she said in our formal interview that we shot in her living room.

Like the other Maureen, Sullivan told us that she had been abused by a family member and then her mother shipped her off at age twelve to what she was told was an "industrial school." But there was no schooling, only hard labour in a laundry.

She drove with us to the nearby village of New Ross, where the old laundry still stands behind a church — a disused, dingy, yellow stucco building, with the windows bricked up.

"If you weren't doing the sheets quick enough, they'd come over and hit you and box you in the side of the face. Or your hair would get pulled," she said. "I often collapsed. Many a times, I collapsed."

We walked across the road to another cemetery, a picturesque spot with a panoramic view and a bleak undercurrent of past wrongs.

"The horror always stays with you, it never leaves, your life is, part of your life that is destroyed," she told us.

Maureen Sullivan, a Catholic from birth, is a Catholic no more — not even Christian.

"I've totally went against it."

The only high Irish churchman who would speak to us was a retired bishop named Willie Walsh, who was known as a relative progressive. It took some negotiating to get his agreement to an interview, given that he did not want to be portrayed as a spokesperson for the Church.

To meet him we had to make a three-hour drive to the west, to Ennis, in picturesque County Clare — coincidentally, not far from the home of my cousin Sheila and her husband, Tom (Suzie's parents).

To give Kirk a break, I made my debut driving on the wrong side of the road, the experience made all the more thrilling by the misty weather that made keeping on the road on a dark night an exercise in guesswork. We arrived alive, although I was gripping the wheel so tightly I virtually had to pry my fingers off.

In a neat bit of irony, we were booked into the Temple Gate Hotel, a former Convent of Mercy — and also, in the view of some locals, the site of a laundry. For our interview we were able to rent a room that was a former chapel in the convent.

I contacted Bishop Walsh because he was already on record as one of the few high officials in the Irish Church to speak out with regret about the priestly abuse of children. Although he was never involved with a laundry, he seemed genuinely regretful of the abuses.

"I think certainly a recognition, a recognition that wrong, serious wrong, has been done, but, and I think that must come, not just from Church, I think society as a whole, I think we have a society being in serious denial," he said.

The Irish government had at least launched an inquiry into the affair, but the organization that represented the order of nuns that ran the laundries would not talk to us, only offering an anodyne statement: "This is a sad, complex and dark story of Irish society that extends over one hundred and fifty years. We are willing to participate in any initiative that will bring greater clarity, understanding, and justice for all the women involved."

The words "we're sorry" were omitted.

I asked Maureen Taylor in our Dublin interview whether she ever expected an apology.

"It's not going to happen … not from the nuns, no."*

Interviews in Ennis completed, we made the long drive across the island to Dublin. Once again Kirk trusted me to take the wheel for the final leg. I only managed to have one outraged Irishman lean on his horn on the outskirts of the capital as I innocently cut him off. When the blaring hit the ten-second mark, Kirk shouted an encouraging, "All right … that's enough."

Aside from a few pickup shots the following morning, we were essentially done, free to have a traditional Irish Saturday night out on the town. An online search revealed that the Merchants Arch Bar was the "most authentic pub in Dublin." Good enough for us.

Their traditional Irish stew, washed down with a pint of Guinness, and then another pint was truly fine — so was the singing, a mixture of Top 40 hits and old Irish tunes. The warmth of the food, the stout, and the atmosphere made it one of the best nights ever in the land of my great-great-grandfather. I wonder if old Mike Mallen ever went on a pub-crawl in the capital, and ate so well, before he got on the boat to Canada.

I was thoroughly satisfied, but Kirk wanted more. Another pint was ordered, then a jaunt over to the nearby Temple Bar, which we had been told was the place to be.

It was standing room only, but we wedged our way inside. My award-winning cameraman colleague continued ordering round after

---

* Just over a year after we did our story, the Irish taoiseach (prime minister) Enda Kenny stood in the Parliament, the Dáil, and said, "This is a national shame, for which I say again I am deeply sorry."

round and they kept disappearing down my throat, even as my eyes grew heavy and the room began to spin. There were conversations with Brazilians and then two young Canadians — all very innocent and largely unintelligible, given that all the participants by this time were completely shit-faced.

It was an old-fashioned bender, the likes of which I had not experienced since university days. At 3:00 a.m. we hailed a cab, which brought us back to the hotel where we stumbled up to our rooms and into bed, regretting that we had already planned to start shooting again at 9:30 a.m.

At least I had the foresight to pre-write the stand-ups I needed to deliver on Sunday morning — although my puffy eyes may well have betrayed how much my head was throbbing. Kirk was a trouper, although his hands seemed to shake a bit more than normal, and he seemed to have difficulty finding the right focus — probably because his eyes were not exactly working properly.

Dublin left its mark on us, and not just because of drink.

The story of the Magdalene Laundries made me look at the land of my ancestors in a more nuanced way.

When I returned to London that afternoon, Isabella was already frantically cleaning because we were about to mark a milestone in our time in the U.K. — our first guests.

Iris was a Dutchwoman Isabella had met and befriended years before when they were both dancers in Montreal. Mario was a Quebecois who had fallen in love with Iris and moved with her back to her hometown in the Netherlands, where they now ran the gasoline station that had been founded by her father.

Isabella had not seen them in decades, but had always kept in touch. This would be my first meeting with the glamorous, gorgeous performers who were now small business people in an unheralded Dutch town an hour's train ride north of Amsterdam.

They booked into a hotel a couple of blocks from our Buckland flat, and we were to meet them for dinner at the Belsize Kitchen, a cozy bistro in the neighbourhood. Naturally, I was delayed at the bureau by logistical complications with my story. When it was finally put to bed, I hopped a taxi to the restaurant and rushed in the door, starved, just as they were paying the bill.

I ordered a beer, inhaled the half-eaten plate of pasta that Julia had left behind, and started to learn the story of Iris and Mario.

She was tall, blond, long-legged, and during her Montreal dancing days attracted the attention of Pierre Trudeau, who asked her on a date even though he was old enough to be her grandfather. She went, but nothing happened.

Filial duty drew her back to Holland, to take over the gas station from her aging parents. There, she drew on her rare combination of creativity and practicality to run a small business in a provincial town.

Mario was lean and ripped, still in incredible shape at age fifty-nine. He also drew famous eyes in his youth back home — Rudolf Nureyev once expressed an amorous interest, to no effect.

Mario was also a joker. He told us that upon arrival at Heathrow a humourless border agent was giving an unnecessarily hard time to a black man ahead of them in line. After a pointed interrogation, the agent ordered the man to step aside and waved Mario ahead. To which the smartassed Canadian cracked, "YES, SIR!"

Border agents as a breed are not known for their appreciation of irony. Mario had already been waiting for an hour in the lineup for non-EU passport holders. He was now treated to a further, steely-eyed interrogation to make his welcome to the U.K. all the more pleasant.

He cared not at all, more pleased with his act of defiance than upset at the ensuing delay.

Iris and Mario were beautiful, charismatic, and utterly in love. Our table was full of laughter. I had never met them before, but we were friends immediately.

The warm glow of the evening dissipated when we arrived back at the flat. Just outside our door, the ceiling was cracking. The renovation had begun on the floor above, with incessant banging, and the old plaster was starting to show the effect.

"I'm scared," whimpered Julia. "I don't want it to fall on my head."

I told her it would never happen, but resolved to complain to the property managers and the landlord.

Isabella continued her frantic cleaning the next day, knowing that we would be having Iris and Mario for dinner that night. She did her best, but there would be no disguising that we were living in an overpriced dump, with plaster on the verge of a cave-in.

We noted that our hosting skills, never the best even at home in Toronto, had atrophied into complete incompetence in London. We would be serving our guests pasta with sauce from a jar.

Luckily for us, Iris and Mario were completely unpretentious and just happy to have our company — as we were with them. They arrived with a bottle of fizzy, sweet, and undrinkable wine as a gift. They were non-drinkers and asked only for water. The bottle sat in our fridge for months before I threw it out.

We sat down at our new Ikea table only to discover that I had neglected to set out cutlery. No matter — Mario hopped up and grabbed utensils for us all. The mundane food, the crappy wine, the poor service — none of it mattered. Once again, we laughed all night long.

We learned that Mario had a bit part in a movie from the eighties, *Jesus of Montreal*. Out came the laptop — we searched out a video clip, and there he was: a smouldering, bare-chested dancer doing a hot number with a lithe partner dressed only in a bikini and pumps. No wonder Nureyev was eyeing him.

Isabella and Iris were constantly reminiscing about their Montreal days. The giggling was constant. Julia was utterly smitten. After they left, she was still so excited she took forever to fall asleep.

On Friday I managed to finish at a reasonable hour for a change so that Isabella could join them to see the musical version of *Ghost*. Mario was soon to be auditioning for a Dutch production of the show and they wanted to check it out.

On Saturday we hosted them again, this time for brunch. Once again, we were bumbling hosts. We did not even own a coffee maker, only the tiny *macchinetta del caffè* stovetop gadget that we had inherited from Isabella's Uncle Giorgio and which I had yet to figure out how to use.

And when they walked in the door, I realized we had almost no food. No problem, they said, tea and toast would be fine. Before we knew it, they were both in our crappy little kitchen making mounds of toast.

Iris finally admitted, almost apologetically, that Mario would probably like some eggs. This I could handle and I demanded that they stay seated while I scrambled some.

They had to catch a midafternoon flight, but Iris had her heart set on seeing the Crabtree & Evelyn shop on Regent Street, so we all schlepped onto the Tube and headed down. As Mario and I had not much interest in fragrance and fancy soaps, we had a quick look around, then stepped outside while the three ladies indulged themselves.

We must have looked like locals because a middle-aged couple approached asking for directions in broken English. Their accent was clearly Quebecois. Mario of course understood them perfectly, but had no idea how to direct them. I took advantage of my imperfect understanding of French to assist, and immediately started running out of words. As I struggled, Iris emerged to take over and translate into perfect French. It seemed that the Dutch gas station owner spoke both English and French better than her husband.

With departure time approaching, we power-walked over to Gordon Ramsay's restaurant at Claridge's — not that any of us wanted to drop a month's rent for a meal at the (soon to be closed) outlet of a celebrity chef, but Iris just wanted a picture. We hustled back to the flat to pick up their bags, called them a taxi, and got them on their way to the airport, all of us resolving that we needed to go to the Netherlands to visit sooner rather than later.

As I sat down on the sofa to catch my breath, I unlocked my iPhone for the first time that day to see what was happening in the world. At the top of the Twitter feed was a picture of a cruise ship lying on its side off the coast of Tuscany. Hmmm.

The *Costa Concordia* struck a rock off the Isola del Giglio, ripping a hole in its hull. It then grounded itself as frantic passengers scrambled ashore.

Within seconds, an email arrived from Vancouver, where they were just waking up on a Saturday morning: we needed to get to Italy ASAP. I took a breath and told Isabella.

"Do what you have to do," she said.

A quick check of flights found one to Rome at 8:00 p.m., and another early the following morning.

"Sunday, Sunday, Sunday," urged my wife.

Sunday it was, mainly because it would take time for Dan to get into the bureau to pack his gear.

Isabella was remarkably calm, given that I had been back in London barely a week since the Ireland trip.

"Well ... at least it's just Italy, not a war."

In an attempt to be a dutiful husband and father, I ran out to the grocer's to stock up for my wife and daughter before abandoning them again.

Chapter Nineteen

With only a couple of hours sleep, we caught a flight that left Heathrow before dawn.

The sun rose as the west coast of Italy came into sight. Dan, one seat ahead of me, said, "Look, you can see it."

Sure enough, down beneath some wispy clouds we could make out a white strip just beside the island of Giglio. As we learned later, you could actually see the *Costa Concordia* aground from space.

Our first priority was to find survivors of the shipwreck, Canadian survivors preferably, and once we recorded their interviews, get on the road to the site of the accident. Conveniently, everyone was being temporarily housed at Rome's Airport Hilton, so we did not have far to go after getting off the plane.

Passengers were not hard to find. They were wandering around the front of the Hilton, many wearing hotel slippers and borrowed robes, carrying their few belongings in plastic laundry bags. TV cameras were already pointed at some of them.

We asked everyone in sight if they were Canadian, with no luck. Every time we heard someone speaking English, they turned out to be American. We interviewed a Romanian man named Daniel, a merchant seaman by trade, who had some training in maritime safety.

"All the staff on deck was terrible," he told us, one of our first indications of how poorly the crew handled the disaster.

A personable American couple from Washington, D.C., Jeannette and Tom, told us a horror story. They had hopped into a lifeboat, only to have it stuck, high above the water, tilting precariously as a crewman tried to figure out how to lower it.

"We thought it was somewhat negligent, unfortunately. Hate to use that word," said Jeannette apologetically, as though she had anything to apologize for.

Other U.S. citizens I overheard in the corridors were already planning the great American response to disaster: a class action lawsuit. Who could blame them? You could see in their faces that they were exhausted, shell-shocked, with fury growing by the minute.

The cruise company had set up a flip chart in the lobby with information for passengers. Many had already written nasty notes about the Concordia's captain, Francesco Schettino.

I was having no success finding Canadians. One man had already been quoted in the initial reports, but repeated calls to his room got no answer. I found the names of two other Canadians staying at a nearby hotel, but no answer there either.

My stress level started to rise: this was the kind of story where reporters tear out their hair, fearing that the competition will get a compelling interview that they miss. As I searched for the number for the Canadian Embassy, we got a tip that CBC was already there, speaking to survivors. The Corp had a local stringer who was several steps ahead of us.

Fuck.

Dan and I flagged down a taxi and screamed through the quiet Sunday streets of Rome into the centre of the city. Our driver was not equipped with GPS and had to pull out an old-fashioned map book to find the address, all while the clock ticked and our prospects looked bleaker.

When we arrived our CTV friends Ben and David were already there. They had landed a couple of hours after us, but had gone directly to the embassy. They told us that the people I had been calling for hours had just emerged a few minutes earlier, declining an interview, saying that they had already spoken to the CBC.

I buzzed the door. No answer. I phoned the embassy and got voice mail. I emailed Foreign Affairs in Ottawa and got the usual maddening response: "We cannot facilitate interviews."

My blood was rising to a boil. While an Ottawa bureaucrat six time zones away was telling us staff could not help arrange interviews, it seemed that staff inside the Roman embassy was doing just that for our friends from the public broadcaster. Meanwhile, we stood outside with our thumbs up our arses, unable to access the interviews we desperately needed.

Here is where the job of a reporter can be less than admirable. We were searching for people who had endured a traumatic event. Passengers had died on that ship. I always kept their feelings in mind, but at times like this the number one priority is to find the people we need to interview and sensitively, but persistently, persuade them to go on camera to share their near-death experiences.

Succeed and you are a hero with the producers. Fail, while the competition gets the story, and you look for the nearest hole to crawl into.

After thirty futile minutes of waiting, a couple in their sixties emerged from the embassy. Dan and David scrambled their cameras onto their shoulders, Ben and I approached with microphones in hand.

The man raised a hand. "We'll talk to you … but later," he said. Although he could have easily told us to piss off, his tone was friendly. Lawrence Davis even gave us his room number at the Hilton and promised that he and his wife, Andrea, would indeed grant us an interview later in the evening. I wanted to believe him.

It was clear that we would not be driving to Isola del Giglio that night, so we went back to the Hilton, checked in, and I started writing my story. Fatalistic, I did a script without the Davises — even as I called their room repeatedly for progress reports.

Finally the call came from Dan, who was waiting downstairs: they were on their way down. It was eight o'clock, already dark in Rome but still time to get the essential element for our story and file.

We agreed with our CTV friends to share the interview on the lawn out front, because they did not want to go through the process twice. Lawrence Davis was remarkably genial about the whole thing. Andrea was understandably suspicious. She was walking with difficulty and I noticed that her feet were swollen and scabbed.

She gave Ben and me a penetrating look.

"This is just one interview for one story, yes?"

"Absolutely!" said Ben and I simultaneously.

She took our business cards and asked for our guarantee that they would not get any more calls, either at the Hilton or when they returned home to Calgary. Who could blame them? But of course our guarantees were worthless.

The Davises were enjoying a late supper when the *Concordia* went aground and started listing. It was like a scene out of *The Poseidon Adventure*. Tables started sliding over to the walls and panicked passengers ran for their lives. A crewman told them to go to their staterooms — advice that the Davises immediately recognized as stupid.

They ran on deck and found chaos.

"I told Andrea to stay away from open doors, because people were flying by like bowling balls, hitting walls, fracturing limbs," said Lawrence.

The sea was rising to their knees, with no lifeboats in sight. But they could see the shore just a short distance away, so they jumped. It was not the North Atlantic, but the Tyrrhenian Sea in January is brisk. From their vantage point, the giant cruise ship appeared to be tilting over on them, so they swam for their lives.

"I shouted at Andrea, 'Paddle, paddle!' So we kicked and swam, kicked and swam."

Adrenaline pumping, hearts pounding, they scrambled up the rocks and coral, Andrea's bare feet shredding in the frantic escape.

She pointed down at her ruined feet. "I didn't even notice. They were just these things at the ends of my legs."

While the *Concordia*'s crew were fumbling, the Giglio islanders were already springing into action, despite the late hour. As the Davises stumbled ashore, bleeding, soaked, and chilled, the locals were ready with blankets and loaned clothing. The shipwrecked passengers were brought to a church for shelter and warmth.

"This is the first day of the rest of my life," said Andrea. "We were just so grateful for everyone's support." She clutched Lawrence's arm. "And my lionheart for pulling me along the way!"

The wary Andrea had delivered a golden, sincere TV news moment.

I asked her what she thought of the *Costa Concordia's* handling of the disaster.

She pressed her lips together. "I don't think you would want to put that on the news."

Lawrence showed us his watch, which had stopped at 12:15, the moment they jumped ship. He was still wearing it, almost reflexively, but planned to throw it away.

The Davises were veteran cruisers and had planned to take another one in the Caribbean in a few weeks. Not anymore.

Interview over, I shook their hands and sincerely wished them well. Solid citizens, the Davises. Admirable people who had prevailed with grit and dignity when caught up in a lethal clown show.

And, of course, I was endlessly grateful to them for giving me an incredible story. Vancouver was thrilled. I was relieved, but faintly dissatisfied. In truth, most of my day's efforts were futile. I only stumbled onto the most important part of the story, not through any journalistic skill, but through a bit of good luck.

In the morning, we drove two hours north to Porto Santo Stefano, the jumping-off point for Giglio. Normally sleepy in January, it was teeming. There were satellite trucks parked along the port and dozens of reporters and camera crews prowling for any useful interviews.

Our immediate need was a boat to the island. The ferry had already left and would not be back for hours. We walked up and down the docks, searching for an Italian mariner who wanted to make a nice fee from a Canadian TV crew.

I spotted a blond reporter, Swedish it seemed, chatting with a guy wearing a wetsuit — evidently one of the divers searching the wreck. His English was rudimentary and he was clearly reluctant to speak to a reporter, but she was doing her best to charm him. Reflexively, Dan put his camera on his shoulder, ready to roll — but the diver held up his hand, smiled, and shook his head.

Just then, a boat pulled into the dock with several camera crews aboard. Looked like our ride had arrived. Captain Stefano Donnini normally made a living taking divers out to Giglio but was now reaping a low-season windfall shuttling both coast guard officials and media out to the disaster scene, and charging a premium.

The price would be lessened if there were more crews going, but sadly there were only five of us, and so our share was €340 — steep for a twenty-minute ferry ride, but the cost of doing business. We gratefully climbed aboard.

Whatever you think of cruise ships, floating palaces of excess consumption that they are, there is no denying they are imposing sights, towering maritime edifices — when upright. The *Costa Concordia* was now a mortally wounded behemoth — still gleaming white, but sprawled unnaturally on the rocks of Giglio. We could not take our eyes off it.

Dan rolled all the way in to the island, each shot more spectacular than the last. I took advantage of the view to shoot a couple of stand-ups with the wreck as a backdrop.

The docks at Giglio were teeming with reporters, salvage crews, and locals who were busily opening up their restaurants that had been closed for the season. We were on a tight deadline because Captain Stefano needed to head back to the mainland within an hour.

Our Swedish friends had been there the day before and had good advice for the best location, so we shared a cab for the short, bumpy ride out of the village and out to the most favourable viewpoint.

As we hiked down to the shoreline, I grabbed a quick interview with a local named Mario, who luckily also spoke some French — a good thing since my Italian is rudimentary at best, whereas my French is borderline functional. In a fractured, trilingual interview I managed to get him to say that everyone on the island knew the *Concordia*'s captain had made a mistake, because of the rocks that are just offshore.

With the clock ticking before the departure of our ride, we barely had time for Dan to grab a few more shots from shore and to knock off another stand-up before we headed back to the docks.

On the run to the mainland, I interviewed Captain Stefano, who had years of experience in the waters around Giglio.

His English was ungrammatical but powerful: "I think it was a crazy captain. When you make navigation to the coast you need a little ship."

All in all we got a much better story than I had expected when the day began.

Our home base would be the San Biagio Relais, a homey and cute hotel in nearby Orbetello. Unfortunately, it had sketchy internet service, meaning we would need to have our story done early to allow for slower upload.

As I started writing, there was an email from Isabella, saying she was pissed off and sad. "I'm sick and tired of being left on our own. Sick and tired. First you're in London for five months while we're in Canada, then Greece, Egypt, Ireland, and now Italy."

I felt my guts wrench. We had barely arrived and there was pressure to leave — and I could not blame her. I had already been considering a quick departure, given that Dan had rolled his ankle while shooting on Giglio and was now limping badly.

With a deep breath, I composed a note to Vancouver, gently suggesting that perhaps we could consider pulling out the following day.

"Wait a minute," came the immediate response from the producer. We got on the phone immediately, where I described in general terms the complications, saying Isabella was not feeling well.

"Does she have to go to the hospital?"

"Well … no, but it's tough being the sole caregiver in a new city."

"Oh, Sean …" she said sympathetically. "Stay one more day, okay?"

"Okay," I murmured.

This is why so many foreign correspondents are single … or divorced, I thought. Generally speaking, if you take the job you must expect to be sent somewhere and to stay there until the story is done. In my single days, it would have been a grand adventure. Now, happily, I was not single, which was so much better in so many ways. I suffered less loneliness in a foreign country, but being a husband and a father also brought demands on my time and presence.

The satisfaction from the day's work had now evaporated into guilt. I emailed Isabella the decision.

Her response: "Work wins again. Yippee. Hope you're having a great time. Bye."

Fuck.

It was ten o'clock before the story was safely delivered, but fortunately there were a couple of little restaurants open nearby. Dan limped and I moped as we walked into Trattoria La Pergola, a family-run place where I noted that a lovely half-litre of wine cost a mere €5. I drank it.

The next morning we found a cheaper lift out to Giglio. A guy named Luca agreed to take us and another TV crew to the island for only €140 each. Prices were dropping.

The main harbour was closed as we arrived, tied up with salvagers coming in, so Luca brought us to another landing a few hundred metres to the south. On the way in he pointed out the rock that the *Concordia* hit — the end of a shoal running out from Giglio.

"*Ha colpito l'isola* [he hit the island]," observed Luca, shaking his head in disbelief.

This was not to be a day of much newsgathering. The harbour was lined with live trucks and I was booked to do a series of hits for morning shows from coast to coast back home. It is a curious ritual — you answer roughly the same questions from different anchorpeople from Halifax to Vancouver.

In the end, the only original video we shot was a fresh stand-up. The larger portion of the day's story would be filled with elements from agencies — a common procedure for smaller operators like us.

The principal news of the day was the release of a recording of a phone conversation between a coast guard captain named Gregorio de Falco and the *Concordia*'s hapless skipper Schettino in the desperate minutes after the ship went aground.

It emerged that Schettino had gotten off the ship ahead of many of the passengers — he claimed that he had fallen into a lifeboat by accident. No one was buying it and he was already being painted as a tragically incompetent boob, who guided the ship to disaster in part because of a misguided attempt to impress his dancer girlfriend.

Captain de Falco became an instant and admired celebrity because of the way he barked at Schettino to get back aboard and do his job leading the evacuation.

New and sensational chapters were being written about the *Costa Concordia* every day.

Back at the hotel, the email from Isabella was at least neutral rather than angry as she noted that all the women in her sewing class were talking, enthralled, about the disaster. Encouraging, given that the latest word from Vancouver was that we would likely be staying until Friday.

Couldn't argue. It was an incredible story.

By Day Three we had figured out the cheapest way to get to Giglio was to arrive in time to take the scheduled ferry at 10:00 a.m. We pulled up at the docks at 9:20, and I strolled across the street to the ticket office. As I stepped up to buy, the agent looked at me with wide eyes and pointed to the sign that said departure was actually at 9:30. I looked at my watch: 9:30.

She quickly issued two tickets, shaking her head that we had no chance. I ran across the street to the dock. My eyeglass case fell out of my coat pocket and I stopped, and pirouetted to pick it up with all the grace of a hog-tied calf. It was a moment when I felt fifty-four. Dan was standing by the gangway, where he had convinced a couple of crewmembers to wait. They hauled up the ramp behind us as we hopped aboard.

The ferry was packed, both with journalists and tourists. As we approached Giglio, everyone scrambled over to the starboard side to get a view of the hulk, smartphones and news cameras alike capturing the spectacle.

The tragedy of the *Costa Concordia* had become a macabre tourist attraction, an unforgettable view, but I kept reminding myself that there were still unrecovered bodies aboard.

The media circus had grown even larger at the harbour, with multiple interviews and live shots underway simultaneously. One-stop shopping for reporters.

A slender young man named Kevin Rebello was drawing much interest from camera crews. It turned out that his brother, Russel, a waiter, was among the missing — last seen helping passengers on the listing deck, even as the captain had already gotten off. Kevin had flown in to witness the salvage efforts and to personally remind all who would listen of the human cost of the accident. Russel's picture had already been posted on Facebook, along with others who had not been accounted for.

Kevin told me that he still was optimistic his brother would be somehow found alive, but in his heart he surely must have known he was gone.

"It's very difficult. I don't know where I'm getting this courage from," he said. Next to the ship itself, the image of Kevin Rebello standing on the pebbled shore, looking out at the wreck, was the most compelling of our time on Giglio.

Officially, the Italian Coast Guard was saying that they were operating on the premise that there could still be survivors aboard. Their spokesman, Filippo Marini, could not do interviews in English, but told me in French that "absolutely, there is still hope."

The Italian representative for the salvage company was also making himself available at the harbour, and I managed a couple of questions in English about the challenge of moving 2,400 tonnes of fuel off a ship that was damaged and on its side.

The hulk kept shifting, forcing them to periodically stop work for the safety of the crews.

Meanwhile, the disgraced Captain Schettino was standing in front of a judge on the mainland, claiming that he did not deliberately abandon ship early, but, rather, fell into a lifeboat.

His story was that he had steered the *Concordia* close to the island in order to stage a salute to a former crew member who was now living on Giglio.

"But I made a mistake," he testified. "I was navigating by sight because I knew the depths well … I ordered the turn too late."

No shit.

But some nuance was creeping into the narrative of the incompetent captain. It seemed the *Concordia* had staged a similar manoeuvre just a year earlier with no mishap — and no complaint.

This would be our final day on location. Our friends from the opposition network had already headed back to Rome to fly out. The story would carry on for much longer, but there was no longer a need for us to be first-hand witnesses.

We went back to Pergola that night for supper, and with my rudimentary Italian I attempted to engage the owner in a little conversation, managing to discern that the place had been in his family for decades, and that business had been particularly good the previous few days, thanks to the media circus in town, but that it would shortly be back to the usual off-season sleepiness of January.

With unjustifiably growing confidence in my Italian, I asked him to recommend a dessert. He pointed me to the house specialty. I asked him to describe it, but all I could understand was that it was *E'buono*. He was right, it was good — some kind of chocolate ice cream thing.

The drive back to Rome the following morning was easy, and much faster than the trip up, which gave me more time to buy presents in a modest effort of reconciliation for my latest departure. Leonardo da Vinci Airport offered many gift opportunities and I opted for food: a nice chunk of pecorino Romano cheese, some pesto, a tray of mini-Nutella jars for Julia, and a couple of small bottles of wine. The latter may well have been more for me.

Sure enough, Julia screamed with delight at the Nutella bonanza and Isabella appreciated the wine and cheese. I immediately regretted not buying more. The homecoming was relatively smooth, considering the frosty communications of a few days earlier.

But there was a surprise waiting for me at Fuckland Buckland: Isabella pointed to our fake fireplace in the reception room, which had begun spewing out a dusting of little bits of rubble over the carpet. She'd witnessed their arrival earlier, as the workmen upstairs were busily pounding away. It was the latest ominous sign from the renovation that was underway over our heads, joining the cracks in the ceiling plaster just outside the door to our flat.

A complaint to the management company produced a blithe assurance that there was absolutely positively no chance of any plaster falling, but just in case they would ask the landlord above us to install some "battens" (new word for me) to assuage our silly fears. Said battens had yet to make an appearance.

Isabella now sent pictures of the detritus emerging from the fireplace to the property management company. They responded with the usual level of helpfulness that they had no jurisdiction within flats.

I now called the new upstairs landlord directly. He was effusively apologetic, saying he had arranged for his cleaning lady to come and clear up the mess in our flat. His plan, he said, was to do only minor renovations before moving in himself and that he had always lived in Belsize Park and looked forward to becoming our neighbour.

He sounded like a genuinely nice bloke.

But when Isabella met and quizzed the cleaning lady a couple of days later, it became apparent that Upstairs Landlord was yet another London bullshit artist. He was constantly buying, renovating, and flipping flats, with a team of workers on retainer going from job to job.

We could see that his guys were hauling a huge amount of wood upstairs. One day, Isabella decided to investigate, knocking on the door and asking the workers if they minded if she looked around, that she had a genuine interest in renovations. The guy who seemed to be the leader of the work crew looked wary, claimed to speak little English, and said a tour was not possible.

"What's wrong?" he asked, clearly worried she was there to complain about more damage below.

Even standing in the doorway she could see that the whole place had been gutted. Some "minor renovation."

Chapter Twenty

Julia was born after nine years of marriage and after a stressful period when we seriously began to doubt that we would ever have a child. Knowing that she would likely be the only one, I took four months off to soak up the experience, to try to learn how to be a father at forty-seven and, in theory, to establish a bond. In her early months and years, Isabella and I shared the duties of taking her to bed.

But the London experience changed things. First, I disappeared across the pond for five months, leaving Isabella as a single mother in Toronto. Even after they arrived, my long hours and trips meant that mother and daughter were often solo. Julia now often gravitated more to her mom.

In an effort to spread the parenting around, Isabella organized a daddy-daughter activity at the Little Hands sewing school where they both took courses. Run by a German expatriate named Astrid (who had married a Brit), it was a wonderful little gem on a Belsize Park side street — and it quickly became one of Isabella's and Julia's favourite places in London. For Isabella, sewing at Little Hands in the company of a diverse group of fascinating women had become a gentle, meditative antidote to the trauma of being uprooted from the life and career she had built back home.

Crafts, in truth, are not my thing. My family is full of people who are adept at working with their hands: both my brothers are talented builders who carried out major renovations to their homes, and my late mother was a prolific knitter and woodcarver.

I am the runt of the Mallen litter when it comes to building — inept, and often laughably incompetent. A summer job as a carpenter's assistant while in university ended colourfully when the boss fired me after I managed to put the roof of a cottage on crookedly. To this day I can see him standing on the frame of the building, swinging a sledge-hammer and shouting "FUCK" with each blow as he attempted to pound out my mistake.

Aside from reattaching the occasional button on a shirt (usually stabbing myself multiple times), sewing had never been a part of my life.

But this was my daughter and here was a chance to share an activity with her at a place she loved. The task of the day was to make stuffed creatures out of old socks. In the process, I would be making my debut at the controls of a sewing machine. I eyed it warily, imagining how I would explain in the emergency room of the Royal Free Hospital how I had managed to sew my thumb to a stuffed sock.

I was by far the oldest person in the room, the only male, and by some margin the clumsiest seamstress. But I did not care and neither did Julia, who had great fun mocking my misadventures with the machine, rolling her eyes with a big "Oh, Daddy" at each screw-up. I seemed unable to keep the thread properly attached to the needle, in no small part due to my fear of injury, and regularly had to send a rescue plea to the twentysomething woman who was leading the craft. She patiently advised the old guy how to put things right.

Somehow by the end of our two hours I managed to produce a stuffed tube with buttons for eyes — crookedly configured, of course, in a salute to that long ago askew cottage roof.

The daddy-daughter reunion tour continued the following weekend when her friend Zoë was to have a birthday party that started in the pool at Swiss Cottage Leisure Centre. My task was to bring Isabella's and Julia's swim gear and meet them in the lobby as they were coming from sewing.

With supreme confidence in my courier abilities, I arrived at the agreed time and place with the packages, then headed to the men's change room while they went to the ladies'.

The party was to be held in the kiddie pool where, awkwardly, I was the first to arrive. Nothing like being a middle-aged guy standing by the side of a pool full of little kids, being eyed suspiciously by the staff. Normally I would have Julia by my side to verify that I was there for legitimate purposes. Not now.

So I hopped into the pool for partial cover.

"Sir, I'm afraid you have to wait for the lifeguard to arrive," warned a staffer. Rules are rules in London, even if the water only came up to my waist.

Out again, now not only ill at ease, but dripping wet.

"Uh … I'm here for the birthday party," I explained to the staff guy, who appeared unconvinced and kept a careful, skeptical watch on me.

After a very long couple of minutes, other parents started arriving with their kids, along with the lifeguard, which give me licence to get back into the pool. The party commenced, with me as bystander because my wife and daughter had not yet arrived. Minutes passed. Anxiety rose.

After about a quarter of an hour, I realized that something was clearly wrong. Then: there they were at poolside, Julia sporting a new black one-piece bathing suit, shaking her head at me, Isabella staring daggers at me. Instantly I realized the issue: I forgot to pack Julia's suit.

"You only had ONE THING to do. Just one thing," said my wife. Turns out that once it became apparent I had neglected a key ingredient for a pool party, my daughter's swimming costume, she had to run up and down the stairs of the leisure centre several times to try out the new ones for sale at the front desk, then scramble to a bank machine for cash.

While I was now effectively a grey-haired turd floating in the kid's pool, Isabella jumped into entertainer mode for the other children. She has a knack for amusing small children, this time pretending to be a monster and drawing huge screams and giggles.

After a few minutes of silent contrition, I made my way over to Julia.

"Okay, you get to splash me in the face three times for forgetting your suit." She administered my punishment with great enthusiasm.

After an hour of watery fun, the party adjourned to Roxane and Dave's nearby flat, where I saw that they were scarily adept at organizing food and entertainment for the girls — mainly due to Roxane's talents as a chef: her job before she devoted herself full-time to her two daughters. She devised a craft that enthralled the girls: building towers out of marshmallows and toothpicks. The birthday cake she had made for Zoë was a work of art — decorated with a marine theme, complete with a jumping dolphin on top.

Chatting with Dave, I learned that they had enrolled their two girls in the Village School in Belsize Park for the fall — a place I had never heard of. The change of ownership at the Royal School was bringing not only renovations, but also a changed mandate — it was to become a school for older girls in the fall, meaning all of Julia's classmates had to make other plans.

We were still uncertain as to whether we would even be staying another year, but, in the meantime, had accepted an offer to have Julia go to a school owned by the same education conglomerate that had bought the Royal. The news that Zoë, one of her best friends, would be going somewhere else was a complication — especially given that we had also become close to the parents.

Several deadlines and decisions were about to converge on us: the future of my work, a school choice, and also whether to vacate Fuckland Buckland. I had already had an initial conversation with Vancouver about doing another year, in which I gently broached the topic of having the company pay for Julia's school — something I had learned was a basic element of most expatriate deals.

Coincident with the complications of domestic life was my planning for our next big trip: Russia. I was going there to cover the presidential elections that were to bring Vladimir Putin back to the throne that he never truly vacated.

For two months I had been working my way through the inscrutable bureaucracy of the foreign ministry in search of journalist visas.

Russia was one royal pain in the ass for the uninitiated. It started with an agonizing call in December to someone named Marina in the

Foreign Ministry. She had rudimentary English and minimal interest in being helpful, or maybe it was the Russian way of showing affection.

After several tortuous minutes, I discerned that we needed to send her our photos along with letters of assignment from head office and also fill out an online application that asked us the name of our Moscow hotel and to list every single country we had visited over the last ten years. I wondered why they didn't also demand my shoe size, whether I preferred boxers or briefs, and to submit a book report on *War and Peace*.

I screwed up the online part twice before finally getting it right. For the hotel, I just consulted Google Maps for the closest brand name property to Red Square. Only afterward did I check the actual room rates, which started at $700 U.S. per night, slightly above our usual budget (well, catastrophically above), but I decided to worry about it later — a choice that I and the budget people back in Vancouver would eventually regret. A reporter with more experience with the Russian ways later told me that he just made up the name of a hotel for his visa. If only I had known.

Marina in turn would send an "invitation" to the Russian Embassy in London, where we would go through yet another layer of bureaucracy to get the actual visas. By February, we actually succeeded in getting the required document, only to discover that we needed to separately apply for two more accreditations: one to cover the election and another that would authorize us to shoot in polling stations.

With a deep breath, I picked up the phone to call Marina in the Foreign Ministry again. After another session of mutually poor communications, I learned that for the election accreditation I needed to email more photos to her, along with a scan of the visa. She read her email address to me twice, with ever-decreasing interest and comprehension. Naturally, it bounced back when I tried sending it, and when I called back there was no answer — Russian Foreign Ministry bureaucrats evidently wrap up their workday shortly after lunch.

By this time, though, we had hired a fixer to work with us during the campaign. I asked him to get us the right address, and to explore the procedures for the polling station accreditation. For the latter, he advised that we needed yet another letter from head office — but this one needed an official seal with the logo of the company.

This touched off a massive search across the network in Canada for the keeper of the Great Seal of Global Television. I never knew that there was a Great Seal of Global Television. But, in fact, one existed, in the hands of the legal department in Calgary. So: the letter was written in Vancouver, couriered to Calgary, where the Great Seal of Global Television was affixed, then FedExed to me in London, where I in turn shipped it off to the Kremlin.

At this point I concluded that perhaps I should stop mocking Russian bureaucracy.

I had developed an appreciation for its ability to stymie any kind of useful activity, but I was to learn that it had further weapons in its inscrutable arsenal. Our fixer found the correct email address to submit our accreditation application, but days after having sent it, Ministry Marina emailed that she had not received it. It seemed that the ministry's address for receiving accreditation applications had a filter that prevented it from receiving applications. A Kremlin version of Catch-22.

Marina gave us a fax number, but it rang endlessly — the machine clearly having been briefed on the proper protocols for frustrating foreign journalists. By this time, it was Friday night and I was about to be away on vacation for a week, so I left all the information in the office for Dan and Stu to FedEx to Moscow on Monday morning.

As for me: the ski hills of Austria beckoned.

Chapter Twenty-One

The lengthy breaks in the British school system are not only a huge headache for parents, they also reminded us of the class divides. Most parents of kids at the Royal were several tax brackets above us. We heard of vacations at five-star resorts in the Maldives. A very friendly mother told me about family ski resorts in the Alps, which, upon checking, would cost me roughly the value of a new car for a week.

But as we were living in Europe, if only for a year or two, we were determined to go somewhere. Luckily, I had the equalizing factor of my travel writing, which I exploited for all it was worth.

Our Canadian friends Roxane and Dave were avid skiers. Dave was particularly passionate, and had even developed his own spreadsheet of potential resorts in the Alps, breaking down the average temperature and expected snowfall. Organized people that they were, they determined early on that they would be going to a family friendly resort in Austria called Serfaus.

Knowing how much Julia enjoyed Zoë's company, I got to work on generating a travel story. Emails were fired off to the local tourism promotion people, explaining how much I would love to bring the story of Serfaus to a Canadian audience, adding links to stories that I had already published to verify my credentials. Oh, and uh, by the way, do you, uh, offer any support for visiting journalists with commissioned stories? At times, it's occurred to me that such requests quite resemble an elegant form of begging, but in fact the tourism agencies get publicity that is easily worth far more than the costs of subsidizing a reporter's trip.

My efforts paid off with a few nights free at a nice hotel (a four-star, compared to Roxane and Dave's five-star), some lift tickets, rentals, and lessons for Julia. It was a score.

Getting to Serfaus was a bit tricky: fly to Frankfurt, transfer to a regional flight to the small city of Friedrichshafen on the north shore of Lake Constance, stay overnight, rent a car, and drive two hours across the border to the resort.

We were flying Lufthansa, so we counted on German efficiency to ensure we made our connections. But we did not account for the challenges of flying out of Heathrow. It is always up to the brim of capacity and a stray twig on a runway can cause backups that resonate all over Europe. So it was that a "ramp problem" caused us to take off forty-five minutes late.

Had we been on time, we only had seventy minutes to make our way through the vast Frankfurt airport to our connecting flight. We scrambled off the plane and started to run, only to encounter a lengthy lineup at passport control.

"We're screwed," I observed.

My wife's Italian heritage, however, taught her to pay little heed to queues.

"Come on," she ordered as she led us to the front and talked her way into the line.

More running. We arrived at a security checkpoint where my carry-on bag betrayed me. Forgot I had a bottle of water on the flight.

"This is mine now," barked a stern Frau who ordered me to go through again.

Isabella and Julia ran ahead and were waiting for me at the gate with my boarding pass. The connecting flight was late, so we made it — unlike all our bags.

Upon arrival at Friedrichshafen's little airport, one piece of luggage never appeared. It was not a tragedy, given that we were already staying overnight anyway, so we headed into the town and the hotel that I had booked online.

The next morning, baggage now complete, GPS led the way out to the highway and got us on the road to Austria. I welcomed Europe's sensible decision to drive on the right side of the road, but on the highway was always conscious to stay in the slow lane, having heard of Germanic lead foots. The time passed quickly and the scenery grew more and more spectacular.

As we approached Serfaus the road became a winding series of switchbacks headed up and up.

"Are we going to the centre of the earth?" asked Julia.

"I think I'm getting dizzy," said Isabella.

My hands gripped the wheel, knuckles whitening.

Then, there it was: a picturesque Austrian village, surrounded by mountains. If I was not concentrating on my driving I might have been tempted to step out, spin with outstretched arms, and croak "the hills are alive."

I had been warned that cars were not allowed inside Serfaus. In fact, we were allowed to drive to the hotel, the Drei Sonnen (Three Suns), but then the car stayed parked for our week. Serfaus was the definition of quaint Austrian, with cute alpine architecture, snow piled high on either side of the road, and impeccably dressed skiers clumping along in their ski boots.

It was already late afternoon, and after checking in I was immediately keen to start exploring. My ladies were less enthusiastic, even though I was the one that did all the driving while they relaxed.

Our compromise was to allow Julia her requisite swim time in the hotel pool, after which she reluctantly agreed to hike fifty metres down the street to the Patscheider ski store, where our equipment rentals had been arranged.

It was a model of friendly Germanic efficiency: within minutes all three of us were set up with our gear, which would be delivered to a satellite operation at the base of the hill where we would be catching the cable car up the mountain the following morning. It was the first in many lessons on how the Austrians know their skiing.

Dinner was in the Drei Sonnen's homey restaurant where I predictably ordered Wiener schnitzel and loved it. We all slept a little too soundly.

The first day of skiing is inevitably awkward and stressful. In an unfamiliar resort, there are the logistical issues: finding where to go to pick up the gear, getting it on, and negotiating unknown runs.

With that in mind, I asked Isabella and Julia to get up a bit early. Vainly.

"I'm tired," moaned my daughter as she tightly pulled the covers over her head. I asked sweetly for her to get up, then cajoled, then moved onto dire threats of withheld treats. I told them we needed to leave by 9:15 a.m. At 9:45 they dragged themselves out the door.

Serfaus has a permanent population of about 1,100 people but the ski trade allows it to have what they bill as the highest, and shortest subway in the world: the Dorfbahn. It runs a mere 1,280 metres through the centre of the town, ending at the base station.

We arrived at the height of ski hill rush hour. The Dorfbahn station was packed and when the train finally arrived, the crowd surged forward to get aboard, skis, poles, and elbows askew.

"Stop pushing!" screamed a man behind me. "There are children here."

Curious that he would shout his warning in German-accented English, given that we were likely the only native English-speakers in the station. All was well, however, and there were no casualties.

The ski depot was easy to find and our equipment was indeed waiting for us. But the boots that slipped on so easily at our leisure the night before were now unbending slabs of plastic that refused to accept our feet. I helped Isabella first, mindful that her bad back makes it difficult to bend over. Then Julia, jamming her feet into the boots and struggling to close the clasps.

Sweat was pouring down my face before I even attempted to put on my own. Now drenched, we lined up for the Komperdell cable car that would carry us up to the main ski area and the school. These kinds of transports are not for the laggards. The car slows down slightly as it swings through the station and you are required to promptly slide your skis and poles into the racks outside and step aboard. I carefully scrutinized the veterans doing it ahead of me in line so that I would be prepared, but still managed to crack under pressure and fumble the skis. The observant attendants calmly, with patient smiles, lifted them out of my hands and slipped them expertly into place.

We were aboard.

Julia's class was to begin at 10:15 a.m. We stepped off the cable car at 11:00. I asked a resort employee the location of the ski school and he pointed to a series of huts about fifty metres down the hill.

All the way en route to Austria, Julia protested that she did not really need lessons because she had already studied the sport back in Canada, and she brushed aside my warning that those lessons happened when she was four years old and were on the pimple-sized hills of Ontario. These were real mountains, the land where the sport was born.

Now I asked my expert skier daughter to snowplow with me the short distance down to the school area. She travelled approximately eighteen inches before tipping over. I picked her up. Fall. Pick-up. Fall. The weeping began.

"I DON'T WANNA SKI!"

I took a deep breath, reminded myself that she was only seven and that I was her father. Off came her skis and mine and we walked down to the school, with the gear over my shoulder.

There were literally hundreds of children from toddlers up to teenagers at the school, all expertly organized into their own outdoor classrooms. More Austrian ski efficiency. A couple of quick questions led me to her instructor, Peter. Her tears were now dry, but the lip was still slightly quivering as I handed her over.

Peter knew his stuff, cheerfully calling out advice and instruction in both German and English.

"We try to make it fun," he told me. "The kids learn much better."

By this time Isabella had joined us and we agreed that she should stay in the school area for a bit to ensure Julia was okay while I took a couple of quick and easy runs to warm up. When I returned, we would ski together, presuming our daughter did not want to get on a plane back to London.

My skiing abilities are modest at best. A few lessons as an introduction, coupled with sporadic excursions over the years meant that my skills were at a low intermediate level, allowing me to swoosh down easy hills with only moderate fear of disaster, while managing to enjoy the scenery.

I quickly learned that the rating system for difficulty in Austria is somewhat higher than back home. An easy run in the Alps looks much more like an intermediate in Ontario. The difficult ones appeared suicidal.

With shoulders clenched and technique shaky, I managed to make my way down to the two easiest runs adjacent to the ski school, while managing only one ungainly fall — more like a humble tip-over than a spectacular tumble.

Breathless and thighs tingling from the effort, I made my way back over to the ski school, only to see an ashen-faced Isabella trudging back up the hill, toting her skis in a tangled mess over her shoulders.

"I just had a horrible experience," she puffed, dropping the gear in the snow.

It seemed that rather than waiting for me, she decided to try a run on her own. Isabella was at best a novice, with the added complications of a chronically bad back, which limited her exercising. Predictably the "easy" runs that I found challenging with my modest skill level were disastrously hazardous for her. She fell repeatedly, was terrified by the slope, and reasoned that it would be better to just take her skis off and walk back uphill to the school.

Thus concluded the first morning of invigorating alpine sports in the Austrian Alps. We were both exhausted, and she was borderline traumatized.

Meanwhile, the kids were ready for their lunch break. Julia bounded over to us with a broad smile, telling us how much she loved ski school and could we extend the lessons to a full week? Another reminder of the resilience of seven-year-olds.

I learned later that there were approximately eighteen thousand people skiing in the Serfaus-Fiss-Ladis region that day. But the area is so massive, the runs so numerous, and the transportation so efficient that the hills did not seem crowded. By contrast, it seemed that all eighteen thousand people decided to have lunch in the various restaurants at the same time.

We were supposed to be eating with Roxane and Dave and their kids. But finding seats was next to impossible, and we ended up at separate tables. While Isabella and Julia held the seats, I trudged through the mobs to line up for food. Balancing it all on a tray while clambering in ski boots through the crowds, I managed to deliver our meal without mishap: a burger, a plate of spaghetti, and a couple of soft drinks that cost a mere €28.

"It's the wrong kind of sauce!" carped my daughter. I ended up with the pasta while she ate my burger, and Isabella contented herself with some salad and whatever was left over from the rest.

With Julia safely and happily delivered on time for the afternoon session at ski school, Isabella and I headed out onto the slopes together, with me insisting she stick to the bunny hills to avoid further mishap. Given the challenges for a beginner of riding lifts, we opted for a T-bar up the shorter hill. Approaching the top, she asked how to get off.

"Just let go," I advised calmly.

"HOW?" she demanded frantically.

At the designated drop-off spot, she hung on grimly, fearfully; body writhing as the spring pulled farther and farther out. She only released her grip when she was dumped face first into a snowbank. The T-bar snapped violently back into place, swinging around crazily in a lethal arc that would have concussed anyone unlucky enough to be in range before continuing on its journey back down the hill.

As I helped her back to her feet, she looked at me — a failure as a T-bar instructor — shooting daggers from lasers flashing beneath her snow-encrusted eyebrows. A woman who had followed us on the lift, expressed concern for Isabella's condition, and then gently but pointedly observed that her dismount technique was a hazard for anyone in the immediate area.

Chastened by our alpine incompetence, we headed warily out onto the bunny hill. With five-year-olds zipping by, adept and unafraid, she managed to make her way carefully down the run a couple of times without mishap. Then, another mistake: I suggested if she used similar caution she could probably handle the easy run that I had tried earlier.

Seeing her level of fatigue, I immediately regretted it, reversed my position, and strongly advised that it would be better if she just called it a day and signed up for a lesson the following morning so that she could get instruction from someone who knew what they were doing. By this time, though, she was determined to try. Nothing I could do or say would dissuade her.

It was instantly clear that it was far beyond her capabilities. I advised her to snowplow in a zigzag back and forth across the hill to control her speed, but she was too tired, too inexperienced. Every few feet she would tip over. Fall. Fall. Fall. After the umpteenth tumble, she was so exhausted that I had to haul her back to her feet, with a gentle remonstration: "Fuck, you are a maddening woman!"

When we finally reached the bottom, drained, sweating, and sore, she observed, "I hate skiing."

We picked up Julia from her lesson and her comment was, "I love ski school!"

Ah, the Alps.

The best part of the day was the swimming and the most welcome sauna back at the Drei Sonnen.

Day Two saw more morning torture with our daughter, who, despite the professed love for ski school, loved staying in bed more. Once again we did not leave the hotel until 9:45, but given that we now knew the routine we were able to get up the hill somewhat faster.

Still, Isabella was late for her lesson and the instructors had to ferry her up the hill in a snowmobile to join the group. Her teacher was Czech — there were many East Europeans at the ski school, the money being much better in Austria than in their homelands. Gradually she started to get the hang of things.

I tried skiing with Dave and Roxane on supposedly moderate runs, but found myself regularly on my ass. He was expert and she was more capably intermediate than me, but both showed typical Canadian patience with my uncertain performance.

As I got my ski legs under me, I became more ambitious and rode the Planseggbahn chair all the way up the mountain, ears popping, lungs struggling ever so slightly for breath in the thinner air even though the high point, called Plansegg, was a mere 2,376 metres.

The view was glorious — truly alpine. I'd consulted the piste map in advance and was going to take a long, long blue (easy) run called Zanbodenabfahrt, which Google Translate tells me means

"Zanbodenabfahrt" in English — although the *fahrt* part could be read as "run," as in ski run.

It was easy only in the Austrian terms of reference, the first part being fairly steep with me being forced to sit down a couple of times as a defensive measure. But then it opened up into a wide and gentle run that could not be more perfect for my limited skills. I liked it so much I went right back up the lift again.

The second time around I handled the steep parts better, but my legs were already tiring, and by the time I reached the bottom the technique was growing ragged with thighs screaming and skis wobbling.

It was a good time to break for lunch. Now forewarned, we arrived earlier at the eating area and all managed to get a table together. With the help of an expert teacher, Isabella was feeling better about the sport but wisely decided to recognize her physical limits and only ski a half day, saving the remaining part of her lesson until the next day.

Meanwhile, Julia was thriving, and was on her way to surpassing us both in skill level before graduating from grade school.

Although I was slowly starting to look more at ease on the hills, my wife informed me that my appearance was crap. Having done little skiing in the past few years, I had no proper ski jacket. Appearances meant little to me, as I was content to wear an old muddy-green thing that I had had for years. It had the benefit of being paid for.

Isabella shook her head at the sight from the moment we knew we were going on a ski vacation, regularly advising that it needed to be replaced rather than have her face the humiliation of accompanying a low-life bum in an Old World resort village.

I did not really want to spend the money on a new jacket but did not resist heavily when she hauled me into a shop on the main street of Serfaus where we picked out a dandy black number with green trim and I rang up €299 on the Visa card.

"Don't you dare say 'feel better?'" she warned as we stepped out of the store.

The words were already in my mouth, so I wisely demurred and just said, "I'm glad you finally agreed to let me buy this."

Although my old green jacket did have much sentimental value and I really did not think I could afford €299, I had to confess that

I felt somewhat less like a slob in my new one and wore it endlessly for years to come.

I was a whole new man in classy alpine skiwear the following day. It was snowing a bit at the base of the hill when I dropped off Julia and Isabella for their lessons. Dave and I rode up the Planseggbahn and were dropped off in a whiteout. He, being a former ski patrol guy in the Rockies, was unconcerned and advised me that the trick to negotiating fresh powder was to keep the skis closer together. Had I been able to stand up with my skis close together I might have tried it.

Not wishing to hold him up, I bid him farewell as he disappeared into the white haze en route to a red run. I pointed my boards down my old faithful Zanbodenabfahrt. Within seconds the winds picked up, the marginal visibility declined to zero, and I was in trouble. This must be what it is like to be trapped in a blizzard on Everest.

I slowed right down, not wishing to blindly ski off a cliff. My breathing became laboured, my quads were burning. Traces of fear crept into my gut, but I kept going, minimizing the speed. Whenever the whiteout lifted slightly I could see other skiers doing the same.

I realized that I still had my backpack, having foolishly neglected to hand it over to Isabella, who had already wrapped up her day. In my struggles I started falling again. A bottle of iced tea flew out of the pack's mesh holder. In one awkward tumble, I managed to do a face plant, leaving my skis uphill of my head — an impossible position for regaining your feet. I rolled over on my back, trying to get my skis downhill, remembering partway through the manoeuvre that our $2,700 camera was in the backpack that was now beneath me.

It was with no small relief that I reached the bottom, resolving to take a lesson myself at the beginning of our next ski vacation.

With our free lift tickets and rentals now at an end (and our bodies feeling their age after three intense days on the slopes), Isabella and I resolved to spend a leisurely day in the village. Not having to worry about dragging Julia out of bed, I slept in blissfully, awakened only by booms resonating throughout the valley — avalanche removal crews, I guessed.

We strolled over to Murmli Park in the centre of Serfaus. Murmli the marmot is the mascot of the region. Throughout the ski school, loudspeakers would play an incessant ditty celebrating the friendly rodent. A guy in a marmot costume was working the crowd of kids all day long, a Teutonic version of Mickey Mouse on skis.

In my interview with the Serfaus tourism representative, I asked why they chose a marmot, hoping there would be some ancient legend from the time of the Visigoths of a heroic rodent who saved the valley from imminent disaster — something to enliven my travel article.

"Because we have lots of marmots," she responded cheerfully. Okay, so Murmli would not be part of my story.

The eponymous park, however, was a charming celebration of winter, with a little toboggan run for the kids. We met Roxane there, who had already thoughtfully rented a *rodel* for her kids, which she shared with us. It was a ball riding down the gentle and neatly groomed slide and a pleasure to stand aboard the magic carpet for a free ride back up to the top — much as I enjoy the Canadian tradition of trudging up a frozen slope, dragging a toboggan, lungs exploding, feet slipping out from underneath you.

This would be our day to spend with our Canadian friends. Dinner together was planned, but we hit a snag when the suggested restaurant told us reservations were impossible. To the rescue came the genial owner of the Drei Sonnen, Franz Lechleitner.

"Your friends will be our guests," he said in limited but winning English. Franz was an exemplar of rural Austrian hospitality.

In our stay at the hotel, Franz told us a little about himself and the region. For centuries, the region was a rustic backwater, downright impoverished after the war, populated mainly by hard-working, simple farmers who scratched out a basic living. Like most Austrians, however, these farmers were born with skis attached to their feet and were expert downhillers in the wintertime.

"In my time I can remember when it was a little village with poor farmers who each owned a few cows," Franz told me in the lobby of the Drei Sonnen.

As Europe and the world embraced skiing, Serfaus transformed itself into a money magnet for skiers willing to pay for what the locals had always enjoyed as a birthright.

Franz started out as a butcher, but in the early nineties he and his wife, Irene, saw that hospitality was the local growth industry and built their little hotel. Every night Irene would stop at every dinner table with a warm greeting in her limited English. If they wanted to expand, they surely could have filled a larger place but to their credit chose to stay small.

"If a hotel gets too big, it's like a factory, not a family," said Franz.

On this night, the Lechleitners were hosting their gala dinner, which meant Strauss waltzes playing throughout and glasses of Prosecco handed out for a toast to the guests, to Serfaus, and to enjoying winter.

Sadly, Isabella was confined to the room with a splitting headache, leaving me to host our guests. Also, since the festivities delayed dinner a bit, Roxane had to leave early with their younger daughter, who was past her bedtime and fading. But Dave and I carried on with the older girls, long enough to be able to sample the chocolate buffet that topped the evening.

Friends, if you ever go to Serfaus, drop by the Drei Sonnen, say hello to Franz and Irene, and give them my compliments.

Isabella's headache was receding by the time we returned to the room and we talked about how to spend our final day in Serfaus.

Julia's tears of the first day were already a distant memory as she was now utterly devoted to ski school, so much so that she asked if she could do one extra day. The tourism people paid for three days of lessons, but if she did one more she could take part in their fun races and get a medal presentation. We gladly paid up.

As if to justify the investment, our daughter surprisingly bounded out of bed, ate her breakfast promptly, and allowed us to get to the hill thirty minutes *early*.

The Murmli song was blaring in German, something about "*SOOP-ER MOORM-LEY … dah da dah*," the guy in the rodent suit was waving and shaking hands, and the kids were all shwooshing down an easy run complete with an authentic-looking finishing line and a medal ceremony for all.

Despite the warm feeling and the medal around her neck, Julia mysteriously managed to develop a grumpy humour and in the treasured family photo we have of her parents beaming with the Austrian Alps in the background, she stands forever preserved as sour-faced.

One more swim at the Drei Sonnen pool, a quick stop at a ski shop to drop €199 that I could not afford on a pair of ski pants to match my nice new jacket that I also could not afford, and we bid farewell to lovely Serfaus.

Chapter Twenty-Two

Nine days after our return to London, Dan and I were on a flight to Moscow.

Somehow all the proper paperwork made it through the Russian bureaucracy and we were fairly certain that we could at least get into the country. Our flight was packed and I was seated next to a massive Brit, who had a head that was entirely shaved with the exception of a tuft of hair at the base of the skull that suggested Attila the Hun. A taste of what was to come perhaps.

Moscow has several airports. We landed at the busiest: dumpy Domodedovo. At passport control, the idea of an orderly lineup was a foreign concept. Far better to form an unruly arc fanning out from the agent, a rabble that never seemed to advance, only compress inward. The arrivals displayed all the jollity of zombies recently risen from the grave, with weary, dead eyes that suggested they had seen all of this before and were resigned to its hopelessness.

As a good Canadian, I gradually edged forward, my courtesy rewarded with a constant flow of Russians elbowing ahead of me. After approximately an hour in the mob, I found myself standing in front of the passport officer. She looked about twenty, although her listless eyes appeared to have seen decades of dreary Russian history.

She opened my passport to the visa, stared at it for a moment, looked at me, down to the visa again, then me, then shook her head, showed it to the officer beside her, who took it, followed the same routine, then walked it over to his adjoining desk. I moved in front of his space and opened my mouth to speak, reasoning naively that he was going to help me with whatever problem had arisen. Up came his hand, wordlessly telling me to shut up and wait.

A supervisor arrived, a large, grim woman who scrutinized my offending passport, shook her head in disgust, and disappeared with it.

Great.

A minute later she was tapping me on the shoulder and pointing me toward a side office where a younger guy of better humour explained to me in broken English that my visa listed me as British, which was problematic given that my passport was clearly Canadian. There was no point in asking why the faceless bureaucrat who issued the visa did not note that the nationality on the visa did not match the passport. He pointed at the word in question: "Британская." Not speaking or reading Russian it could have listed me as donkey.

"No problem. I fix," he said with an un-Russian grin. Five minutes later I was on my way, a nice improvement on the two and a half months it took to get the screwed-up visa.

Now I had to return to passport control where the mob of arrivals had dwindled to a mere three. The officer sadistically found a means to check every comma on the documents of the people in front of me, just to add an extra element of exquisite torture to my arrival in Moscow.

I met Dan at luggage pickup. He had gotten through only minutes ahead me, also delayed by an erroneous visa.

"It listed me as a girl," he said.

Another mere thirty minutes dealing with the carnet for his equipment at customs and we emerged from the labyrinth into the arrivals hall and found a taxi stand. The ride into the centre of Moscow took the better part of an hour — hyperspeed by local standards. It can take twice as long if traffic is bad.

The outer reaches of Moscow in late February have all the charm of any dreary North American suburb: grey, with the few people on the streets uniformly grim-faced. But as we approached the centre, the buildings grew grander, the people better-dressed.

Moscow's heart often sees swanky shops next door to dumpy greasy spoons, evidence of how Russia has both fabulous wealth and grinding poverty, often within spitting distance of each other.

Our hotel, only a short walk from Red Square, was luxurious, as it should have been for the price we were paying. I still had not gotten around to advising Vancouver about the cost issue.

Our local fixer was not Russian. Emmanuel was a tall, elegant Parisian who had moved to Moscow ten years earlier. Over coffee he explained that he came in search of adventure. Given that he arrived with little knowledge of Russian, he most certainly was an adventurous spirit. He freelanced for various French, Belgian, and Swiss publications, and did seem to be well-plugged into the local political scene. He also brought a Frenchman's sardonic view to the loopiness and edge of Russian society.

Inevitably, our first shoot had to be at Red Square to get scenic visuals. Equally inevitable was the briefness of the opportunity. Dan barely had placed his camera on the tripod when a cop came over to advise that a special permit was needed to record news video on the square. As it was unlikely to be granted before year's end, we opted to walk over to a nearby bridge that offered a perfectly fine panoramic view, without the need for paperwork.

Emmanuel had gotten wind of a stunt by the Putin forces to launch a charm offensive on the Moscow Metro: young people were to hand out one hundred thousand tulips to subway riders, just to highlight the warmth and cuddliness of the ex-KGB strongman. We dropped off Dan's news camera at the hotel and headed out with the DSLR, which was less likely to draw frowns from officialdom.

Revolution Square station (*Ploshchad Revolyutsii*) was drab at the entrance but grand below — one of the many elegant Metro stops built by the Stalinist regime between the wars to demonstrate that Communists have taste. Under the grand arches we found clumps of millennials standing around with armloads of tulips. But they were just standing there, unsure what to do next, until a party functionary arrived and gave them the cue to start spreading the love.

Emmanuel advised that the giving of flowers is a big deal in Russian culture, and sure enough, many of the Metro riders, particularly the women, were charmed by the gesture. Of course, given that they were coming indirectly from Vladimir himself, it was probably wise to smile broadly and thankfully.

As they were working for the boss, there was no issue in shooting them and doing interviews. They were all holding heart-shaped signs with poetic slogans like "Love, Not Meetings," a Putinesque elbow to the head of his opponents.

Nineteen-year-old Ivan struggled a bit when I asked him (via Emmanuel's translation) why he liked Putin. Finally he came out with: "I was able to get an education."

Twenty-seven-year-old Evgenia, who appeared to be the leader of the jolly troupe, told us, "My family's life changed after he became president. Before, we didn't even have enough food to eat."

With the arranged event duly recorded, we went in search of the undecided. On the street above the station, several vendors were selling their wares on the jammed sidewalks. Emmanuel doubted they would talk to us, given that they were acting illegally, but two of them readily spoke up.

A woman told us that she planned to vote for Putin: "He's a good guy … but the result is already decided, so it doesn't really matter."

The man standing next to her shook his head: "Everything is hard. I'll vote for Prokhorov [the billionaire owner of an NBA team]."

We trolled for more streeters as we walked back to the hotel and came up with a young man named Anton who spoke English: "I won't vote for Putin. Too much corruption." But he, too, recognized the inevitability of the so-called race.

With that, we declared a lunch break. A great thing about having a Parisian fixer was his recognition of the importance of eating well. Dan would always tell me that he would be satisfied with the Moscow outlet of Burger King, but I considered it a sacred duty to fully exploit our expense account and always sample the best of local cuisine whenever we were on the road.

Emmanuel recommended a Caucasian joint in the neighbourhood, with hearty Central Asian fare. It was dark, rustic, with heavy wooden tables — a perfect setting for a tasty stew, full of huge chunks of meat still attached to the bone.

With stomachs full, we hailed a taxi to take us to the next interview that Emmanuel had set up. Masha Lipman impressively straddled

east and west, working for the Carnegie Endowment and contribut-
ing to the *Washington Post*, while also editing a reformist magazine in
Moscow. As we set up for the interview, she explained how the publication was shut down — "collateral damage," she called it — because it
was put out of business the same day that the Kremlin pulled the plug
on a TV station that had been too critical of Putin.

Lipman believed that, although Putin would certainly win the election, his time could be running short. His opponents were heartened
by the big protests that followed the corrupted parliamentary votes a
couple of months earlier.

"His legitimacy of course has been eroded by this. His power is
weakened. He no longer has an aura of invincibility about him," she
said. Lipman made her point elegantly and convincingly, but later history showed Putin had not lost his touch for crushing opponents and
consolidating his grip.

State media were certainly still firmly on his side. There was fawning Putin coverage every day while his erstwhile opponents received
little airtime. Although polls showed him well above the 50 percent
mark that he needed to avoid a runoff, the opposition were still out
there trying.

Emmanuel arranged a shoot that evening at a gathering organized
by the Russian United Democratic Party "Yabloko," a centre-left group
that supported freedom, civil rights, and more engagement with the
West — none of which proved to be much of a vote winner in the
Russian political climate of the day. Yabloko no longer had any seats in
Parliament. Although no threat to Putin, Yabloko's presidential candidate was disqualified by election officials just to ensure he would not be
able to stir up any trouble.

Yabloko was holding a meeting to train election observers, hoping
to at least document the expected fraud. The meeting room was full,
but it made for weak television — just a few earnest speakers address-
ing an audience of earnest idealists.

As we started to shoot, there was an email from Vancouver: they
did not need a story from us that night, which meant an earlier end to
the day, but left an empty feeling. We wanted to file. I resolved to work
the video into future stories as we headed back to the hotel.

Moscow had a taxi culture unlike any I had ever seen. There were the clean limos that you could arrange through the hotel, which were ridiculously expensive and took forever to arrive. And there were the gypsy cabs, which were everywhere and instantly available.

By everywhere, I mean everywhere. All you had to do is raise your arm and within seconds a guy would pull up and offer a flat-rate ride that was a fraction of the regular cabs: usually three hundred to four hundred rubles, although you often ended up paying five hundred because the drivers rarely had change for a five-hundred-ruble bank note.

Emmanuel discouraged the use of the gypsy cabs, given that many if not most of them were sketchy operators: no taxi licence, crappy cars, and questionable drivers. But we decided that since we were travelling as a group of three men we would probably be fine, and that taking one would save the company some money on our otherwise pricey mission to Moscow.

Outside the Yabloko meeting, Dan barely raised his arm before a beat-up compact squealed to a halt. The driver pounded on his trunk to open the rickety lid. Dan deposited his tripod, slammed the trunk shut, and held up a hand that was now black from the grime. We piled inside the heap as he looked for a place to wipe it off.

Our guy had evidently been sleeping in his vehicle and not indulged in a shower for some time; as a result the car was suffused with the fragrance of rarely washed socks and underwear. Despite frigid temperatures, we lowered our windows in a vain attempt to dissipate the aroma.

The driver screamed out from the curb, weaving in and out of traffic, waving his arms, and yakking at Emmanuel. Knowing we were Western reporters, he was anxious to give his opinions on the political scene. He was a Communist, a true believer, who thought Russia had slipped into mediocrity with the fall of the Soviet Union.

Emmanuel struggled to keep up with the translation of our motormouth's monologue while we all attempted to minimize breathing to keep out the smell and simultaneously held on for dear life as his jalopy lurched around corners with a suspension that was built in Brezhnev days.

When he screamed to a halt in front of the hotel, Dan gratefully handed him a wad of rubles and we said a brisk *"Do svidaniya"* as we scrambled out and inhaled the comparatively clean air of a March Moscow night. Our first Russian Communist stank, and not only as a driver.

Westerners do not appreciate that the spirit of Communism is alive and well in Russia, even if no longer officially in power. The commies would typically finish second in the presidential races, often a distant second, but they were a force.

The next day we attended a news conference with the current leader of the party, Gennady Zyuganov. A former propaganda apparatchik from Soviet days, he had managed to not only keep the Communist movement alive but had given Boris Yeltsin reasonable competition in the nineties' elections.

Zyuganov exuded all the charm of a concrete block — his face in a permanent scowl, his voice a low rumbling monotone. Given that he was likely to finish second, and we would never have access to Putin, the room was packed with reporters, both Western and Russian.

Zyuganov intoned how things were so much better under Communist rule — that modern Russia had devolved into a dangerous, corrupt place, rife with economic inequality.

With not a hint of irony (it might involve a smile), the heir to Stalin promised to be a champion of a free press if he should ever win power.

Emmanuel brought us to a power lunch joint only a block from the hotel. It was all chrome, glass, and money, with flush businessmen served expensive meals from beautiful wait staff. He flashed a winning smile at our server, who giggled with delight.

Our fixer explained that Russian women are easily charmed by Western courtesy because Russian men tend to be so brusque. As we ate our lovely, expense account meal, he regaled us with stories of the expected fraudulent electoral tactics. It seemed that evidence of the old adage "Vote early, vote often" would be in view in the election, as many paid operatives would likely be casting many ballots in many places for the same guy.

Our next interview was with Vladimir Ryzhkov, a poster boy for the new Russia: smooth, well-groomed, English-speaking, and relatively liberal, the Putin critic was in big demand from the Western media in town for the election. We met him in the lobby of one of the luxury hotels, where he squeezed in a quick interview in between meetings with foreign election observers.

Ryzhkov's cellphone kept ringing incessantly as I tried to engage him in conversation while Dan set up for our interview. A representative of the observers stood off to the side, openly impatient that a Canadian TV crew was delaying him while a passel of dignitaries was kept waiting.

Finally, he shut off his phone, apologized with a winning smile, and gave us the full attention a media-wise Western politician understands instinctively. Like most opposition leaders, he claimed that Putin's power was eroding.

"If Putin will be so-called re-elected, protests will go on, two, maybe three years because people are tired of him and want change," he said.

Mikhail Prokhorov was also drawing much attention from foreign reporters, mainly because they actually knew who he was. The billionaire owner of the New Jersey Nets NBA team was seeking the highest office in his homeland, with lots of money to pour into a campaign that had to date yielded polling numbers south of 10 percent.

His news conference was jammed with cameras — high-priced communications consultants swarming the room, slick posters stuck up everywhere.

At six-foot-eight in an expensive suit, Prokhorov was easy to spot when he strode into the room. He had the best advice money could buy, but his answers were vague, unquotable. He refused to speak any English, as it would be a sure vote loser. The billionaire's exact motivations seemed unclear. Oligarchs who challenged Putin often came to unhappy ends, so he was choosing his words carefully and we all wondered exactly what kind of game he was playing.

With a couple of hours of downtime before our next adventure, we split up: Dan back to the hotel for room service, Emmanuel off to do his own work, me to explore the neighbourhood in search of lunch. Moscow is tricky to negotiate for visitors who do not speak Russian and who do not know where to look. I second-guessed myself, fearing that I was playing restaurant roulette before finally settling on a joint called My My, a couple of blocks from the hotel.

It was a cafeteria-type place that at least had some English translation on the posted menu. I asked a server, "Borscht?" She shook her head impassively, which I took to mean they were all out. I pointed at what appeared to be some kind of dumpling stuffed with spinach, which she plopped onto a plate and handed over with hospitality techniques evidently learned in the Gulag. It might have been a yak testicle for all I knew.

I picked up a little dish of what I presumed to be a complementary sauce. The cashier pointed at it with a head shake but I was determined to pretend I actually knew what I was doing. She shrugged. It was some kind of sickly sweet custard that in no way matched the main course, so it was left uneaten. But my yak ball was not bad at all. Even better, it did not make my ass explode, which would have made the rest of the day's work awkward.

Putin supporters, although seemingly the majority, proved to be tricky to locate. After many phone calls, Emmanuel arranged an interview with one of his more glamorous admirers. Tina Kandelaki was both the host of her own TV show and a former cover girl for the Russian version of the lad's mag *Maxim*.

In early evening, we trekked to her office, which resembled a fashion magazine's digs. Her assistant answered the door, a tall young woman who herself had the look of a supermodel: slender, sky-high heels, and a jawline so sharp it could cut paper. She served us tea and chatted while we waited. Although she would have been perfectly at home on a Paris or New York runway, she told us that she voted Communist in the parliamentary elections. The Soviet Union collapsed when she was a baby, but she believed there were many aspects of the old system that were admirable.

Then Kandelaki bustled in, apologetic for her lateness, saying she had been asked to check out some of the latest allegations of electoral fraud. She oozed TV host: perfect figure, perfect dark hair, lips painted a perfect bright right — a bundle of energy, talking about five things at once, asking our impressions of Russia, and delivering opinions a mile a minute in English that was barely understandable.

Her admiration for Putin seemed more practical than fawning.

"You can agree or disagree, but he knows what he's going to do."

She believed that despite the expected dirty tricks and the pre-ordained result, Russian democracy was showing signs of maturing.

"The next election will be with real competition, with a different class who want to take up power."

"A real democracy?" I asked.

"I hope so, yes."

We sampled Russian democracy, 2012 style, the next day.

Our small view of voting showed many Muscovites believed in the process enough to show up and cast a ballot. The halls were jammed at the polling station we attended at a school. (Our headaches over getting accreditation were justified — without it we would not have been allowed inside.)

In plain sight were some of the ninety thousand webcams that Putin had ordered installed as a nod to fighting fraud.

A young opposition party observer named Philip Miklashevsky looked at them, shrugged, and said, "It doesn't make a big difference."

Fraudsters, he noted, would need to be supremely dumb to do something illegal in sight of the cameras.

A Putin voter told me with a straight face that he thought the election would be clean, offering a ringing endorsement: "I'm voting for Putin because things didn't get worse under him."

As we exited, we bumped into a livid Margarita Vladimirovna as she stormed out, declining to cast her ballot, proclaiming loudly that the election was not fair and the voting was badly organized.

Back at the hotel, I started writing my story and incorporating the news from around the country. Turnouts were reported to be high, to the delight of the Putin forces, but observers noted many instances of the so-called carousel voters — people bussed from polling station to polling station to cast multiple ballots.

There was also a welcome outbreak of satire: the protest group FEMEN showed up at Putin's polling station minutes after he voted, stripped to the waist to reveal the slogan "We steal for Putin" painted across their bare bosoms, and made a joking attempt at taking his ballot box.

Seconds after the polls closed at 9:00 p.m., the Great Man was declared the runaway winner and he appeared on stage at a giant rally near Red Square. There appeared to be tears running down the tough guy's face as he proclaimed that his victory was a defeat for those who would destroy Russia.

We made the short walk over to the rally so that we could use the happy winners waving their flags as a backdrop for my stand-up. Clearly, many had been toasting the result with several hits of vodka.

We went to bed knowing that the result was not so newsworthy as the expected reaction. We wondered whether Russians would rise in the streets as they had after December's tainted parliamentary elections. The authorities were not going to make it easy. Even before the polls closed, hundreds of police appeared at the entrances to Red Square in a blunt message of warning.

While pro-Putin factions were given permits for several rallies at choice locations around the city the day after the election, the opposition got exactly one: for Pushkin Square. Naturally, this was where we and the world's media would descend.

We met for a coffee the morning after the election to work out a plan for the day. But first, Dan had some news: turned out that he had been propositioned by a couple of prostitutes in the lobby of our expensive hotel — they lured him over with broad smiles when he walked in after a pre-bedtime cigarette. He declined.

Emmanuel's jaw dropped. He had heard of hookers working hotels in Moscow, but never at one of the pricier joints. Hard to imagine it being tolerated so openly in the lobby of a luxury hotel in New York, London, or Paris.

Our first challenge in advance of the rally was to find expert analysis of the election result. Being a small player on the international scene, we were having trouble getting phone calls returned. Emmanuel advised that we head to the studios of RIA Novosti, the government-controlled news agency. Sure enough, the lobby was a pundits marketplace, with multiple interviews underway.

We waited in line for our chance with Nikolai Zlobin, a genial, shaggy academic who was gleaming with sweat by the time our turn came. He took no notice of drips hanging off his nose and cheerfully advised us to fire up the light and ask our questions.

Zlobin believed that Putin's real challenge would come not from the critics shouting in the streets, but from his own supporters. The president-elect made many expensive promises that could be difficult to keep.

"I suspect some of his loyal people will turn against Putin because they feel deceived," he said. "This is bigger problem I think because they have money and influence."

We rode the Metro to Pushkin Square for the opposition rally and found the station jammed with protestors. Their mood was not improved when the escalator stopped partway on the long journey to the surface, leaving hundreds immobilized, elbow-to-elbow. As the minutes dragged on, some guys in the crowd barked loudly at unconcerned transit cops who were leisurely strolling down the adjacent stairway.

Finally, the escalator came back to life and we emerged on the square. It was dusk. The place was teeming: live TV trucks parked haphazardly around the edge, protestors making their way in to join the show. There was a nod to security as we all had to pass through metal detectors to get in, but the erstwhile guards showed little interest.

Pushkin Square was filled to the brim. There were young people carrying posters depicting Putin in impossible sexual positions and older Muscovites proudly displaying the hammer and sickle, their nostalgic "I told you so" statement that things really were better when Brezhnev and gang ran the show.

As we filtered through the crowd, looking for a place to set up our tripod to record some of the speeches, there was a stir ahead. Someone important had arrived and was drawing the attention of several cameras.

It was the billionaire Prokhorov, who just that morning was pictured with other opposition leaders seated around a table with Putin in a show of unity, despite the dirty tricks. He strode right toward us so I stuck a microphone in his face, asked what he was doing at the anti-Putin rally, and was rewarded with a brief clip in English.

"After ... comments after the meeting," he said, caught off guard. Not exactly a revelatory statement, but at least something.

As the sun set, the temperature dropped and our teeth were chattering despite all the body heat. They were a well-behaved group, mostly middle class and educated, ready to make reasoned arguments but unlikely to storm the barricades of the Kremlin. After listening to the usual suspects make the usual criticisms of Putin, the rally-goers started streaming out.

We lurked around the edges, searching for trouble, and stumbled upon a skirmish. A more hard-core group was making noises about marching on Red Square, but the cops were having none of it.

The riot squad blocked the street that led to the city centre. A few protestors made a show of squeezing past, but got nowhere. The cops by Russian terms were relatively restrained — no one was clubbed, but several of the more persistent guys were given the bum's rush down the stairs to the Metro.

Dan captured some of the roughhousing, which I knew would make our story. Instinctively I walked into the middle of it, iPhone rolling, and was caught in a squeeze, then spurted out backward as the riot squad marched ahead. I flipped the video back on me for a dandy vlog as I gave a play-by-play description of how the cops were telling us all that it was time to go.

As far as I could tell, no blood was shed and the rally was petering to an end. With deadline approaching we hopped on the Metro back to the hotel to file. Things livened up afterward as the cops arrested a few diehards who refused to vacate the square, including some of the opposition leaders.

But the popular rising against Putin never really happened, even though video cameras captured some carousel voters who admitted to casting as many as five ballots.

Our final day in Moscow was quiet, a feature on Russian emigration already largely shot and written. We got some scenic video just outside Red Square, amidst a touristy outdoor market. I negotiated with a vendor to buy a nesting doll of Russian leaders, from Putin back to the czars. We agreed on a price, which he then upped as soon as I handed over a note and asked for change. Emmanuel looked at me and shrugged as the vendor impassively refused to budge off his new price — our fixer making the point through gesture that one must expect to be fleeced in a place like this.

For lunch, he took us to a restaurant called Uzbekistan, which, strangely enough, featured Uzbek food. It looked like a place out of the *Arabian Nights*, with plush sofas for seats, carpets hanging from the walls, and rooms named after Scheherazade and Ali Baba. Emmanuel said belly dancers were featured at evening meals.

We were served an Uzbek dish called *lagman,* a spicy mutton stew, accompanied by a huge loaf of bread in the shape of an oversized donut. We ripped off chunks like Taras Bulba and dipped them in our bowls. Exotic and delicious.

With that, we said farewell to Emmanuel, Dan returned to the hotel to start editing, and I took advantage of a couple of free hours for a bit of sightseeing. Most of the Kremlin museums were closed, but I did get into the armoury for a look at some royal jewels and regalia. The State Historical Museum on the opposite side of Red Square was a huge, slightly dusty tour through Russian history. Uninspiring.

It occurred to me that we had seen only a pinprick of this giant nation, scarcely getting out of central Moscow during our short visit.

After editing our final story, Dan preferred to stay at the hotel to pack his gear, but I could not resist a small night on the town. A couple of friends from the CBC invited me to meet them at a bar, so I ventured out alone, paying for a more expensive hotel taxi to minimize the chances of being hijacked to Tashkent.

The cab arrived at the appointed address, but there was no bar in sight. The driver spoke no English but had been given the address and name by the doorman at the hotel. He pointed to the darkness between two buildings. I thought for a moment about the wisdom of walking down an unlit alley on a cold Moscow night, but took a chance and survived. The entrance was just around a corner and my friends were inside a funky place full of what appeared to be students and young professionals, observing the traditional Russian custom of getting hammered on vodka.

They ordered another round, with glasses of cranberry juice on the side to quench the fire. I made the mistake of sipping my shot glass and was immediately reprimanded for a gross faux pas. In Russia, one always gulps down the entire drink. Another round was ordered to correct my form. And another. And another. Moscow spun slightly.

We called it a night before causing too much damage to ourselves. The CBC Moscow correspondent did me the courtesy of translating for the gypsy cabbie I waved down so that I had at least a shot at getting back to the hotel. The driver quickly became confused, so I just repeated "Bolshoi, Bolshoi," knowing that the theatre was only around the corner from our place. This he could find.

Swaying only slightly, I stumbled into the hotel lobby where, sure enough, two exceptionally friendly women of a certain age fixed me with a warm smile — apparently the same working ladies who had earlier introduced themselves to Dan. I smiled back and kept walking to the elevator.

Midnight in Moscow and it was time for one more sleep before getting on the plane.

Chapter Twenty-Three

We sprang for the more expensive hotel taxi to get us to the airport: five thousand rubles for a crazed driver who risked life and limb, swerving in and out of lanes in an unnecessary race that against all odds ended with our safe arrival.

Domodedovo was as chaotic on exit as it was on arrival, carry-on bags scattered everywhere as we made our way through security. I was left with about five minutes for shopping and opted for the safe choice: a stuffed Russian teddy bear for Julia.

Moscow was minus ten degrees when we left. London was nine degrees and raining when we landed at Heathrow. Thanks to the time difference, we arrived at noon, allowing me to get home in time to pick up Julia at school. She melted me immediately with her patented run and jump into my arms. There really is nothing better.

But within minutes she was pissed after I denied her request for a Nutella crepe. Crepes had grown into negotiable currency in her first months in London. Every afternoon there was a lineup of kids waiting outside the kiosk opposite the Hampstead Tube stop getting their after-school treat. For Julia, it was a key element in assuaging the challenges of adapting to a new country. If we allowed it, she would happily eat a Nutella crepe every single day. We agreed to limit her consumption to one a week. I reminded her that she had already had her ration for the week, but strong-willed seven-year-olds are not known for keeping agreements that involve limiting access to sweet treats.

"YOU'RE RUINING MY LIFE!" she wailed.

Julia was becoming noticeably more difficult to handle, showing early signs of teenaged defiance, less willing to listen.

Several stressful strands of our London life were now converging.

I was in negotiations with Vancouver for a possible second year, all contingent on whether the company would pay for Julia's schooling. And contingent on whether my wife and daughter would even agree to stay. Despite their not infrequent outbursts to the contrary, however, they seemed to be slowly relenting, slowly growing to actually enjoy London, to accept the arguments I made when I got the job, that it is a grand city with many charms and that this was a once-in-a-lifetime opportunity.

Julia had learned that wearing a uniform at school was not fatal and that it was possible to eat at a cafeteria without being poisoned by exotic foods such as "jacket potatoes." Isabella had made friends, was enjoying her time at Little Hands where she could pursue her long-held desire to improve her sewing skills, and was generally coping with being forced to abandon a much-loved job and move to another country.

Gradually we came to an understanding: if the company would pay for Julia's school, we would stay another year.

With our bargaining position in hand, I spoke to the same two people who had hired me, explaining how we had grown to love the place and I loved the job, but the economic realities were tough and most expatriate deals included paying for education.

They listened sympathetically but with no commitment.

Even if I was able to get an increase in my expense allowance, there were still critical issues to be dealt with. Isabella's patience with Fuckland Buckland was at an end. Every time she pointed out the flat's many deficiencies, and this was several times per day, I would respond that if my posting was extended, we would definitely look for something better. For now, it had the advantage of being only ridiculously overpriced as opposed to the ruinously overpriced alternatives in the neighbourhood. I pleaded with her to delay any precipitate action until we learned the status of my contract.

And there was the not-so-small matter of Julia's school. The new corporate owners of the Royal had promised minimal disruption, but key staff members were already quitting for new, more secure jobs. The building was in the midst of massive renovation, surrounded by scaffolding, with Julia's class moved out of the building into a drafty, cold portable with minimal space. The homely but venerable and welcoming Royal was being transformed, the name soon to disappear as it morphed into a school for older children.

When the chair of the parent council had had enough and pulled her girl out, Isabella took over the position and jumped into the fray, trying to hold the new owners' feet to the fire to properly maintain the place. When her outrage peaked, she and her new American friend, Carolyn, marched into the office of our MP, the redoubtable Glenda Jackson, and demanded she do something. The two-time Oscar winner listened gravely and intoned in her mellifluous voice that she would look into it. Jackson later wrote a letter, to little effect.

Julia had secured a place in another of the corporation's schools for the fall, but her teacher, Miss Eisele, told us that she feared it might be too big for our daughter — she would be in one of several classes in her age group, with no guarantee that any of the friends she made at the Royal would be in hers.

In sum, we did not know whether we were staying in London, where we would live, or where our daughter would go to school.

As if that was not already enough, the sky fell in.

It was now March. The daylight hours were growing noticeably longer, almost making you forget the bleakness of December when darkness fell at 4:00 p.m. There were days that were downright mild. No one moves to London for the weather, but I welcomed a winter where I rarely had to put on a heavy coat.

As spring approached, the blossoming fellowships with other expatriates helped carry us through the cascades of teeth-grinding frustrations. To her everlasting credit and to our collective benefit, Isabella had worked hard to nurture friendships in London — through the school, through her sewing classes and her singing group. Among the best were Carolyn and Jon from New Jersey. Their older daughter, Addie, was a classmate of Julia's, an astonishingly bright girl who had already read all of the Harry Potter books and was becoming a rare and treasured commodity: a friend who was an enlightening and positive influence. Julia shunned the Potter books at home, but Addie's enthusiasm was turning her into a Hogwarts fanatic.

Her mother, Carolyn, was both wryly funny and unassuming, belying her Ivy League law degree and sharp mind. She had given up a career as a corporate lawyer in favour of motherhood and a passion for clean, whole food that she expressed in an elegant blog.

London is replete with expatriates. The lucky ones build friendships to help each other survive the experience. We were lucky. Carolyn, Jon, Roxane, and Dave, and a few other parents from the Royal, were now fast friends, our children equally drawn to each other.

So, when Carolyn had to return to the U.S. to be present for her mother's surgery, Isabella was keen to show support, offering to pick up her girls after school, give them supper, care for them until Jon got home from work, and even sleep over to assist with the morning run.

At first I was dubious, thinking it all a bit too much. But soon I understood that it was a fine and good thing to do, an investment in a friendship that sustained and lasted.

Jon negotiated with his employer to get mornings free and gratefully told Isabella that the sleepovers were not going to be necessary. But Julia had already set her heart on it, so they agreed to do one night. She packed three bags, enough for a week's vacation: stuffed animals, toys, dolls, and even a few clothes.

On Day 2, I joined them after work for supper at Carolyn and Jon's apartment, a meal prepared by that other key member of our expatriate band, our Calgary friend Roxane. Something about being fellow foreigners in a great city of the world brought out the generosity in us all.

There was to be no sleepover this night, but Julia displayed adroit methods of obstructionism in avoiding our calls to go home. We knew Jon was desperate to get his kids to bed, but our daughter continually ignored our calls to get dressed — lying on the ground, finding new things to play with. Both of us were on the verge of blowing up before we finally got her out the door.

All was forgotten upon arrival at Fuckland Buckland.

I slipped my key into the front door and expertly wiggled it just so, in order that it would not jam — a skill learned through several weeks of trial and error in which I was frequently trapped outside with an armload of groceries.

Flicking on the hallway light, I admired again the Ikea shade that we had bought at our own expense to disguise the bare bulb. It gave us a clear view of the hallway that was growing filthier by the day, thanks to the renovations upstairs. The dirt-coloured carpet was now coated in a thick layer of construction dust.

More cracks had appeared in the ceiling above our door, the ancient plaster suffering from the incessant pounding from above. We had taken little comfort from the assurances of the building management company that it was in no danger of collapse. It was now two months since the renovator had promised to put up battens to assuage our foolish concerns of danger, and they had yet to arrive.

It had been a long day and Julia was going to bed late for a school night, so it was with some weariness that I opened the door and flicked on the light.

Our jaws dropped.

The grand reception room was a shambles. A huge patch of Victorian-era plaster had given way in the ceiling and collapsed. The dining table, sofas, and carpets were layered with rubble.

Our laptops, rashly left open on the dining-room table, were coated with a thick layer of dust. The same dust storm had turned the puke-coloured carpet the same shade of dun grey as the hallway. The overhead lighting fixture had swung from its position in the centre of the ceiling and gouged a divot out of the wall — in exactly the spot where my beloved daughter's head would normally be positioned as she watched television.

"What the …?" was my Shakespearean comment.

Julia screamed, "MY LIFE IS RUINED!"

She ran into the closet, emerging with an umbrella that she opened to protect against any further calamities from above.

"I DON'T WANNA LIVE HERE ANYMORE. WE'RE GONNA DIE!" she wailed, cowering under her bumbershoot.

Isabella was euphoric, seeing it as our ticket to break the lease and escape.

"YES! Now we can get out of this dump!"

I saw her point. But also saw no reason to celebrate.

"Uh … I'm thinking this is just going to be one giant headache."

I got on the phone with Upstairs Landlord, told him what had happened, and said I would forward pictures. He sounded as stunned as us, told me not to bother with the pics, and added that he would be there first thing in the morning.

Each step into the room revealed a new aspect of the catastrophe. Both our laptops were covered in dust and bits of rubble. The bright red rug Isabella had bought at Ikea to give the room a splash of colour was now a dusty grey. I took a long look at the dent in the wall that was gouged out by the light fixture that would have clobbered Julia had we not been out for the evening. Shock began to turn to anger.

We forwarded pictures of the disaster to friends back home, the landlord, and the building management company, which had so patronizingly told us that there was no way the ceiling over the door could collapse. I reminded them of the promised battens that had never appeared.

There had been no sign of cracking in the reception room ceiling, no warning of the imminent cave-in. It was only Isabella's generous offer of help for a friend that had us out of the flat when the sky came tumbling down.

Sleep was impossible. Julia was too frightened to be in her room alone so she crawled in between us. As she snoozed, Isabella and I stayed up for hours talking about the implications of what had happened and a plan of attack. But we were in a foreign country, with only a passing understanding of our rights.

Somehow, I dozed off for a brief, unrefreshing sleep. I awoke before dawn and stared blankly at the ceiling for a time, wondering what the fuck could possibly happen next. Radiating out from one corner of the ceiling was a crack in the plaster. That's what the fuck could happen next.

We needed to get someone official to declare that the flat was dangerous and uninhabitable, and in the meantime the guys upstairs needed to stop work before they brought down more disaster upon our heads. I fired off an email to Upstairs Landlord, asking politely that his workers down tools until we sorted out the potential dangers, a message I passed along to his guys when I heard them arriving. They looked at me blankly, shrugged, and carried on up the stairs. Within minutes their hammering continued.

Stepping over the rubble, I made my way into the dust-covered kitchen to make a bit of breakfast for us all. Isabella took Julia to school while I awaited Upstairs Landlord.

He arrived, grim-faced, striding past me into the reception room to survey the mess.

"Have you asked your guys to stop working?" I asked.

"No."

"I think you should tell them to stop."

"No."

Fuck this.

"Then I'm going to have to call the police."

Boom. The floodgates opened to reveal all that had been churning in his mind overnight.

"Then call the police!" shouted Upstairs Landlord. "No insurance company in the world will cover that ... we weren't even working when it came down."

The ferocity of his response put me back on my heels. I managed to blurt out something about how we just wanted our costs covered for the damage and our accommodations while we searched for a new place.

"No ... no way," he ranted.

Now, I found myself trying to calm him down.

"I suppose this is stressful, but we're not trying to gouge you. We just want —"

Another interruption: "I'M NOT STRESSED BY THIS," he screamed. "You want, my guys can clean it up and patch it in a day. What's stressing me is that you're trying to use me to get out of your lease!"

Now I became pissed, reminding him that we were the ones who had the ceiling cave in and that it was only luck that had us out of the place when it all happened, otherwise we might all be in the hospital. This did not cause the conversation to flow any more fruitfully. After a few minutes of back and forth he strode out.

I sent an email to Isabella: "Huge argument with Upstairs Landlord." Her response: "We need legal advice ASAP."

I placed a green garbage bag over a dusty chair, brushed the detritus off my laptop, and Googled: "legal advice Camden."

The first place that came up said that due to budgetary reductions its hours had been slashed — not open until 1:00 p.m. I called the second legal clinic and got an answering machine that advised they opened at 10:00 a.m. It was already 10:10.

My political instincts kicked in and I looked up the local Camden councillor. Turns out that these are only part-time jobs, but I managed to get through to a sympathetic assistant, who promised to call a "building control" officer, who would come to inspect and if necessary shut down an unsafe workplace.

By this time Isabella had returned. A friend from her sewing class put us in touch with a lawyer, who gave a quick and free consult over the phone: very difficult to break a lease, even in the face of this kind of catastrophe, but we could make a claim in small claims court for our damages.

As she talked, stray pieces of plaster continued to drop from the ceiling. We started coughing with all the dust in the air.

By now her jubilation from the previous night had been replaced with cold anger.

"I thought if our ceiling fell on us that people would want to help."

She called the police, who promised to arrive within the hour, then they called back to say they would not be coming but would forward our case to Camden building control — the same people the councillor's assistant contacted.

I sent out another email to friends and colleagues, complete with a photo gallery:

"Here's what you get for $3,450/month in London: cracked ceilings, drafty windows, cacophonous rattling washer-dryer, filthy common area, lady downstairs who plays the same music every night at 11:00 p.m. and who thinks English neo-fascists have great ideas, and now, the *coup de grâce*, a collapsed ceiling in the living room."

My Queen's Park pal Randy wrote back immediately: "You should dust more. Maybe buy a Swiffer."

Some eighteen hours after I had emailed him about the disaster, the landlord finally picked up a phone to call.

"I'm sorry but it appears your flat is ruined," I advised. He admitted that he had never spoken to Upstairs Landlord, despite all my reports of cracked ceilings and debris falling through the fireplace.

I told him that we now wanted to leave the flat as soon as feasible and asked if he would be willing to allow notice of less than two months, given the calamity that had befallen us. He bobbed, weaved, changed the subject, and when I persisted, claimed that he needed to check with his estate agent. My bullshit detector moved into the red zone. He was not going to budge, but did not want to say it.

In early afternoon, the official from Camden Building Control arrived on the scene, displaying all the decisiveness of a career bureaucrat.

I wanted the flat declared as dangerous and unfit for human habitation, but he hesitated. "Well, the reception room would certainly appear uninhabitable," he declared tentatively, gazing at the pile of rubble, the hole in the ceiling plaster and the bits that continued to fall. No shit, Einstein.

But he seemed dubious about the rest of the flat, despite the cracks in the ceilings both in the master bedroom and outside the door in the hallway, despite a ceiling collapse in the bathroom the year before, and despite the plaster avalanche that had just befallen. I explained that I was not a structural engineer, but two collapses with other cracks showing might possibly suggest there was a risk of another.

When we persisted, he asked for a broom and used the handle to probe the bedroom ceiling. With a gentle touch, it poked right through the plaster directly above our bed.

"Hmmm," he observed, evidently unconvinced unless it all caved in right in front of him.

"Well, it's up to your landlord to call a surveyor to get a professional opinion."

I dialed the landlord's number, got him on the phone, and handed it over to Mr. Building Control, who in turn advised our landlord that he needed to call in a surveyor immediately. It seemed, listening to one side of the conversation, that our landlord was in no particular hurry, clearly not intimidated by this flaccid functionary from local government.

We heard a commotion in the hallway outside. Upstairs Landlord's workers were busily putting up drywall over the cracked plaster over our door. This would be the work they had promised to do two months' earlier, work that the building management had said was merely to put our foolish colonial minds at rest because there was no chance in hell of any plaster falling.

Mr. Building Control went out to talk to them and then upstairs to Upstairs Landlord, returning with the renovator's complaint that we were the real problem in the whole affair — that we were obstructing his efforts to conduct repairs in our flat.

Ah yes, of course, clearly it was entirely our fault that the plaster in our overpriced, crappy flat collapsed and we were so sorry to be of such inconvenience to the lying, flat-flipping scoundrel, and we must certainly apologize for ruining the day of our absent, uninterested landlord. Utterly unreasonable of us to expect some kind of restitution and support after having the apartment rendered uninhabitable, our laptops possibly wrecked, our furniture and belongings despoiled, and our lungs filled with toxic dust.

After I picked my jaw up off the floor, I pushed him for some kind of official declaration that we could not safely live in the place. He remained doubtful of the dangers in the bedroom. It was too much for Isabella. She grabbed the broom, hopped up precariously on the bed and furiously poked at the ceiling, easily creating several more holes to reinforce the point.

Out of breath, red of face, and teetering on the mattress, she glared at Mr. Building Control and said, "SEE?"

Unimpressed, he said he would write a report on what he had observed.

Our journey through British bureaucracy and what might laughingly be described as the justice system for tenants had led us exactly nowhere. The pounding above continued, our landlord was evading responsibility, the contractor who had caused the cave-in was blaming us, and no one seemed to give a shit. Oh, and we had no place to stay.

Searching for temporary accommodations proved tricky. The bed and breakfast down the street was booked, as was another nearby hotel close to the Swiss Cottage Tube stop. How was it that no rooms could be found in north London on a Tuesday in March?

Finally, I found a discount hotel near the Belsize Park Tube that had a room for two nights. I stayed in the ruined flat to pack while Isabella went to pick up Julia and Carolyn's girls at school.

While she was out, she started firing email rockets, arguing that we should refuse to allow Upstairs Landlord to start repairs until we got satisfaction on our demands.

"I don't think it helps our cause to be obstructive," I responded with what I thought was a reasonable tone.

Her response was fiery: "BACK OFF! I'm busy with the kids and if you give me a hard time, I'm packing up Julia and flying to Toronto."

I took a deep breath, filling my lungs with the toxic dust, trying to keep my head from exploding. It was now early evening. I took a taxi with our bags to the hotel and checked in. No sign of my wife and daughter, so I went down to the hotel, ordered a Guinness-and-meat pie, and had a morose, solo supper.

They arrived in a foul mood.

"We should immediately stop paying rent," said Isabella. "This is all negligence."

Julia was disobedient and defiant. I offered to sit beside her on the bed and read Harry Potter to her before sleep time.

"There's no room, Daddy!" she complained, squirming as I attempted to make space. Immediately, I was pissed and barked at her, prompting little girl tears. Now regretful, I relented, moved off to a side chair, and opened the *Philosopher's Stone* to read.

But stress and lack of sleep left me feeling exhausted, drained, and beaten up. Halfway down the first page, my eyes became heavy, my reading deteriorating into near gibberish. I looked up to tell her I could not continue, but she had already passed out.

At last the day ended. What a fucking day. Sleep was lousy. There was now officially too damn much happening at once.

In the morning, we somehow managed to get Julia off to school, then rushed up to Hampstead to check out a school where she might be able to go in the fall, "might" being the operative word given that I did not even know if Global would renew me, whether we could get out of the commitment to the corporate owner's other school, or whether we would even have a place to live.

After a flash tour of the school, we walked across the street to an estate agent — the same guy who showed us the late, lamented Upper Park Road place that we (I) declined. Once again, we had to launch into the mug's game of flat-hunting in London.

At Isabella's request, his supervisor had a look at our Fuckland Buckland rental agreement, in search of a means of escape. He found a clause that allowed us to break the lease if the apartment could be rendered uninhabitable, but said it would be of little use, given that once repairs were made it would soon be habitable again. Habitable, that is, in the fucked-up, overpriced London fashion.

As I had taken the day off work to deal with our converging crises, I was able to join Isabella for the Julia pickup at the Royal, and to get a taste of trailing spouse culture. I was the only man in the schoolyard, joining the moms to chat while we awaited the emergence of our children.

All listened sympathetically to our tale of woe, and added similar anecdotes from the London housing scene. All their husbands had far better deals from their employers; all made far more money than me.

Back at the hotel, Isabella got a call from her lawyer friend, who gave a detailed briefing. It seemed we had a case for claiming negligence against our landlord, perhaps enough to force him to let us out of the lease and cough up some damages. Isabella made an appointment to meet with the lawyer the next day to talk about drafting a threatening letter, a service that would cost us £400.

I pulled out my laptop and started writing, figuring that I could be just as threatening as a lawyer, minus the fee. My wife was skeptical, preferring that we spend the money to craft our threats professionally.

At eleven o'clock, she had an inspiration. "I'm calling our landlord," she announced.

It took three tries before anyone at his house picked up the phone. His wife, who was not inclined to put her husband on the line.

"I'm sorry, but this is an emergency," Isabella insisted, until the landlord's wife finally relented.

For thirty intense minutes, my wife calmly, firmly, and in a businesslike fashion kicked his ass all up and down the sceptered isle.

"This is negligence," she stated simply, and then went on to list exactly why. The landlord was clearly trying to dispute the point.

"Don't interrupt," she barked in a stern teacher's voice.

And so it went. Hearing only her side of the conversation, it was obvious that he was resisting, but she did not back down, citing the lawyer's advice and persisting with plain common sense.

At times it got heated, but finally he seemed to relent, with the notice possibly reduced to a single month. He probably just wanted to get off the phone.

By the end they were pals, with Isabella suggesting that Fuckland Buckland could be easily improved with a few designer touches, allowing him to charge more rent. She even offered to do a consult!

Finally she hung up.

"He was scared," she said.

It was exhilarating to witness her dismantling the landlord, who I always judged to be not a creep, actually a rather nice chap. Just not very interested in doing much to take care of his flat.

I stayed up late to draft a letter summarizing our demands, while Isabella scanned the web for alternative accommodations.

Once again, sleep was a casualty.

In the morning I ran back to the flat to get clothes because I was planning to try to get back to work. Upstairs Landlord's guys were removing our furniture to be cleaned while they started repairs on the ceiling.

Before I could head into the office we had to check out another possible school, the Village School, because that was where Julia's Canadian pal Zoë would be going in the fall. It was a beautiful old mansion, just off Haverstock Hill, with a lovely little playground. Promising.

From there, we needed to check out a flat that Isabella had already spotted: a three-bedroom place just around the corner from Fuckland Buckland. It was a roomy ground-floor flat, with three cans and lots of light.

We stepped out front after our tour and an intense discussion broke out on a park bench.

"I like it and I want to put an offer in right now before we lose it," Isabella declared.

It was a dizzying £795 a week, a massive increase in the rent that we already could not afford.

"That's what it costs to live here."

At this point we had not even confirmed that our landlord would let us out of the lease, despite Isabella's verbal battering of him. Belsize Park was spinning as I weighed financial disaster on one hand with an angry, determined wife on the other.

"I will not lose this flat," she said.

"Mommy, Daddy, I WANT TO GO," said Julia, utterly uninterested in the whole affair.

Walking down to work was a relief. As I collapsed into my chair, seeking solace in watching news reports on how the world was falling apart, an email arrived from our landlord. He had agreed to let us go as soon as we found another place. I quickly, gratefully responded, telling him not to worry about our demand that we be refunded a week's rent. No sooner did I press send than I realized I was an idiot, that of course he should be returning our £500 for the week that we could not use the flat, and immediately fired off another note saying we would definitely need the money.

Meanwhile, Isabella was furiously negotiating with the estate agent and landlord for the new place. The agent claimed there was a competing offer from an American family, an offer that had just been improved. All a lie, I was quite certain.

"I think we've lost it," said Isabella in an email. But only a few minutes later the agent advised that the flat was indeed ours, for £775 a week, far beyond our means.

Time to just accept that London was now officially a financial disaster.

The new landlord flatly refused to give us an open-ended break clause. Isabella managed to negotiate a one-time window to get out of the lease. If it did not work out, we had one day in July where we could give him two months' notice that we wanted out.

It conveniently dovetailed with our potential return date to Canada, depending on what happened at work.

Except: I got a call from my Vancouver supervisors. They were ready to make a decision. They asked once again: was the cost of schooling a deal breaker?

"We're already in deficit every month," I said.

One producer seemed hesitant, but then the other jumped in decisively. "Okay. We think you're an asset to the program and we'd like you to stay. We're going to pay."

I could scarcely believe my ears. I was getting a second year in London. I called Isabella with the news.

"O … kay," was her restrained response. At least she did not dissolve into tears.

One issue settled.

As I put my story to bed in early evening, she called me: the hotel was refusing to let them into the room, even though I had confirmed we could stay another night.

I ran out to the high street, flagged a taxi, and raced up to meet them, finding them sitting in the nondescript lobby as Julia did her homework.

Steamed, I walked over to reception.

"Oh, we just needed you to pay for the room," said the hotel woman blithely.

"You kept my exhausted wife and daughter waiting because you needed payment? Why didn't you just ask her for her credit card?"

"Oh. They said they wanted to wait for you here."

Another London liar.

The next morning, Saturday, we moved over to the B&B down the street from the flat. The only available room was on the top floor, just underneath the rafters, the can was down a flight of stairs. Not the Savoy.

The estate agent for the new flat was pressuring us to get all the papers signed right away and the money handed over. We had promised Julia we would take her to the pool, but it had to wait. It was an unhappy, cranky, crying girl who we dragged to the agent's office, but we could scarcely be angry. The kid had been through a lot that week.

The agent looked drained. He had a head cold that kept him dabbing at his nose with Kleenex. It seemed that he had a demanding landlord and now a demanding tenant. Isabella insisted on reading every clause of the agreement, quizzing the agent about each clause.

She spotted the requirement for a "professional cleaning" for when we move out. Knowing the state of disrepair of most of the flats we had seen or lived in, she found it an insult to demand that we pay hundreds of pounds for cleaners when we could perfectly well hoover the place ourselves.

"I'm not signing."

"You're not signing?" said the agent weakly, trying to control a dribble of snot from his nose.

"I'm not signing."

I chose wisely to not remind her at this moment how she had been adamant two days ago that she was not going to lose this flat.

I ventured: "It's standard, Isabella. All London rental agreements have it."

She was doubtful, but finally relented.

Then came the time to pay up: six weeks rent for the larceny that they call a deposit, plus the first month's rent in advance. I realized belatedly that our U.K. bank account did not have sufficient funds, a transfer of money from Canada having not yet been processed. No problem. London estate agents are happy to take your credit card. My balance burst through to an impressive new high.

But it was done. We had a new place. Now we just needed to move. Again. In two days.

That night an email arrived from the Royal: two of the senior staff people were leaving to take new jobs, not waiting for the official takeover by the conglomerate. Isabella was livid.

"London is so corrupt. I just want out of this fucking city."

I laid on the lumpy bed, staring at the ceiling as she ranted and I added up the converging calamities:

- ceiling falls in
- nasty negotiations with our landlord and the landlord above
- need to find new flat and move
- need to find new school
- school seeing staff desertions
- only my work situation had been recently resolved

If this were a prizefight, the referee would stop it, seeing me hanging off the ropes, bleeding and semi-conscious, thoroughly pummelled into submission by London.

But it was not a fight, there was no referee, so this palooka carried on despite the risk of brain damage.

The next morning an urgent email arrived from Isabella. I needed to get back to Buckland pronto. It seemed that Mr. Upstairs Landlord's guys were there with our freshly cleaned furniture and were grumpily claiming that they had been kept waiting. As I flagged down a taxi, she forwarded a snippy note from Upstairs Landlord where he groused that his guys had been standing around since 7:00 a.m. Of course he had neglected to inform us that he wanted to deliver our stuff bright and early. Lacking psychic abilities, we somehow missed the message.

It was part of a growing pattern of snippiness from him, complaining that we were not giving him proper access to our flat for the cleanup. All bullshit. Despite Isabella's murmured threats, we let them in whenever they needed.

He was perhaps tuning in to the reality that it really should have been our landlord covering all our costs.

Upon arrival, we ran upstairs to find furniture being moved in and Isabella in the bedroom with the door closed.

"You deal with them," she said grimly.

"We've been waiting since 7:00 a.m.," groused the lead mover, parroting the boss's line.

The words formed in my mind: "You can kiss my Royal Irish arse [a lovely James Joyce insult] for not being psychic."

But facing three large, grumpy guys with my furniture in their hands, I settled for the more prosaic, if safer: "You gotta give us notice, fellas."

I told them to just put the stuff down in roughly the right spots, just wanting them out.

Fuckland Buckland was now clean as a whistle, with new ceilings in both the reception room and our bedroom — although Upstairs

Landlord grumbled about the mysterious holes in the bedroom ceiling, suggesting darkly that we should be the ones paying for that damage. I neglected to respond directly, focusing only on the couple of holes created by the guy from the council and somehow forgetting to include the detail of the further aeration perpetrated by my wife.

A friend of Isabella's from Toronto, an interior designer who had often advised us, sent her a note suggesting that it was a bit kooky to abandon the flat, now that it was all fixed up. It gave us a moment of pause. But only a moment. The money was spent on the new place, the Buckland folks now thoroughly alienated, and our minds made up.

Chapter Twenty-four

Our final week in Fuckland Buckland flew by in a flash of tension, improvisation, and emotional swings.

My patience with Julia, my gorgeous if willful seven-year-old, was worn to a nub. One morning she was particularly obstinate, refusing to get out of bed to prepare for school. I snapped, getting in her face and hissing, "GET READY NOW OR I SWEAR I'LL CARRY YOU TO SCHOOL IN YOUR PAJAMAS!"

There was a stunned pause for a beat before she began to wail. I stomped out to the bathroom and was instantaneously overcome with guilt. I rushed back into her bedroom where she was being comforted by Isabella, knelt down in front of her, my eyes now welling, and sputtered out, "I'm SO sorry!"

She immediately stopped crying and stared, puzzled.

Isabella: "Don't cry! You're scaring her."

Later that day, Isabella texted me: "You should know that Julia is telling all her friends that she saw her daddy crying."

"Excellent," I responded. "Don't know if I'll include that part in the book."

"Not funny."

An estate agent phoned, wanting to show Buckland to a prospective sucker tenant. It reminded me that we had not actually gotten confirmation from our landlord that he would carry through with the promise to refund a week's rent. I called him. The conversation began cordially enough, but quickly deteriorated. He was peeved that Isabella had recommended in an email to Upstairs Landlord that he might want to consider suing our landlord to recover costs.

"That wasn't right," he snipped. "I'll just have to THINK about whether I'll refund that money to you." The tone was exquisitely English snark.

My hands were forming into an Italian salute but my telephone voice was conciliatory, verging on pleading. He still held our £3,000 deposit as ransom, and until we got that money back I did not want to provoke him further. He left the issue hanging. I swallowed my "I'll see you in fucking court" response — saving it for later.

As I hung up, an email from Isabella popped up on the screen. She was scouting out the new flat, now suddenly second-guessing her haste and determination, wondering whether we could afford it, predicting that it would certainly bring a whole new set of problems.

"Just don't go there," I advised, remembering how she had demanded we move quickly to bid on the place.

I was getting my head around the reality that it was far beyond our means, reasoning that we would only be in London for another year and that the extraordinary rent would only lead to the equivalent of a new car's worth of debt.

If only …

It is extraordinary how quickly human beings can accumulate stuff. We had been in Fuckland Buckland for less than a year, but now as we packed, the boxes of belongings kept growing. I made multiple trips to buy more boxes. It was crucial to have everything packed and organized because the movers were charging by the hour.

Moving day was a Tuesday and we seemed to be ready. Two remarkably slight and excruciatingly slow movers showed up at the door to pick up our stuff.

The boxes we had carefully packed were all made to stack and move on trolleys. But our guys chose to carry them out one at a time at a leisurely pace.

I gently suggested, "Perhaps if you use a trolley you could transport a few at a time."

"Ah no, mate. By the time I got the trolley up here, we'd already have moved them," he responded with the calculating logic of a guy being paid by the hour.

So I pitched in, lugging boxes out to the truck at roughly double their pace.

And then came the sofa. Ah, the sofa. Our Ikea hide-a-bed that Isabella insisted we buy so that we would be able to accommodate our many visitors from Canada, the visitors who had yet to arrive. This would be the same sofa that was delivered in boxes and assembled INSIDE our flat.

After nearly killing myself moving a massively heavy sofa bed in my student days, I had resolved to never ever buy another one. But my wife insisted. Needed to be ready for the mythical visitors, you see.

Now as our skinny, leisurely, paid-by-the-hour movers hoisted the back-breaker from Sweden, I watched in horror as they attempted to guide it through the door and failed. They turned it every possible angle and still it would not fit.

I instructed them to set it down and that I would remove the bed apparatus while they continued to saunter out with our boxes.

I was not present when the bed was assembled — we hired a guy to do it for us. So now as the clock ticked I worked frantically to figure out how the damn thing came apart. In a masterwork of Swedish engineering, the bolts were not only well-hidden but ingeniously situated so that you could only turn them a millimetre at a time, this while splayed out on my back underneath the heavy metal bed that threatened to either amputate a finger in the mechanism or collapse upon my sweating brow, ending my London misery in an epic furniture fail.

For fully thirty minutes I writhed beneath the never-used sofa bed, as the amiable movers sat and watched, having finally brought all our boxes out to their truck.

Finally, it was free! We lifted out the bed and they grabbed the shell of the sofa that I thought must certainly now be able to be manoeuvred out the door. Certainly fucking not.

They gently edged it around the corner until the space dwindled to nothing. It was wedged.

"Maybe we can bend it just a bit," I suggested, perspiration now pouring down my face.

I pushed a bit harder.

Crack!

A bolt was starting to rip through the particleboard frame at one end. Fuck.

We brought it back inside and I unbolted one armrest. At last it was dismantled enough to be freed from Buckland.

The drive to the new flat took all of thirty seconds. The unloading somewhat longer thanks to our genial mates from The Sloth Moving Company of North London.

The final piece was the carcass of the sofa bed. Our new flat was on the main floor, the door a direct line from the entrance to the building. A piece of cake, surely.

No.

The sofa was once again wedged, necessitating the removal of the other armrest before it would deign to enter our new place. The moving guys helped me reassemble it. No extra charge. One side of our sofa bed was now slightly rickety, but it was more or less holding together.

At last it was done. Escape from Fuckland Buckland complete (pending the return of our deposit/ransom from the landlord).

We collapsed on our scattered furniture and took a breath. After a few moments of blissful silence there was a loud beep. Then another one. The source was on the wall just inside the door: a keypad for a security service. I pressed a few buttons in an attempt to disable it, but the periodic beeps kept coming.

We were now paying approximately $5,400 a month in rent for an apartment equipped with a beep that would wake us up every minute.

It was at least a huge, bright place, with a giant reception room, a spacious kitchen, three bedrooms and bathrooms, and even access to a backyard.

Isabella and Julia went to bed early, but I was motivated to start putting our things away and getting organized as quickly as possible. The covers for our sofa had been cleaned by Mr. Upstairs Landlord after having been doused in dust in the ceiling collapse. I removed them from the plastic bags in which they were transported and started pulling them onto the cushions. It was a struggle to jam them in. Once again my brow was moist with sweat as I wrestled with them. The covering for the main sofa frame was just not fitting anymore. I looked at the cleaning tag: "Dry clean only." Sure enough, he had put our coverings in the wash and shrunk them.

I had managed to stuff the cushions into their diminished coverings, but now they were so compressed that they left large gaps between each other. I gave up on the cover for the sofa, leaving it partially installed, one side hanging open with the zipper partially done up. The effect was akin to putting a tutu on an elephant.

At breakfast the next morning, Isabella noted that the door to the freezer did not seem to be closing properly. There was a gap around the edge even when I leaned hard on it. Terrific.

Although the flat was a nice, airy space and located in a prime neighbourhood, the owner had opted for cheapo finishings. The fridge and freezer were both bar-sized, stacked inside a unit where the exterior doors were poorly installed. The kitchen cabinets appeared to have been bought at a second-hand shop, and the floor was a battered hardwood, sorely in need of refinishing.

In London you can pay a pile of money and still get crap.

Having just moved in after the Buckland fiasco, I was determined to make the best of it. At least it was big.

But a couple of hours later, Isabella texted me at work: "I just spotted mouse droppings around the fridge."

Seconds after I walked in the door that night, she declared, "I'm out of here! I can't stand this!"

By "here," she meant London generally and our pricey new flat in particular.

I checked out the fridge/freezer unit and sure enough there were little globules of dried mouse shit in the containing cabinet. I recalled the lease form that demanded tenants pay hundreds of pounds for a "professional cleaning" upon departure. The landlord's obligation for a "professional cleaning" before moving in seemed to neglect the detail of removing rodent scat from food areas. Not to mention removing the rodents.

I opened the poorly sealed door to the freezer. Already a thick layer of frost was forming and our food was covered in arctic snow.

Each new discovery was punctuated by the occasional beep from the home security system.

I emailed the New Landlord — a German expatriate who worked for an international bank. He promised to hire exterminators for the mice and suggested that I call the home security company to disable the alarm system's beeps.

The cleanup of mouse shit, evidently, was to be left to us. I vacuumed up the droppings, washed the infected area, and made a note to remember it all when the time came to move out and we faced the demand for an expensive professional cleaning.

I phoned the company that installed the alarm.

"Do you have the security code, sir?" asked the woman on the line.

"If I had the security code I could disarm the beep myself. It was installed by the previous tenants."

"Well then, we shall send out an engineer," was her cheerful response. An engineer's visit, of course, would cost us — unless we were actually signing up for the service.

"Can I get a quote, then, on how much the service costs?"

I was transferred to the sales department.

"To quote you a price we would need to send a salesperson to talk to you about it," said the sales guy.

"I don't want a visit. I just want a rough quote over the phone."

"I'm afraid we can't do that, sir."

My voice started to rise: "You can't tell me over the phone how much this costs?"

"Uh, well. Perhaps I will have another of our sales staff ring you," said the suddenly flustered sales guy.

The call never came. The beeps continued.

I left behind the mouse shit, glacial icebox, and mountainous rent the next morning to hop on a train with Dan to Southampton. The one-hundredth anniversary of the *Titanic* was approaching and I had been assigned a story on the great ship's port of departure.

Southampton has a maritime history that goes back two thousand years, to the days of the Romans. But the city itself was blandly modern, with a particularly ugly housing estate near the port. We have to have some sympathy for the lack of heritage buildings because it was bombed heavily during the war. Southampton was strategically important, not only because of the marine trade but also because it was the home of a Spitfire factory. Only a few remnants of the ancient city remain, fragments of old buildings.

The shell of Holyrood Church was just a short walk down the street from our hotel. Within the walls is a small memorial to the *Titanic* crew. And here is an essential element of the disaster's story that is usually overlooked: 685 of the 1,517 people who died were crew members. Four out of five crew members came from Southampton.

No single place felt the disaster more keenly than this ancient port city. The dramatizations focus on the captain, the Astors, the well-heeled passengers, and the unfortunates in third class who died in much greater numbers than the rich folk in first. But many of the victims were working-class folk from Southampton.

Those who had gotten jobs on the *Titanic* felt lucky. There had been a bitter coal strike that had kept most ships in port, with thousands of mariners left without work.

I visited the Grapes pub, where the three Slade brothers gathered to hoist a few in celebration of their new jobs on April 10, 1912, the day of the *Titanic*'s departure. In one of history's many ironies, the boys had a few too many, showed up too late and too lubricated, and found that they had lost their prized positions to other guys who had been lingering at dockside. A rare example of how getting hammered can save a life instead of ruining it.

Two years after the sinking, a memorial was opened to the *Titanic* engineers — a bronze of the winged Nike, goddess of victory, above carvings depicting the men who kept the great ship moving. Incredibly, one hundred thousand people showed up for the dedication.

We interviewed David Haisman in front of the memorial as he told the story of his mother. Edith was fifteen years old when she sailed on the *Titanic* with her parents, Thomas and Elizabeth Brown, en route to the New World to set up a hotel business.

He told us that when they heard the bump as the *Titanic* hit the iceberg, Thomas went up to the deck to investigate. He returned to tell his wife and daughter to dress in warm clothes, put on their life jackets, and come up top. He left his life jacket behind.

"My mother always told me she never saw her father look so sad as they saw him on the deck, puffing a cigar as their lifeboat was lowered," said Mr. Haisman. "He cupped his hands and called out, 'I'll see you in New York.' That was the last they ever saw of him."

"I'll See You in New York" is the title of the book he wrote about his mother, a story he loved to retell. Their American dreams sank with the great ship, Edith and Elizabeth returned to their native South Africa. Edith ended up marrying a Brit and, amazingly, moving back to Southampton where she raised ten children (David was the youngest) and lived to the age of 101 — one of the oldest *Titanic* survivors.

When Peter Boyd-Smith was a boy growing up in Southampton, few people spoke about the disaster, the memories too raw even decades after the sinking. Entire working-class neighbourhoods were decimated, hundreds of widows and fatherless children left behind.

We spoke to him in his memorabilia shop, Cobwebs, where *Titanic* items were among the biggest sellers. The interest is endless, verging on bizarre. Easy to understand why an actual ticket for the fateful voyage would be a prized collector's item. Boyd-Smith showed me one that he was about to send to Sweden for an exhibition. But odd and slightly creepy were the pieces of coal that had been hauled up from the wreck at the bottom of the Atlantic.

Boyd-Smith was also a contributor to the library of books on the *Titanic* — his paints a picture of the disaster through contemporary accounts: newspaper articles and official reports. I bought a copy and got him to sign it.

Southampton would be sharing the limelight for the *Titanic* anniversary. Belfast, where the ship was built, had opened a glittering new museum — a sore point for some in Southampton. They were also getting a museum, called SeaCity, that would tell the story of their long maritime history.

But Belfast got a substantial EU grant for their institution. Southampton taxpayers had to foot the bill for theirs.

A taxi driver ranted about it to me: "I don't know why we have to keep kissing Irish ass after they bombed us all those years!"

I decided best not to tell him my name is Sean.

David Haisman was more sanguine about the anniversary's impact on his hometown. "I think it'll do a bit of good for Southampton," he said. "It'll remind us of all those people who died. Poor people, most of them. They deserve to be remembered."

Back at home. Early Saturday morning we were awakened by the sound of our door buzzer. The exterminator had arrived. His task was urgent because the droppings around the fridge were not historical artifacts. While I was in Southampton, Isabella had a rodent encounter: one night in the kitchen she saw movement out of the corner of her eye. She turned to see a mouse staring up at her before it darted away. She warned that if the mice were not gotten rid of she would leave.

Exterminator guy listened to our story with professional interest, nodded, and advised that the solution was to spread baits and to close up holes under sinks and elsewhere to eliminate their entry points.

As he started to work, New Landlord arrived on the scene — our first meeting. He was a slender, bookish young German. He and his French wife had previously lived in the flat before moving out to a nearby house with their two small children. He likely made a salary that was a multiple of mine, although he was twenty years younger. Investment banking is far more lucrative than journalism.

New Landlord handed me a fob to disable the security system. Sure enough the beeping stopped, only to resume anytime we opened the door.

"Hmm," said New Landlord. He promised to see if he had written down the code somewhere at home.

I showed him the freezer, now in its own mini ice age. Somewhere beneath the frost a chicken breast was now completely encased in ice. There was a narrow ice cave in the centre, enough perhaps for a single Popsicle, but it was quickly closing in.

"Hmm," said New Landlord. "The door really does seal." He pushed on it, then leaned into it with all his slight weight. As he stepped back, the door slowly swung open again.

He pulled out one of the freezer drawers to demonstrate its many benefits. Several large chunks of ice fell out onto the floor and shattered. "Hmm. I'll try to get my handyman to drop by to have a look."

If it was the same handyman who installed the cabinetry where every door hung at a different angle, I despaired of a prompt solution. The freezer needed to be replaced and clearly we were in for a long battle to get it done.

Our experience of collapsing ceilings and calamitous rents for crappy places was only a variant on the broader theme of the challenges of finding housing in the world's greatest city.

One of the enduring mysteries of London is how so many people can afford to live there. Even with my housing allowance, even with our Fuckland Buckland dump, we were stretched into deficit. And now with our move to MouseShit Manor we were tipping perilously into the red. The struggle for affordable shelter is among the ongoing narratives of the city, with conflict inevitable.

There is a subculture of squatters, who choose to occupy vacant buildings both to give a roof over their heads and to make a point about class divides. Their message appeared to be: use it or lose it. Fascinated, I decided to do a story.

Dan and I met a group of them in a gutted row house on the south side of the river. They were happy to talk to us, on the proviso that we did not reveal the actual address.

A young woman named Rueben Taylor met us at the door and gave us a tour.

She told us the place had been empty for two years before she and a couple of friends moved in a month before. "For all these properties to lie vacant and rotting while people are being forced out of their homes seems completely unfair," she said.

The walls were all bare to the studs, a single hose brought water up from the basement, and the electrical supply was a fire hazard of cords running off an extension plugged into the single working outlet. Their food was salvaged from grocery store dumpsters. Living off the land in London.

This brand of squatting, the kind where it happens in vacant properties, was not a crime in London. Owners must resort to civil remedies to evict their unwanted visitors.

"He hasn't taken us through the civil procedures," said Rueben.

"Has he said, 'please leave'?" I asked.

"That would be the automatic reaction."

"And your answer is?"

"Do you have an immediate use for this property?"

The other side of the story was embodied by two retired nurses from the Philippines, Lilia and Amelita. Dan and I took a taxi far to the north side of the city, where I knocked on the door of their modest house. There was no answer and I was about to walk away when Lilia opened it a crack to ask what I wanted.

"I'm a Canadian journalist," I responded, with all the kindness I could muster. Being Canadian tends to reassure.

"I want to talk to you about the squatters."

Warily, she invited me inside. The tiny living room was sparsely, modestly furnished, with a small Christian shrine the dominant feature. These women were the opposite of flamboyant.

Their nightmare played out when the sisters were away for a month, visiting family back home. They got a call from a London neighbour, advising that unwanted visitors had moved into their home. Seven "Romanians" were how they were described. Whenever anyone came to the door, they would use the sisters' family name, having read it off their mail.

Because this was not a vacant house, merely one where the owners were away on vacation, police could intervene. They were called and the squatters evicted, not without complaint about the injustice of it all.

When Lilia and Amelita returned to their home, they found thousands of pounds worth of damage. Jewellery was missing.

For fifteen minutes, I gently negotiated with Lilia to tell her story on-camera. She was unwilling until I agreed to not show her face. I called in Dan from the taxi and shot the sisters from behind.

In a soft, tremulous voice Lilia said the experience made them ill. "We can't sleep, knowing strangers had slept in our beds," she said.

In a city with so much opulence and wealth staring you in the face, the sight of those two wronged nurses sharing their pain in their modest house has stayed with me. As has the image of the political squatters in the bare-walled joint that they were occupying.

Back in our slice of the London housing comedy show, April Fool's Day came and went in a blizzard of packing and cleaning. It was the first anniversary of my accepting the job as Europe Bureau Chief, but there was no celebration. We were busily preparing for a return to Canada for Julia's month-long Easter break.

With departure time looming, we scrambled into a taxi to Heathrow, leaving the vacuum cleaner in the centre of the reception room, hoping that in our absence the poison would kill the mice, the landlord would fix the freezer, and that pigs would learn to fly.

For me, it was a brief visit home. Enough time to see how the two guys staying at our house had put away a few of our less-decorative appliances (my big coffee carafe had disappeared beneath the sink) and replaced them with more fashionable gadgets — an espresso machine, a soda water maker. Our place was remarkably tasteful and clean.

The guys were busily searching for a new house to buy, but had been continuously outbid. I hoped that they would take their time because we needed their rent money and their care of the place.

After a whirlwind visit with family, it was back out to the airport, my giant blue suitcase jammed with more necessities for living in London.

When I heaved it onto the scales at the Air Canada check-in, the agent's eyes went wide. "Whoa! That's definitely not getting on the plane."

It seems we had managed to exceed the weight limit for one bag, so much so that they would not take it even if I paid for excess baggage. Off to the friendly and overpriced airport luggage store to buy an expensive and remarkably non-durable duffle bag to split the load.

Upon return, there was an email from our Buckland landlord. In the latest turn of the flat saga, he was now asserting that he should withhold £200 of our deposit, claiming that his place was not cleaned perfectly, that there were a couple of grease spots on the cheapo venetian blinds in the kitchenette.

Meanwhile, no sign of him refunding the rent we paid for the week when we were forced to live elsewhere.

With the assistance of Isabella's American lawyer friend who she had met at sewing, I composed a response. Not only did we expect to have our deposit returned in full (his claims being spurious, silly, and downright shitty), he should be

- refunding a week's rent;
- paying for the repairs to Isabella's laptop;
- covering several days of my pay, given that I had to take vacation days to deal with the disaster; and
- paying us a total of £1,779.69. A nice round number.

I thought, briefly, about forgoing the pay claim before deciding that I was in a mood to be litigious.

The landlord responded a day or so later with a note that began, "Many thanks for your email" (those Brits have an obtuse way of saying fuck off). Out of the boundless kindness of his heart he was prepared to refund the deposit in full and forget about his claim of £200 worth of damage to his £10 blinds.

No mention of the £1,779.69.

Our lawyer friend read his email and said, "It was clearly written by someone who knows he has the upper hand." She advised that we remind him of his written promise to refund the rent, and if he still stonewalled, to forget about it. "Small claims court is for those who have nothing better to do with their time."

Chapter Twenty-Five

Travelling remained a healthy distraction. No sooner had my two ladies arrived back in London than we were packing our bags for a long weekend in the Netherlands, visiting Iris and Mario.

For our Dutch adventure, we would be taking the Eurostar train to Brussels, then renting a car — all made a bit cheaper because Global paid for my ticket, since I would be staying in Brussels upon our return to do an interview with the secretary general of NATO.

We would stop en route to Iris and Mario's at the famous Keukenhof tulip garden. Isabella wanted to use the opportunity to shoot another of her "Julia's Europe" travel videos — a decision that risked a stress-out, given that I would be the cameraman and barely knew how to use the camera.

The famous gardens grew up around the grounds of the seventeenth-century Keukenhof Castle, the name meaning "kitchen garden." The Dutch may not be known much for their cuisine, but they know their tulips. And marketing. They also know, and value, their friends, having sent shiploads of bulbs to Ottawa after the Second World War as a gift to Canada for sheltering their royal family.

In 1949, enterprising Dutch tulip marketers transformed the formal castle gardens into a showcase for their product. And now, for eight weeks every year it is the place to go for floral tourists.

Arriving May 11 was a bit late. Keukenhof was off its peak, but still offered a lush riot of blooms for us to see and video. They have about 350 different kinds of tulips and they plant seven million bulbs every year. Each by hand. The gardeners must have spectacular benefit coverage for chiropractic and massage therapy.

We got to work on the video, taking the traditional approach when one is surrounded by manicured floral beauty by snapping at each other. It was Isabella's baby and having done hundreds of lovely design shows, she took command, hoping I could deliver a useable product.

I carefully framed my beauty shots, working methodically to ensure I did not screw up due to my unfamiliarity with the camera.

"Sean, you need to speed it up," she pleaded. I could not match the pace of a real cameraman, which she needed but we could not afford. Our London move had pulled her out of a director's job where she excelled. The travel videos were an attempt to keep her hand in the game.

"Jason would have been great at this," she said, referring to the young videographer she worked with in her previous job.

"Clearly, I am not Jason, but I am reasonably confident that I can shoot straight and keep Julia in focus," I responded.

We had Julia pose in giant Dutch wooden shoes and to point out the names of the different varieties of flowers that we were discovering.

Isabella approached a gardener named Hans to ask why he was cutting the heads off the flowers. He willingly explained in a nearly impenetrable accent that they had gone off their blooms and that trimming them preserved energy in the bulb below. But we did not have a proper microphone, counting on the camera mic. Hans patiently allowed us to ask the same questions multiple times in the hope that I could capture some sound that might be usable.

The afternoon flew by. By five o'clock we still had not gotten Julia's shot in front of Keukenhof's windmill, nor had we done our interview with the PR person.

"We can't go to the windmill. No time," Isabella declared. In Julia's Dutch video there would be no windmill.

"I want popcorn," demanded Julia. "I want to go on the zip line!"

Filmmakers have to pace themselves when working with seven-year-old talent, even if it is their own kid.

We gave her a few minutes on the zip line as the Keukenhof's patient PR person, Annemarie, waited.

Having gotten her popcorn and playtime, Julia was a true pro at her interview, keeping her written questions in her lap and showing astounding concentration for a Grade 2 pupil. Annemarie answered with enthusiasm and smiling good humour.

Sadly, we were close to the exit road on a windy day and without a proper microphone.

"None of that will be usable," observed Isabella.

A working visit to a world-famous tourist attraction can be a trial.

Iris and Mario's home was an hour's drive away, on a country road outside the town of Schagen, north of Amsterdam. The GPS did its job and brought us directly to their door just before dusk. It was a sixty-year-old farmhouse, with a giant thatched roof and rows of modern windmills spinning in the distance. There was a sign in their front window: live, love, laugh.

Even though their life seemed prosaic, running a gas station in small-town Holland, putting in eighty hour weeks as small business people, there was something about their openness, sense of fun, and lack of pretension that just made us feel good about being in their presence.

Their place came with a couple of acres of land, and an old barn that Mario had transformed into an airy man cave. He proudly showed off his beer fridge, an old Coke cooler from the gas station. It was full of pints, even though he drank perhaps a couple a year — leftovers from a recent visit from his family.

Iris and Mario cooked up a huge load of spaghetti and we sat for hours around their table talking and laughing.

The next day, Saturday, our hostess became our Dutch tour guide, driving us to an antique windmill named *Hoop* (Hope) — one of the devices that pumped the water out of the polders centuries earlier. All the land where we stood was once under the sea. We cajoled a cranky Julia into posing in front of it for our travel video.

Iris brought us into the heart of Schagen, a neat, middle-sized city that traces its history back more than a millennium but has been notable only for a cattle market, a notorious nineteenth-century murder case, and a twenty-first-century innovator named Johan Huibers, who built a replica of Noah's Ark, which he toured around the Netherlands.

As we strolled around, Iris reminded me that it was the day before Mother's Day. She helpfully distracted Isabella so that Julia and I could pop into a shop to buy some appropriate chocolates.

The travel video still hung over our heads as we searched for photo ops. In a grocery store, Isabella spotted a giant chunk of edam cheese and dragged Julia over to pose in front of it. By now both of them were cranky and it turned into an ordeal. It was unlikely to make it into the final product, given that Julia looked like she had just been told she was being sent to reform school.

Escaping from that situation, we set off for the shores of the North Sea where we met Mario because he wanted to show off his passion for kitesurfing. It was a clear, blustery spring day at the beach.

"Not windy enough really for kitesurfing," said Mario with no irony. "But I'll try."

Sixty years old, but without a trace of fat, and he was about to let a kite drag him along the bounding waves of a famously rough sea while somehow keeping his feet on a little surfboard. He admitted to taking a few tumbles when he first tried the sport but now had the hang of it.

"How dangerous is it?" I asked.

"Couple of people die in the world every year. But no one here in a while."

He explained that the biggest hazard was to have a rogue gust of wind lift a kiter airborne like a gonzo Mary Poppins, blow him over the dunes, and smack the hapless sap into the wall of a building in the adjacent village.

Mario managed to keep himself on the board on the sea.

"Sean, you've got to try this!" he urged. I smiled, nodded, and said nothing.

We piled back into Iris's car because she wanted to show us one of the great feats of Dutch engineering. A short drive to the north was the Afsluitdijk, which Google Translate tells me means "enclosing dike." It is a prosaic name for a very long dam with a large purpose. Thirty-two kilometres long, it was built in the 1930s across the mouth of the Zuiderzee, the storied bay of the North Sea.

The Zuiderzee had an unfortunate tendency to get whipped up into horrific storms that unleashed devastating floods. A fifteenth-century deluge killed about ten thousand people. Fed up, the Dutch built the Afsluitdijk to bring a measure of calm to the waters. The name Zuiderzee, though poetic and storied, disappeared because it was no longer a sea. Cut off from the North Sea, it became a freshwater lake, IJsselmeer, and the Dutch filled in large portions of it to make more land for themselves.

A highway runs along the Afsluitdijk and our host pulled over in a parking lot partway along to give us a look. On a walkway over the road we could see that the level of the North Sea on the left was several feet higher than the IJsselmeer on our right. The Dutch know water.

Back at the farmhouse, Mario and Iris whipped up another comfort food supper and we lounged in their living room and talked and talked, long into the night. Julia listened with interest to the adults' conversation for hours until she passed out in the easy chair. I carried her upstairs to bed. Isabella talked with her old friends until two in the morning. There is something about the serenity of being able to sit up and blab with someone long after you all should have gone to bed.

In the morning, our hostess was bleary-eyed as she stumbled downstairs. "I never stay up that late," she said.

Small business people do not often get that luxury.

We needed to be on the road back to Brussels by midafternoon, but we sincerely did not want to leave. Our hosts felt the same. Mario is a master entertainer of kids. He took Julia to the back field and let her drive his little garden tractor, an experience that lingered with her forever.

He had not forgotten his determination to have me sample kitesurfing. He pulled out one of his smaller kites, a mere two metres wide compared to the twelve-metre one he had been using on the North Sea. On their field, he stationed me at one end of the lines while he lifted the kite up to catch the wind. I leaned back with all my modest weight, almost parallel to the ground and wrestled with it. The kite largely won, yanking me back and forth, threatening to take me on a Dutch version of Dorothy's trip to Oz.

My first priority was not to die and secondarily I did not want to wreck his kite by crash-diving it into a fence. After several minutes of amusing him and Julia by being yanked around like a middle-aged rag doll, I managed to guide it down to a gentle splat and thank Mario for the experience.

We lingered longer than we should have; our schedule squeezed even more by a last-minute decision to shoot more video.

Down the road from their farm were fields of tulips, the last lingering blooms of the season. Holland's landscapes are pedestrian and unmemorable — hard to be inspired by such flatness. The exception is tulip time. The fields are transformed into vast rectangles of luscious colour. We chose one that was an expanse of bright yellow; a hue so intense that it seemed someone had thrown a giant tablecloth from Provence over the dirt.

It was video gold.

Julia posed for some shots and delivered a few lines to the camera about tulips in Holland in what was likely questionable sound quality and we were done.

There was now little time to spare. We wolfed down a few sandwiches at Iris and Mario's and regretfully said our goodbyes. As we hugged, she said, "You know, even though we've only met once, it seems like we've known each other a long time." True enough.

As we drove away, Isabella said, "You know she has some psychic qualities?"

I normally say "mumbo-jumbo" to such things, but with Iris I was not so sure.

We were lucky that the highways were clear of traffic and the speed limit was 130 km. Julia slept most of the way, meaning we faced no demands that we pull over at the first view of the golden arches. A speedy journey was timely because the GPS gave us the slowest possible route through Brussels to downtown, driving entirely through what appeared to be side streets with endless traffic lights. As the clock ticked ever closer to the train's departure, my search for the station became increasingly frantic, with the GPS reverting to uselessness. Finally, I pulled over, rolled down the window and called out to two young men on the sidewalk: "*Ou est Gare du Midi?*"

They looked at me with sardonic smiles as one of them slowly raised his arm to point at the gleaming glass edifice directly in front of me.

Merci, M. Dickhead.

Now the challenge was to find the parking lot for the rental car. I did a couple of laps around the station, barely avoiding driving the wrong way down a one-way street or onto streetcar tracks before finding the proper entrance.

By this time, both Isabella and Julia were desperate for the bathroom so they piled out of the car while I grabbed the suitcases and ran to keep up. We left the car with a royal mess and a nearly empty gas tank, having spotted not a single service station on our cross-country route through Brussels. The agency later added a $200 gas bill to my credit card.

Naturally the bathrooms were conveniently located at the far end of the station from the Eurostar entrance.

"We can always catch the next train," puffed Isabella as we power-walked through the crowds.

"No you can't. The tickets can't be changed."

"Oh."

As they dealt with the call of nature in the ladies' room, I grabbed a slice of takeout pizza for Julia to eat on the train. When they emerged I advised a brisk walk back to the Eurostar. At the gate, Isabella was suddenly unable to find her apartment keys. I gave her mine so she and Julia would be able to enter our overpriced London flat upon return.

After frantic kisses and goodbyes, I watched as they passed through ticket check-in and out of sight, twenty minutes before departure. They would make it after all. I took a deep breath to slow my heart rate back to something approaching normal and walked over to the taxi stand.

It was a short ride to the Hotel Metropole, a lush old *belle époque* gem. Upon check-in, I kicked off my shoes and plopped myself on the bed. As I stared at the ceiling, the phone buzzed with an email from Isabella: "Close call."

Turned out that we had forgotten the necessity of filling out a U.K. entry card before embarking. She completed the paperwork and they got aboard with a mere three minutes to spare. Glad I was not there to share the experience.

Chapter Twenty-Six

With Isabella and Julia safely en route to England, my primary challenge now, as it usually was upon arriving in a grand European capital, was to find the best possible place to eat on the company's dime. Brussels is not only a government town — the capital of Belgium and home to the EU and NATO — it also has a reputation as one of the world's greatest gastronomic centres, so my expectations were high.

The front desk recommended a place a couple of blocks away, but when I scanned the menu in the front window I decided that it was too pricey to justify to the bean-counters back home. So, I wandered over to a touristy neighbourhood near the market, where shills were standing out front of joints hoping to wave me in.

I settled on Chez Leon, which seemed to at least have a facade of Belgian authenticity. As I sat surrounded by patrons speaking English, it quickly became clear that it must have been in all the guidebooks. No matter. I ordered one of the famous Belgian cherry-flavoured beers, some mussels, and frites. It was all fine and filling, if not gastronomically adventurous.

In the morning, I took a taxi out to meet Dan at the NATO head-quarters on the outskirts of Brussels. It felt like stepping into a time machine back into the height of the Cold War. It had the look of a fif-ties-era army base, with buildings like bunkers, surrounded by barbed wire.

We were there because the NATO PR department had offered an interview with the secretary general in advance of a conference on Afghanistan, to be held in Chicago the following week. Anders Fogh Rasmussen, the Danish politician who occupied the post, was doing a round of interviews that day. We were just after the BBC — somewhat less important in NATO's mind, no doubt.

They offered us the use of their studio and cameras. All we needed to do was provide discs to record it all on. Generally, news outlets are supposed to shoot interviews themselves, but this all made it more convenient for small operators like us.

AFR was lean, high-voiced, and earnest. I wondered if he remem-bered my name or where I came from seconds after I was introduced. No matter. He would at least remember that we were Canadian.

I was hoping to make some news out of a Human Rights Watch report from that morning that criticized NATO for civilian deaths dur-ing the Libya campaign. But Rasmussen sprang a surprise, telling me that he would like Canada to continue its training mission in Afghanistan beyond the planned 2014 pullout date. Sounded like news to me. A call to the Ottawa bureau chief confirmed that the secretary general had told us something that had not yet been reported — a minor exclusive.

As it turned out, the prime minister was giving a news confer-ence back home, and we managed to get a question posed to him on the subject — although my message was garbled, and he was asked about the U.N. secretary general. The PM's flacks told us afterward that his answer would have been the same either way — that Canada had no plans to change plans. Political message tracks are handy that way. Often it does not matter what you ask, they stick to what they had already planned to say.

We shot the requisite stand-up at NATO HQ and headed back to the hotel to file — only to find that NATO's disc would not play on Dan's camera. Big problem. We had an exclusive that we could not play back.

Given that it was only lunchtime, we quickly made the decision to hop the first Eurostar train back to London and hope that the disc would work in our machine in the bureau. The story did not need to be ready until 10:30 p.m. London time, so there was enough leeway. It was rare to get an exclusive on a story like this, so we led the program. No other news organization bothered to pick it up. Our glory was muted.

Shortly after my return to London from my Brussels jaunt, we were back on the Royals beat, this time with a rare Canadian angle. Given the headbanging impossibilities of reforming Canada's constitution, Queen Elizabeth II and her heirs will reign on for the foreseeable future as our distant head of state.

Consequently, our national police force proudly remains the *Royal* Canadian Mounted Police. The connection with the House of Windsor remains strong. When the RCMP gave the Queen a horse named Burmese, it became one of her favourites. She rode the black mare at the Trooping the Colour ceremony for eighteen consecutive years. When Burmese departed from this life, the Queen showed her regal affection by ordering it to be buried on the grounds of Windsor Castle. Richard III should have been so lucky.

Now, a select group of Mounties was designated to fill in at Horse Guards Parade as the ceremonial guard for the monarch. The Household Cavalry, the ones with the silver-coloured helmets shined to a blinding gleam, typically has the duty. Indeed, only once before in their 350-year history have they stepped aside to allow a force from the colonies to do the job — it was a Canadian group the other time, too. So, when the Mounties were tapped for the job, it was a very big deal in the arcane realm of royal responsibilities, symbolism, and pageantry.

For a preview story, we and our Canadian TV news colleagues were invited over to Hyde Park Barracks to see the Mounties preparing for their big day. For our photo op they were in plain blue jackets, saving the red serge for the real thing. And the horses they were using were not their own. This particular duty requires a special kind of training —

the animal must stand still for hours, patiently unmoving while tourists snap pictures, stand beside them, and occasionally pat their muzzle. Would not do for a horse to bite a chunk out of a bystander or to kick a photo bug in the balls. There was no time to train Canadian horses, so the Mounties were atop loaners from the Household Cavalry.

For the benefit of our cameras, a regimental corporal ran the team through their paces. The barrel-chested Brit barked out commands in a hoarse foghorn delivery that for the average person would cause the larynx to leap out of the throat and go flying across the pavement. After a few minutes of trotting around in different formations, the group headed across the street into the park so that they could canter past our cameras a couple of times.

In the distance, I could see some of the Household Cavalry working on their routines, their silver helmets gleaming in the sunlight. One of the spokespeople advised me that these were merely their "knocking around" uniforms, used for training. Some knock-arounds. The helmets were like mirrors. *They must spend most of their waking hours polishing the various elements of their kit*, I thought. No one does uniforms like the British.

Photo opportunity over, the Mounties lined up their steeds — and looked at us. We looked at them. There was an awkward moment before one of the press people pointed out that this was our opportunity to interview them.

"C'mon. We won't bite," said one of the Mounties.

Perhaps not. But interviewing a tall RCMP atop a tall horse is tricky without a step ladder, even if your cameraman is six foot two. From that angle, the camera looks up their nostrils with a bright sky backdrop — an ugly shot.

I explained the aesthetic challenges and he reluctantly got down. I suspect they were all told that Mounties should preferably stay mounted for the TV cameras. The entire group were members of the RCMP's iconic Musical Ride troupe, and uniformly they were bursting with pride, but not quotes. The best any of them could do was a repeated "It's a great honour."

I resisted the temptation to ask about how this was a welcome bit of good publicity for a force whose image had been taking a pounding.

The lead story on the CBC's website that day was a discrimination lawsuit that had been launched against the RCMP.

The next day, we dutifully set up on The Mall to capture their mounted procession to Horse Guards Parade. It promised to be a great shot — a parade of Mounties in red serge cantering down the grand boulevard with Union flags lining the route and Buckingham Palace behind them in the distance. There was also an extra element of novelty: three of the officers were women — an extremely rare sight for this duty.

As we waited, an elderly Brit stopped to chat with us. I will call him Lord Eyebrows due to the caterpillars on his forehead and the archaic wooliness of this attitude. He harrumphed loudly at the news that women ... WOMEN ... would be part of Her Majesty's ceremonial guard on that day.

To her great credit, Ann MacMillan of CBC (a long-time resident of London, married to a prominent English journalist, and a descendant of Lloyd George no less) effectively dressed him down with an explanation that women do in fact know how to ride horses, stand on guard, and occasionally govern countries, including his.

Lord Eyebrows was the exception. Several other people stopped to ask what was happening and were uniformly delighted to hear that RCMP officers, male and female, would be on duty at Horse Guards Parade that day. In spite of ourselves, we could not help but feel an uncharacteristic rush of Canadian pride. For which we all immediately apologized.

For twenty minutes, we stood in the centre of The Mall, the camera people adjusting their tripods to fine-tune the angle for their expected shot. Then, there they were in the distance. At that exact moment, several cops suddenly appeared and chased us all off the street. So much for the glorious image as we rushed off to the sidewalk and the camera people scrambled to capture the procession as the Mounties turned into the parade ground.

On an unusually warm day for London, the Canadians formed a line in their toasty red serge and stetsons, facing a row of Household Cavalry in their silver helmets. The crowds loved it.

An elderly British lady kindly stepped aside so that we could set up our tripod to capture the scene. "This is wonderful! They should have told us this was happening," she said.

The handover ceremony complete, we walked over to the Whitehall side where the Mounties were now standing guard — in a strictly ceremonial sense, given that the Queen's home is way over on the other side of St. James's Park. Crowds were thick on the sidewalk snapping pictures.

The Canadian cops alternated between suppressed grins and nervous glances whenever anyone tried to pat the horses, likely fearing that the ceremonial steeds might be inclined to bite off a well-wisher's finger.

All in all, it was a lovely story.

More true Canadian patriotism ... and pain ... was to come.

Even as we were covering the Mounties, we got word of a profound journey taking place on the continent. A group of Canadian veterans was on a bicycle tour of famous battle sites around Western Europe — all were Afghan veterans, all suffering from post-traumatic stress disorder. The very next day they were to be making a stop at the most famous of all Canadian victories, Vimy Ridge. It was irresistible.

We rushed back to the bureau to finish off the RCMP story while I simultaneously made preparations to get on the Eurostar that night to Lille, which is about a forty-minute drive to Vimy. As Dan was going on vacation, our China-based cameraman, Nicolas, was in London and would be accompanying me to France.

Except: Lille had some kind of convention in town. There seemed to be not a single available hotel room anywhere, unless we wanted to stay in Belgium. We feverishly searched all websites and kept coming up empty. Finally, Dan managed to locate via a web service a couple of rooms at a spa hotel on the edge of Lille. Good enough.

I called the site's 1-800 number to ensure it was properly booked. A pleasant woman with a southern lilt asked if I minded if she called me by my first name.

"Why sure, darlin'!" (Which I did not say. A good Canadian, I answered, "Sure.")

She took all our information, then read it back to me for verification.

"Y'all have a fine time in Layl," she chirped.

I popped home to shower off the sweat of my horsey day, pack a bag, and then hop a taxi to meet Nicolas at St. Pancras International station. This, dear reader, was the kind of day when being a Foreign Correspondent™ can be invigorating.

As civilized as the Eurostar was, I was looking forward to a pleasant, expense account French supper at the spa hotel, and so decided to hold off on eating. A crucial error.

The taxi driver at the Lille station looked puzzled when we gave him the address of the hotel, but shrugged and headed out. It was a long drive. I watched the total climb on his meter as we went through the suburbs to a country highway and arrived at a gate. A closed gate. The buildings behind were dark.

The cabbie slowly approached the gate, expecting it to open. It didn't. He got out and buzzed on the intercom. No answer. We called the number of the hotel. No response.

Now we understood why there were rooms available. The place was closed, but somehow the booking site and the southern belle who so sweetly verified our reservation missed that useful fact.

The driver said not to worry, that surely there must be room somewhere in Lille. He started calling. And calling. *Tous complets. Nada. Niente.* Fuck all hotel rooms.

It was now nine o'clock and my stomach reminded me of the declined meal on the train.

Our friendly cabbie kept making call after call. Astonishingly, he finally found a real room at a golf resort in Arras, the closest town to Vimy. Only one room, but at least it was a double. Despite having only met Nic the day before, we were now going to be roommates.

The already hefty taxi fare now grew into heroic proportions as we got on the highway. Forty minutes and €220 later we pulled up to our accommodations. We gave our helpful driver a nice tip. He handed over his card with a big smile and encouraged us to call anytime we were in Lille. No shit. It was likely the biggest fare of his career.

By now it was ten o'clock and the resort's restaurant was long since closed. So much for my fine French dinner. But at least the bar was open and at least they would make me a *croque monsieur*. Coupled with a tall glass of beer, it may have been the best *croque monsieur* ever. Our room turned out to be a suite, with the bedroom divided from the sofa bed, which Nic kindly volunteered to take. So at least we did not have to listen to each other's snores and bodily eruptions all night long.

Someone, I am not sure who, once said that any Canadian who is able to go should make a point of visiting Vimy Ridge.

It had been my privilege to travel across the English Channel with veterans of the Dieppe raid on the fiftieth anniversary of the mission and watch as they wept at the sight of the shore where so many fought and died so long ago.

I once walked through the Canadian cemetery in Normandy and got a shiver when I saw how many of the gravestones listed young men who fell during D-Day at age nineteen.

But nothing is quite like Vimy.

And nothing would be quite like my first visit.

Outside of Canada it is lightly understood. Most non-Canadian war historians consider the Battle of Vimy Ridge just one operation within the broader Battle of Arras.

But it was a resonant event in our nationhood. Both the French and the British tried and failed repeatedly to dislodge the Germans from the high point. In April 1917, the Canadians did the job. Although the commander was British, it was the first time that all four Canadian divisions fought as a unit and it became a powerful statement of nationalism.

Of course it was a war and the glory was bought with much blood: 3,598 dead, 7,004 wounded. Likely not counted in those numbers were the men who were shattered mentally, who suffered from what was unsympathetically dubbed "shell shock."

Now we were about to relive it through the eyes of modern-day casualties of war. But first we had to get there.

We rushed to a car rental place and started making our way out of Arras through small-town rush hour traffic.

En route, the phone rang. It was one of the Help for Heroes organizers asking if we were still coming because the entourage had already arrived.

"No worries. We'll wait for you," he said when I told him we were minutes away.

We would be the only news crew at the event.

It was a misty morning and we were unable to see the iconic twin monuments until we were almost upon them. When we arrived, Wayne Johnston from Wounded Warriors immediately rushed up to us, beaming, and thanked us for coming. He is hard to miss, with a handlebar moustache waxed out to impossibly straight points, a shaven head, and a forthright readiness to tell you all about his struggles with post-traumatic stress disorder after his time in the former Yugoslavia.

The parking lot was bustling with a couple of hundred people wearing cycling togs, most with British symbols. The twenty-one Canadian riders were badly outnumbered.

But everyone was carrying little Maple Leaf flags. This was Canada's moment.

The Canadians lined the way as a piper led the group to the monument. The pathway is bordered with electric fences and signs warning visitors not to stray. Even all these years later, the surrounding terrain is still full of unexploded munitions from the First World War.

Unless you have ice water in your veins, you cannot help but have a catch in your throat at the sight of that place, particularly if you are in the company of soldiers who served in a foreign land and came back with demons that scarred their lives.

Captain Phil Ralph, a chaplain, spoke: "Welcome to Canada," he said. "This is holy ground."

The Canadians were given pride of place at the ceremony, standing in a dignified line at the front, their little flags planted in the ground at their feet. It mattered little that they were dressed in sweaty cycling togs.

Back in the day when so many fought and died at Vimy and so many other battles, they did not know anything about PTSD. It had not even been given a name, let alone much understanding. Those who came back from the wars suffering from it often had little support or sympathy at home.

"This monument reminds us that this is not new," said Captain Ralph. "But that we are with you."

"Things have gotten better, but that's not good enough. We've always got to strive," Johnston told me.

The service had many of the elements we have all seen on Remembrance Day: someone saying, "We will remember them," a bugler playing "The Last Post," and a moment of silence.

I watched the line of Canadians, many of them tough-looking guys who have seen a lot. Their eyes were streaming.

At the end of the ceremony, the soldiers clasped each other's shoulders, approached the monument, knelt, and laid hands on it for a moment. One rider, overcome, walked away with head bowed, finally dropping to one knee off in the field with a comrade comforting him. Powerful, powerful.

I wondered how men who had already suffered so much trauma could handle such an intense moment.

Wayne Johnston admitted to me that the organizers had worried about it, but in the end, he felt that they were "good tears."

I interviewed Eric Jenkinson, an Afghan vet who came home with issues that were too personal to reveal to me, except to say that they were tough. He is a big guy who would admit that his figure is less than Adonis-like and that a cycling trip like this was a challenge.

"I'd been planning for the physical," he told me. "We'd been biking 350 miles over six days. But the emotional I wasn't ready for."

For him, the tears didn't flow until after the ceremony when the group gathered off to one side and belted out a loud, off-key, and heartfelt version of "O Canada." Even the Brits got misty-eyed at that moment.

"For me they were tears of pride," said Jenkinson.

We finished our interview and I was about to say goodbye when I realized I had failed to pose an essential question. Nicolas moved in close again with his camera.

"Was this experience therapeutic?" I asked. "Or did it bring back memories of things best forgotten?"

Jenkinson was emphatic. "It was very, very therapeutic for me. Quite honestly, this is one item that's off the bucket list."

Me, too, I guess.

It is true: If you are Canadian and you can come to France, you should go to Vimy Ridge.

Chapter Twenty-Seven

The Queen's business card, if she ever had one, would need its own external hard drive to contain all her many titles. For Canadians, it's officially:

> Her Majesty Elizabeth the Second, by the Grace of God of the United Kingdom, Canada and Her Other Realms and Territories Queen, Head of the Commonwealth, Defender of the Faith.

Aside from also being head of state of a clutch of other places, from Belize to Australia, she carries several other unofficial handles:

- British Columbia: Mother of All People
- Jamaica: Missis Queen
- New Zealand: *Kotuku* (Maori for "white heron")
- Nebraska: Admiral — a gag title from the landlocked state (Not sure if she ever visited Lincoln to pick it up.)

The list goes on. When you are queen as long as she has been, people give you stuff. My London posting coincided with her sixtieth anniversary and a host of events to mark her Diamond Jubilee.

Victoria was the only other British monarch to last long enough for a Diamond Jubilee. (George III fell a few months short but did not even effectively reign over his last ten years due to declining health, dementia, and some say madness.)

They held a huge parade to mark Victoria's Jubilee in 1897, but because of her arthritis she could not climb stairs and the service at St. Paul's had to be said outside. Elizabeth, by comparison, was still hale and astonishingly active at eighty-six. She was able to be a participant in an extravaganza that lasted a whole weekend. The biggest event was to be a thousand-vessel "Pageant on the Thames." There were a few Canadian participants, and my task was to prepare a story on a group of breast cancer survivors from British Columbia who would be paddling a dragon boat.

I arranged for our Vancouver crew to shoot interviews with some participants and video of them training, which I would blend in with elements we gathered in London talking about the overall event. It was to be an easy Friday for Nicolas and me — simply take a taxi to the east end to shoot a panoramic stand-up with Tower Bridge in the backdrop and head back to the bureau for a leisurely writing and edit of our pre-view story. Stu Greer was arriving as well to assist with coverage of the big weekend, and was looking to a quiet day of catching up on paperwork.

News intervened.

As I scanned Twitter while we were in the taxi, the headline from the *Sun* tabloid blared at me: "I'll Kill Again." A notorious and sensational Canadian murder investigation now had a U.K. angle.

The gory details included a young Chinese immigrant murdered and dismembered in Montreal, with body parts mailed to political offices. The suspect, Luka Magnotta, was irresistible to the tabloid press (and mainstream, too) because he was also a former gay porn actor, had auditioned for a reality program, and expressed interest in another notorious Canadian sex criminal: Karla Homolka.

Now it seemed that Magnotta had spent time in London a few months earlier. The *Sun*'s revelation was that he had shown up at their offices to complain about a story in which they reported on his alleged tendencies to torture cats. Later he sent the paper an email warning, "In the near future you will be hearing from me again. This time, however, the victims won't be small animals."

Given that there was an international manhunt underway for him, our easy day was about to be turned upside down.

I woke up the folks back in the newsroom in Canada with the revelation.

Nic and I quickly knocked off the required stand-up beside the Thames and I got into a taxi to our live studio location (we could not go live from our office), while he headed back to the bureau to meet Stu, who would now be scrambling after this story. They had to hop on a train to Windsor to meet and interview the *Sun* reporter who broke the Magnotta angle.

My task was to do several live interviews with Global morning shows across the country, effectively just reporting what had been in the tabloid.

By early afternoon I was back in the office where I returned to Plan A and easily finished and delivered my Thames pageant story in plenty of time. Stu and Nic were running flat out all afternoon and were barely able to get their piece done in time.

Stu's Royal weekend was ruined as he immediately headed off to Paris and then Berlin in pursuit of Magnotta (who was caught in the German capital) — a story that ended up winning him an award, which he deserved not only for the journalism, but the fortitude in keeping up a crushing pace.

As for Nic and me, it was back to the grand boat show.

The previous record holder for marine displays on the Thames was a spectacle that was staged 350 years earlier by King Charles II in honour of his new queen, Catherine of Braganza.

The great diarist Samuel Pepys reported that there must have been a thousand boats on the river, which fairly disappeared beneath them.

Among the crowds lining the banks to observe the spectacle and to welcome the king's wife was the king's mistress, Barbara Villiers, who ensured that she not only had a good view, but that the crowds had a good look at her.

The 2012 event would set a new standard for spectacle, if lacking the salaciousness that marked the reign of the louche Charles II. The ever-quotable Boris Johnson, mayor of London, said, "It's going to be a joyful, successful version of Dunkirk."

It would, however, be wet.

Mindful of the massive crowds, Nic and I headed out early on the Tube to Westminster, the closest stop to the Lambeth Bridge, where I had reserved a camera spot, reasoning that it would offer a great view of Big Ben. The trains were jammed, as were all the banks of the river, spectators at least ten deep.

The bridge was just as bad, and I worried that we would be stuck with a view of the backs of people's heads. But then we found the media pen and grabbed the last bit of available real estate next to the rail, approximately two square feet, elbow to elbow with other cameras and civilians, but good enough for our needs, facing east toward Parliament.

The skies were slate, with occasional raindrops and a brisk breeze that made everyone do up their jackets. A perfect day to celebrate English culture.

Beside us were three generations of the Williams family from Essex, who got their prime viewing spot thanks to a relative's connection. The grandfather choked up at the sight of it all, and his grandson had eyes as wide as saucers. He was not alone.

No one does spectacle and pageantry quite like the Brits.

The first sign of the flotilla's approach was a deafening ringing — a floating belfry passed underneath us, carrying several custom-made bells that pealed out an overture for what was to come.

It was followed by the muscle-powered boats, which provided the grandest vista of the day — hundreds of them large and small filling the river. There was the QRB (Queen's Rowbarge) *Gloriana*, a replica of the vessels that were once the maritime limousines of kings, queens, and the occasional defunct hero, like Lord Nelson. *Gloriana* was rowed by a selection of former British Olympians.

We spotted and filmed our Canadian dragon boat, as well as an antique canoe sporting the Maple Leaf flag with the paddlers dressed as voyageurs — thus fulfilling our duty to include fellow citizens in our story.

A crowd of guys on the other side of the bridge started belting out an off-key "God Save the Queen," so we knew the star of the show was approaching. She was riding aboard the royal barge *Spirit of Chartwell*, which actually began life as a luxury Rhine riverboat called *Vincent Van Gogh*.

The Queen and her family passed directly underneath us, offering a brief glimpse of the back of her head before chugging on downriver, where they would be mooring to allow her to watch the entire passing show.

As crowded as our location already was, a Filipino crew now wedged their way in beside us. Their reporter, clearly unaccustomed to English June weather, was bundled up in a heavy coat, gloves, and woolen cap. She shot a lengthy stand-up, without apparently bothering to gather any video of the passing show and then posed for several still shots and selfies.

Nic and I rolled our eyes.

Then we realized this was a once-in-a-lifetime resumé shot and took turns snapping pics of ourselves with the procession below and Big Ben behind. I used my picture incessantly on all forms of social media and it became my calling card for the London assignment.

Important work done, Nic asked, "Do you think we should go?"

Realizing that the pageant was about half done, that the biggest names in the show had already passed, and that in about forty-five minutes approximately 1.2 million people would be all headed for the Tube, it seemed like a good time to beat it.

Lots of others had the same idea and the surrounding streets were teeming. A couple of blocks from the Thames, and still within the no-traffic zone, we spotted a cab dropping off a fare and hopped in.

Asked how he got past the barricades, he simply said, "You just need to know where to go, mate." Part of the cab drivers' "know-ledge," evidently.

No sooner did we close the door than the skies opened into a full-on English deluge.

My favourite image of the day, and the one I used to open my story, was a group of plucky opera singers, all drenched and freezing, with hair plastered to their heads, belting out "Land of Hope and Glory" in front of their monarch. Cannot get much more English than that.

They deservedly won much acclaim, although one paper unkindly dubbed them "the drowned rats."

The pageant was the highlight of the weekend, but there was still one more show to wrap up the Jubilee — an all-star concert in front of Buckingham Palace on the Monday. As is the way with these things, thousands of people camped out all night on The Mall to save a spot. And as is the way with reporters covering these things, Nic and I went down in search of Canadians.

We spotted a woman with a Maple Leaf flag draped over her shoulder, who despite a Cockney accent so heavy that I could barely understand her, insisted that she was indeed Canadian. Due to the language barrier, I had to ask her to repeat her hometown several times before I could discern that it was Burlington, Ontario.

"How's it been here?" I asked, camera rolling.

"Worst possible night to be camping out. Let's just say I'll be happy to get home."

As we worked down The Mall toward the palace, we searched for the tent of the inevitable Bernadette Christie from Grande Prairie, Alberta. The same Bernadette I had interviewed outside Westminster Abbey at the Royal Wedding in 2011. She had asked our Alberta correspondent, Francis, to tip us off that she would be back in London for the Jubilee. Francis met her when she was chasing Will and Kate in Yellowknife, during their honeymoon tour of the Northwest Territories.

Bernadette had a way of making herself ubiquitous at these kinds of events.

I rang her on her cellphone and she directed us to her campsite close to the front of the crowd. As she was giving us directions, I heard a neighbour bark at her to not bring in any interlopers. The campers are understandably territorial at these things.

She made her way out of the sea of humanity to talk to us on the side.

"Why do you do this?" I asked, with genuine curiosity and an element of human concern.

"Because it's so much fun!"

I was scheduled to be live from outside the palace at 10:30 London time, just as the concert was ending and just as the Queen was to light the last of four thousand Jubilee beacons. The tone of the day darkened with the news that Prince Philip had been admitted to hospital with a bladder infection, with much tongue clucking about how he had stood outside for hours on Sunday watching the pageant. The speculation was that he was made ill not so much by the cold and damp but by his stubborn refusal to go below deck to pee.

I made my way down on the Tube and my press pass got me through the hordes of people to the media position off to the side of stage, just as Elton John was wrapping up "Crocodile Rock." I did not have much of a view of the performers but it was a great vantage point to see all the projections on the palace.

The Queen missed the first hour and had a stoic look on her face when she arrived. A comedian on the stage noted her presence with, "You missed Tom Jones!"

The AP producer overseeing my live hit warned I would not be able to do it if the concert was still going at 10:30, given the BBC had the rights to the broadcast. But she had been told definitely by the organizers that the Queen was most certainly lighting the beacon at the bottom of the hour and the music by Royal command had to be done by then.

Somebody neglected to inform Sir Paul McCartney because he was going long. One would have thought he would wrap up with a soulful rendition of "Let It Be," but for unknown reasons had made "Live and Let Die" his closing number, complete with a thunderous pyrotechnical display. He was still singing at 10:30.

However, a couple of lurid crime stories were leading the show (including the aforementioned Magnotta case) and I was to get on the air closer to 10:37. The producer shrugged, smiled, and said go ahead. We would just neglect to inform the BBC. As it turned out, Sir Paul had finished, but the last bit of pageantry still had not played out when I did my bit. My TV job was done.

Moments after I spoke to Canada, the Queen, now no longer suppressing a smile, walked out on stage with Prince Charles. With McCartney, Tom Jones, Elton John, and other loyal subjects as a living backdrop, he called her "Mummy" in his tribute, which drew a look from HM that in an earlier era might have been a prelude to decapitation. But it was a passing cloud and she genuinely seemed to be enjoying herself.

Even the most rock-ribbed republican would have to admit that this was a genuine and large-scale show of affection as the thousands raised their voices in "God Save the Queen" and a giant, waving Union Jack was projected on Buckingham Palace.

If I am ever given the chance on voting on the subject, I would choose to not have her or her successors as Canada's head of state. But the British Royal Industry does put on a pretty impressive show.

Chapter Twenty-Eight

It is well known that St. Patrick drove the snakes out of Ireland. Lower down on his list of credits was his role in bringing surfers in.

The story is convoluted and a bit of a stretch, but involves a legendary race of pagans who, angered at the introduction of Christianity, turned themselves into foals and jumped off the majestic Cliffs of Moher on the west coast — a spot since named *Aill na Searrach* (pony's cliff in Gaelic).

Where mythical heathens once met their end, surfer dudes from around the world are now drawn to challenge the reality of a wave dubbed "Aileen," a monster that only appears about a dozen times a year and that can reach fifteen metres in height.

It was the chance to write about that wave and those surfers (as well as the chance to visit my cousin Sheila and her Irish husband, Tom) that brought us out to Stansted Airport before dawn. It would also be my wife and daughter's first visit to Ireland.

Part of our journey would be the experience of a modern form of Irish culture: airline humiliation. We would be once again flying on the Celtic Tiger of budget aviation: Ryanair. With the fare already rock bottom, I paid a bit extra to check a couple of bags and to get us to the front of the line so we would have a better chance of getting three seats together.

Knowing the strictness of the carry-on regulations, we had carefully packed in advance to ensure all would go smoothly. Sadly, few of our fellow travellers were as well prepared. As with our first Ryanair experience, the lineup for check-in was long and tortuously slow as frantic passengers opened up their overstuffed bags on the floor to madly rearrange their undies, socks, and essentials to try to comply with the edicts of Ryanair policy for carry-ons.

When we finally got to the front, we sailed through — veterans of the trials of budget air travel that we were. But we did not account for the endlessly inventive methods of torture that could be dreamed up by those who will fly you for less than the cost of a bus fare.

At the gate, we stood near the front of the "priority" line and were among the first to be called through to board. Except we would not be boarding. The thoughtful folks at Ryanair pointed us through a door and to a stairway that led to the tarmac. Just ahead of us was a young mother, carrying her three-year-old son who chose that moment to throw a tantrum and refuse to walk himself. She was also burdened with two carry-on bags and a stroller. A triathlete would have been challenged by less.

The service-impaired Ryanair staff paid no attention. Isabella picked up the mother's stroller and I grabbed one of her bags, allowing her to hoist her recalcitrant son and other suitcase and struggle down the stairs — where we were stopped partway down.

Dear reader, you might well ask why the airline would wave us through the gate and down the stairs if they had no intention of letting us board the plane. We can only surmise that it was the result of extensive market research and long, billable hours of consultation with experts in the field of consumer humiliation.

For a full twenty minutes, we were left to stand in a grim, post-industrial stairwell, balancing luggage, cranky children, and sanity with no explanation from Ryanair staff. It could not possibly have any perceptible cost saving for a budget airline. Perhaps it was the result of a monthly employee contest to find the most Kafkaesque method for pissing off your customers as their punishment for being such cheapskates and not flying with British Airways or Aer Lingus.

Shortly before a riot broke out, the door to the tarmac finally opened and we made our way to the jet. The best thing about the flight, aside from the price, was that it was short.

Ryanair's bag of customer satisfaction tricks had one more dandy for us upon arrival at Shannon Airport. The jet did not pull up at a gate — you always seem to disembark on the tarmac, which is fine on a fine day. But it was raining sideways in western Ireland and as a result our budget flight experience was capped by getting drenched as we scurried inside.

"Daddy, are you *sure* you can drive on the left side?" asked my ever-supportive daughter.

I reassured her that I had already done so in Ireland while covering a story back in January and had only been cursed by a total of one driver for my questionable road generalship. She seemed unconvinced, particularly as I kept looking up and to the right to check my rear-view mirror, which was actually on the left.

The rental car came with an installed GPS — a very handy innovation, except that it immediately failed to work — refusing to allow me to input any directions. I went back inside to the rental desk and asked the grizzled, earringed Irishman who had handed me the keys if he could help.

"I have no idea. I'm proudly computer illiterate!" he declared. "You're going to Doolin? Well, there's only one road out of the airport. Follow the signs to Ennis, from Ennis to Ennistymon, Ennistymon to Doolin."

Sounded simple enough, but I still managed to make a left when I should have turned right, which only dawned on me with the realization that we needed to be headed north along the coast but the sea was on our right. After ten minutes in the wrong direction, I turned us around. As it was still pelting rain, it did not matter much — just gave us more of a tour of the area.

Our destination was just outside Doolin: Ballinalacken Castle, a place arranged by the Irish tourism board. It is on a rise that would normally have a panoramic view of the sea, if we were not in the middle of a Celtic monsoon. You do not actually stay in the castle itself, which is a ruined, fifteenth-century tower that stands beside the main manor house.

Ballinalacken was run by the O'Callaghans, now in their third generation of operating the place after buying it from the O'Briens in 1938 — the same O'Briens whose ancestors built the tower. It was a tidy, homey place with a few tasteful antiques and it seemed very few guests.

After checking in, we decided to drive into Doolin to look around a bit. The village was spread out along a coastal road, with clusters of buildings leading to the dock where you catch the ferry to the Aran Islands. Too misty on this day to see the islands, but still a nice seaside Irish village.

As we searched for a place to pull over and explore, Julia asked from the back seat: "Daddy, aren't you supposed to be on the left side?"

As I calmly steered to the correct lane on what was luckily a deserted stretch of road, I thanked my clever and observant daughter.

After a bit of desultory shopping in stores that had an impressive array of Irish sweaters, and one "Made in Ireland" sweatshirt that my wife vetoed, I dropped Isabella at the hotel for a nap and resolved to take Julia to one of the local attractions: Doolin Cave, home of the world-famous Great Stalactite. At an impressive 7.3 metres long, it was billed as the "largest free-hanging stalactite in the Northern Hemisphere." If there is a longer one in the Southern Hemisphere, it must be a dandy.

Julia's interest in it was restrained, but she went along without much complaint. Sadly, the heavy rains had flooded Doolin Cave and it was closed. The young woman at the front desk cheerfully told us to check later because it only takes a half day of dryness to drain the water. We never did make it back.

We met Sheila and Tom for supper at a lovely little seafood restaurant called Cullinan's in Doolin. It was their recommendation that brought us to this part of Ireland — partly to see them, partly to experience the many charms of County Clare, home of the Burren, the Cliffs of Moher, and surfing.

The next day the clouds cleared and the sun came out, although it remained blustery. The first task was to meet a celebrated conqueror of Aileen's Wave. On the main street of the village of Lahinch, next to the

Shamrock Inn, was John McCarthy's Lahinch Surf School where we met Ireland's most famous surfer, John McCarthy.

He had the lean build of a surfer dude, a mop of blondish hair, and the ready smile of a guy who draws joy from the simple pleasures of riding mountainous waves that could squash an elephant.

McCarthy was the first to surf Aileen's Wave beneath the Cliffs of Moher, and gave it its name, drawn from the Gaelic *Aill na Searrach* moniker for the cliffs.

Try to visualize it: McCarthy rode a twelve-metre wave at high speed directly toward cliffs that rise 214 metres above the sea. Aileen only appears ten to twelve times a year, only when wind, weather, and sea combine in catastrophic serendipity to produce monstrous swells with the kind of lovely curling breaks that give erections to surfers and nightmares to normal human beings.

"It's like a Jurassic Park," McCarthy said. "You feel really tiny."

McCarthy and his followers would rush out to catch it, either climbing down a goat path through the cliffs, or towed to the scene by Jet Skis.

"It's not good to wipe out," he said with admirable understatement. "You have to climb up on the rocks and wait for help. Or hike back up the goat path."

Mounted on the wall behind him was a shard of a surfboard, split jaggedly in half — a souvenir of one of his dances with Aileen.

McCarthy was a devout Christian, who said a prayer every time he paddled out to sea to ride the waves. Now thirty-seven and the father of a three-month-old girl, he said he was starting to think about how much longer he would tackle the more extreme challenges of his sport.

"So ... would you like a surfing lesson then?" he asked with a big smile.

Irish Tourism had offered to pay for one. I declined, not wishing to taint my visit to the old country with a calamitous injury. McCarthy explained that I would not be testing Aileen, but rather getting a beginner's introduction on the small waves and forgiving sand beach right in the town of Lahinch.

I looked at Isabella. She looked at me. I said yes. For good measure, we signed up Julia, too, thinking we could turn it into a travelogue video. We were set for two days later, lots of time to change my mind.

We checked out of the Ballinalacken and shifted to Sheila and Tom's house. After spending several years in London, they moved to Lahinch to retire, buying a tiny cottage beside a tidal river on the edge of town. They tastefully expanded it, doubling it in size to a lovely, airy place that they shared with their dachshund, Bailey. In sight were the ruins of Dough Castle, built in the fourteenth century by the O'Connors and now a picturesque part of the scenery on the golf course.

In the nineteenth century, Lahinch was a popular seaside resort town, thanks to a railway delivering vacationers to enjoy golf and the sandy beaches. The rail link closed in the sixties, but visitors kept coming.

It is only more recently that it became surf central for Ireland. Locals say that it has transformed the town into a year-round operation with a nice selection of restaurants and shops benefitting from the ongoing traffic in dudes. The west coast of Ireland is not exactly Maui. But the Gulf Stream keeps the water from ever getting too cold. It never gets particularly warm either — wetsuits are needed even in the summer.

Surfing lesson day began with to Mass at St. Brigid's Church in nearby Liscannor — a modest place "built by the people, for the people" in Sheila's words, dating from the mideighteenth century when Catholicism was still under the boot of the Brits in Ireland.

We sat behind a very large, very fragrant older gentleman. Isabella turned to me, eyes wide, and signalled that she might not get through the service without either barfing or passing out. She did neither, but we all breathed shallowly.

It was a warm, fine day at Lahinch beach, with thankfully only modest waves gently rolling ashore. The Irish passion for surfing was evident as I saw dozens of pale Celts pulling on their wetsuits and carrying their boards out to the beach.

At the McCarthy Surf School's hut, we met our instructor, a tanned, toned dude with sunglasses pushed atop his flowing blond locks. He looked every inch a California beach bum, until he opened his mouth and out came a full County Clare Irish brogue. Ollie O'Flaherty was a local boy who had made good in the surfing subculture.

Ollie was a professional surfer. He made his living partly through teaching, partly through sponsors who paid his way to ride some of the biggest waves in the world, including his local monster, Aileen.

He had just finished third in an international competition after having conquered a fifteen-metre behemoth near Sligo, farther north on the Irish coast.

He brought us to the back of the hut to pick out our wetsuits. This is a garment that has no sympathy for middle age. I like to consider myself relatively trim, but after pulling it on and thinking that it would nicely show off all the weight-training work I had done in the gym I unfortunately caught a glance of myself reflected in a car window. Wetsuit Dad Bod.

Ollie, of course, looked like Superman.

Isabella was busily recording video of everything, but happily was focused more on Julia's struggles with getting into her kid wetsuit, thus sparing me the wifely raised eyebrow.

Ollie had a practised shtick to introduce us to surfing, pulling out a chalkboard to go over some of the basic terms: "stoked," "bro," "gnarly." Death was not among them.

He took the safety advice seriously, telling us that we needed to stay close to him at all times and to stay with the board when we inevitably fell off. The dangers seemed slight, given that he assured us that we would be staying in water that was no more than waist deep.

We practised our techniques on the beach first — beginning by laying on our bellies on the board, pretending to paddle like mad, getting up on one knee and finally to our feet. All very straightforward on dry land.

With that, we picked up our boards and waded into the Atlantic for the moment of truth. I evinced a relaxed attitude, trying to show I was not taking it too seriously when within my heart I was determined to not be an utter incompetent.

Isabella took off her shoes, rolled up her pant legs, and tottered into the twelve-degree water with our $2,700 camera in hand to record the spectacle, hoping more to capture the charm of a seven-year-old girl's adventure than the humiliating flailings of her middle-aged dad.

The paddling part was fine, particularly given an assist from Ollie, who would give the board a push at exactly the right moment. I could feel the board gathering momentum and tentatively got up to one knee and then to my feet — before immediately tumbling over.

I tried again, and again — same result. Because I was officially writing a commissioned travel story, I asked Isabella to break off from the video for a moment to capture a couple of still pictures of my fumbling attempts.

For just about a millisecond, I thought I had it. The board was beneath my feet, I was hurtling (actually gently gliding) toward the shore. The moment was fleeting as I tipped off once again.

As my head popped out of the water, I could hear Isabella: "ARRRGH …!"

She was pointing off to my right where our seven-year-old was expertly riding a wave all the way ashore, a glorious moment for the video — except Isabella was not rolling on it, having focused on a still shot of my failure.

Isabella shook her head, her teeth chattering, lower legs growing numb in the chill surf. I walked over and took the camera so that she could go ashore to warm up and I could make further attempts to recapture the magical scene of Julia successfully surfing. Nothing matched the shot we missed, but she did manage to stay atop for a few seconds — just barely enough for the purposes of the video.

Ollie and Julia gave each other a high-five for the camera to provide us with a visual punctuation point for her success.

In spite of my inability to stay on the board, I had to admit it was all strangely invigorating. Had I not been distracted by the demands of the video, had Ollie not had to concentrate more on Julia, I was confident I could have done it.

"If only I had just a bit more time, I'm sure I could have surfed ashore, too," I told my wife and daughter.

"Yeah. Right," they chimed in near unison. The old guy thinks he can be a dude.

Ashore, we found a quiet place to sit down with Ollie so that Julia could interview him for the video. I had given her a few questions in advance, which she carefully studied as we set up the shot.

She took it all very seriously until the moment she had to start, when the strangeness of it all took over her bright, seven-year-old brain and she blurted out the first question with a manic delivery that suggested someone had jabbed her with an electric cattle prod.

"What's so great about surfing in Ireland?" she shouted, hands waving aimlessly.

Ollie was a good sport, and it was, after all, his favourite topic, so he spoke lovingly (if slightly incomprehensibly, due to his accent) about the beauty and perfection of the Celtic version of the sport.

"We've got amazing waves, amazing scenery, amazing people, amazing lifestyle. Altogether, people have to come to experience what we have," he said as Julia fidgeted and looked off into the distance, with all the concentration skills of your average seven-year-old.

He spoke with particular affection about Aileen's Wave: "There's a perfect flat rock at the bottom of the Cliffs of Moher. When we get big swells, this wave comes in and breaks pretty much perfectly in that one spot every time. So it's probably one of the best big wave spots in the world."

Once she was done, I threw in a couple more questions for my travel story, all focused on the hazards of big wave surfing beneath massive cliffs.

"So many things can go wrong," he told me with a big grin. "The thrills definitely outweigh the scary parts."

Ollie had already broken all his boards that year and boasted of an impressive list of career injuries, from a broken ankle to a gashed forehead. He was a man happy in his work. This was going to be a great story.

Back at my cousin's place, Tom was utterly preoccupied with football. A true fan, he was headed out the following day to Poland to catch some games at the Euro 2012 tournament. But first, Ireland was playing Croatia that night in Poznań so he scrambled to barbecue supper before we all settled in front of the TV.

Tom handed over a copy of the *Irish Times*, which had a front-page picture of some slightly refreshed Irishmen headed to the game with the headline: "Angela Merkel thinks we're working!"

Alas, the Irish were overmatched and lost 3–1. But there was something about sharing a pint in an Irish home, surrounded by sublime Irish landscapes, warmed by real Irish hospitality, that generated a deep satisfaction inside me.

My eyes grew heavy as the game drew to a close. Isabella typically growled when she saw me falling asleep in front of the TV. Not this time.

"Look at you — you're really happy," she observed, accurately.

The moment was fleeting.

My phone buzzed with an email from Vancouver. It was decided that I was to head for Greece in a few days to cover elections that threatened, again, to upend the European Union. A great story for a foreign correspondent, but not such a great scenario for a father — it meant that I would be missing Julia's First Communion.

I told Isabella just before bedtime, after Julia was asleep.

"She's not going to be happy," she warned; clearly she was not either.

Chapter Twenty-Nine

It was only a three-day layover in London before getting on a flight to Greece.

It was thirty-three degrees when we landed in Athens — a hot, angry, and uncertain city.

The Greeks were having their second election in two months, after the first one was unable to produce a viable government. This time the opposition Syriza seemed to have a real chance of winning and carrying through with a promise to junk the bailout agreement that had imposed so much hardship. Once again the EU seemed to be in big trouble because of the sufferings of one of its smallest members.

On the advice of our fixer, Maria, we hired a taxi to take us to the port town of Perama, just to the west of Athens. Once it has been a prosperous place, thanks to shipbuilding. But the industry collapsed, taking most of the best jobs with it. Unemployment was upward of 60 percent, triple the already high national rate. In keeping with a dreary pattern, people started blaming immigrants. It was fertile ground for the neo-fascist Chrysi Avgi (Golden Dawn) party. There were stories of guys in black shirts tearing through residential areas on motorcycles at night, screaming anti-immigrant slogans.

Among Golden Dawn's enlightened ideas was a promise to plant land mines at the border to discourage illegal immigration. Their hammerhead image was vividly reinforced by their party spokesman, a guy named Ilias Kasidiaris, who demonstrated his manhood on live TV by throwing water in the face of a woman representing a competing party, and then slapping around a middle-aged woman who dared to upbraid him. Gallant fellow that he was, Kasidiaris then scurried out of the studio before the cops arrived to arrest him. The incident made for a powerful element in one of my stories.

On this day in Perama there was to be an anti-racism march, a reaction against an outrage committed against a family of Egyptian-born fishermen. One night earlier in the week a dozen or more goons brandishing bats and iron bars broke into their house at 3:00 a.m., trashed the place, and beat the shit out of one brother, sending him to hospital with a broken jaw. One of the assailants was wearing a Golden Dawn T-shirt. There had been no arrests.

A couple of hundred people gathered in a square by the waterfront for their march in support of the victims. I wondered how representative they were, given that Golden Dawn had managed to elect an MP in Perama in the most recent election.

I spoke with a young man named Rabab Hassan, who told me he was born in Greece of Egyptian parents. He said he was feeling the chill. "I'm afraid, afraid, afraid. I'm afraid for my baby because I have a three-year-old. Afraid to be here now. But I can't leave from Greece. Where can I go?"

As we walked along with the demonstrators, Maria pointed out the fish shop owned by the family who had been attacked. She asked around on our behalf and found one of the brothers in the crowd in the square where the march ended. Ahmed was chatting with a few supporters and apparently in no rush to step away from the people who had staged the protest on his family's behalf.

An Australian news crew was also on the hunt for him, led by a reporter with a chiselled jaw and a sour face, one of the very few unpleasant Aussies I had ever met. He was eyeing me warily as we negotiated with Ahmed for an interview.

Through Maria we asked Ahmed if we could interview him at the home that had been trashed. The Australian's pushy fixer, a bald, middle-aged guy, butted in and offered to drive our fisherman to the place. I smiled and shook my head, not wishing to be part of an international media feeding frenzy, but also not wanting to be elbowed aside. It was agreed that we would all meet at the house shortly.

We flagged down a cab and the driver knew exactly where to go.

"He says he just took a crew from Sky News there yesterday," translated Maria.

So much for our exclusive.

We beat the Australians to the scene and found two other brothers who were happy to speak and show us around. Saad Abu Hamed brought us inside and showed the broken windows and clothes still scattered around.

"I was scared I was going to die," he told us via translation. "It makes us sad because we've lived alongside the Greeks for many years."

It was a squalid little hovel. The thugs had not exactly targeted rich folks. I wondered why the Egyptians could not afford anything better, given that they seemed to be running a successful small business.

Out front, Saad showed me their old minivan, battered and windows smashed by the assailants.

The Aussies arrived, with the reporter still looking as if he had inhaled a lemon. Trailing along were a young Italian woman and a guy with a compact camera, anxious to record the same story.

Over her shoulder I spotted Maria standing cross-armed with a wry grin, watching the spectacle with bemusement. The Egyptians had had undoubtedly a pretty rough week, but were now at least enjoying the attention and more than happy to tell their story.

Their misfortune had become a kind of commodity in the international news business — a telling vignette in the Greek election story, one that visiting international reporters swarmed to record. We all need these kinds of compelling human elements in our stories, much like you need good olive oil to dress a salad. We all knew the game and told ourselves we were playing it to the greater good.

Maria knew a nice fish restaurant in Perama, but the taxi driver claimed to know a better one right beside the water. We suspected that he likely got a commission for delivering passengers to the place, but decided to give it a try.

The waiter brought over a platter of dead fish, which he said were yesterday's catch, all perfectly good, but suggested that if we waited five minutes we could get the catch of the day.

One hour and several glasses of wine later, the catch of the day finally arrived. The platter display looked very much like the catch of yesterday, but never mind. I ordered the smallest fish and it was fine. Dan ordered grilled calamari, which was a large load of seafood when it arrived. Maria took one look, saw that it was clearly undercooked, gave the waiter a bit of hell in Greek, and sent him back to grill it some more. She was a native of the island of Lesbos and knew her fish.

On the long taxi ride home, she got into a long conversation in Greek with the driver, then translated for us: "He says yesterday an Al Jazeera crew hired him to bring them to the same Egyptian fishermen's house. They were with him all day, bought him lunch, and in the end paid him one hundred euros. We should have more elections so that foreign journalists can stimulate our economy."

As Dan and I made our way to the Plaka for supper, the streets were filled with cars honking and jubilant Greeks hanging out the windows, shouting and waving the national flag. Although it was election eve, this was no campaign event. The football team had just upset Russia at the Euros to unexpectedly advance. Athenians welcomed the distraction from the world of economics.

Greece could not pay the bills. Unemployment and economic suffering were everywhere. Black shirts were beating up people of colour and winning seats in Parliament. But this was one of those glorious nights like nowhere else in the world. On a rooftop patio, I was served sublime lamb chops, all the more spectacular with the view of the Acropolis, lit golden against a cloudless sky. All around us, the daughters and sons of this ancient nation ate, drank, loved life, and put aside their cares for the moment.

For me it was an imperfect occasion. I wished my wife and daughter were with me to see those sights. Tomorrow morning my little girl would be passing a life milestone without me.

Election day was scorching hot and largely joyless. At a polling station in the Plaka, a Syriza voter told us, "Maybe today we give the world a lesson in democracy." No small irony, given that the Greeks gave the world democracy in the first place.

At another voting spot, we hit a bit of journalism gold: a woman born and raised in Montreal, but now casting a ballot in Greece. "The politicians are not capable of handling anything," Anna told us. "I'm very worried for young children, teenagers, people just starting out with their lives."

I asked Anna if she would prefer to go back to Canada.

"Yes, but my husband doesn't want to go."

He clearly understood, but piped up with a response in Greek, causing her to laugh.

"He doesn't like the snow."

Having stumbled upon some helpful Canadian content for my story, we were finished by early afternoon with nothing left to do until the results arrived later in the evening.

As darkness fell, we searched around the Plaka in hopes of finding people watching the results on TV. There were not many, but we did manage to capture one shot of a woman shaking her fist at the screen when the leader of Golden Dawn appeared.

We returned to the hotel to watch the results in the lobby bar as New Democracy, the old line party, took a narrow but consistent lead. The only real suspense came when a couple of guys in the bar wanted to switch the channel to watch Euro soccer. The bartender intervened on our behalf so that we could confirm that Syriza had fallen short and the Greeks would not yet be tearing up the bailout agreement. Europe could exhale.

Supporters of ND started to gather across the street in Syntagma Square in anticipation of the arrival of their leader and the next prime minister, Antonis Samaras.

A few young partisans tried to get up a rousing cheer, but their rhythm was off, the enthusiasm forced, and it all petered out.

"These guys make me want to throw up," observed Maria, whose sympathies were more to the left.

When Samaras arrived, he was engulfed by a giant scrum. On this night of lukewarm triumph, the crowd was dominated by foreign camera crews, given the paucity of party supporters. I advised Dan to keep on the outskirts, seeing no need to enter the maelstrom given that anything Samaras said would likely be anodyne and would subsequently be transmitted on our feeds where we could easily access them.

Dan hopped up on a rickety plastic chair to get a high shot of the arrival, and to my dismay, I saw the mob edging in our direction. I suggested that he might wish to get down rather than be knocked down, but he was determined to get his shot and instead stepped up onto an even more precarious plastic table, which started to bow alarmingly in the middle. Maria and I each grabbed a side to steady it as I visualized what it would be like to try to catch a six-foot-two cameraman if he were toppled. Luckily the scrum passed just to the side and disaster was avoided.

Samaras was an elegant scion of the Athenian elite, with a Harvard M.B.A. and a perfect knowledge of English. In other words, another product of the class that had so infuriated so many Greeks and led them to consider radical alternatives.

Now he would be getting his turn to clean up the mess. One commentator made the observation of the day: "Hercules was not on the ballot."

But at least they had a government.

After filing our story, an email arrived from Isabella with a glorious picture of Julia at her First Communion. She rarely wore dresses, but Isabella made the milestone special by buying her a saintly frock and a pearly hair band that complemented our little girl's beatific expression. I had missed it.

On the morning of our departure, Athens seemed more or less normal. The heat had eased. The news vendors on Syntagma Square were open for business like any other day, with the headlines moving on to other stories. About an hour before we were to leave for the airport, I strode out of the hotel on a mission. My fatherly absence at a key moment demanded a special, if wholly inadequate, present from Greece.

I walked down Mitropoleos Street in search of jewellers.

Having had her ears pierced, Julia was now building an impressive collection of earrings. My goal was to get her a pair with the traditional Hellenic symbol of eternity, similar to what I brought Isabella back from Athens on my 2004 Olympic trip.

Just a couple of blocks off the square I came upon a familiar storefront. It was the very same shop where I had bought those earrings, eight years earlier. Nick Papadopoulos still owned the place. I had interviewed him for my final story on the Olympics, a multibillion-dollar international extravaganza that brought him little extra business.

As I walked in the door, there was a minor flash of recognition on his face, but he clearly did not remember me and at first I did not remind him. We picked out the present I wanted, and added a ring for Isabella with a Cycladic spiral design.

As I pulled out my card to pay, I said, "Actually we've met before."

He gave me another long look.

"At the end of the Olympics. I interviewed you for Canadian TV."

He beamed and clapped my hand with a hearty grip.

"You were right about the Olympics!" he said. Business had remained mediocre, so much so that he was retiring at the end of the year. It was just too tough to make a living.

Nick wanted to give me a huge discount. I insisted on paying full price, but he threw in an extra little charm for Julia. It was a delightful moment — not so often that a past interviewee greets you with such warmth.

Back at the hotel, the lobby was jammed with TV crews checking out. The circus was largely leaving town.

As the doorman opened the door of our taxi, he wisecracked, "Sorry you didn't get the more interesting story."

The reception back in London was cool, but not as icy as it could have been. Julia liked the earrings. But for as long as I live she will remind me that I had missed her First Communion. And that a neighbour taught her how to ride a bike back home in Toronto while I was playing at being a Foreign Correspondent in London.

I was now determined to be witness to every single major event for the remainder of Julia's life.

The next one was to be a solo performance at the school. She had been practising for weeks to sing an a cappella version of "Breaking Free" from *High School Musical*, and the tune was now fairly drilled into my skull. Isabella coached her with some appropriate gestures to make the presentation complete.

There were only two classes and their parents were seated in the gym for the performance, but still it was a high-pressure moment.

"My heart is just pounding," Isabella whispered in my ear as she grabbed my hand in a bone-crushing grip.

In truth, she was also feeling a bit hungover, having had a rare night out with other Royal parents. It was a lubricated evening that lasted until two thirty in the morning.

Our little girl showed no sign of tension, though — a natural performer, she seemed cool as she stepped up for her moment. I suspected she was nervous inside, but she showed none of it.

Julia belted out her song like a pro, missing some of the planned gestures, but generally delivering a solid performance. Isabella exhaled.

Julia came over to us and I wrapped her in a big hug. "I need to go, sweetie. Have to catch a train."

She grabbed my tie with both hands and glared at me. But this time I had done my duty and now needed to return to work.

Chapter Thirty

To be a Canadian in Britain is to be a walking synonym for boring. We tend to take it with good nature, preferring it to the odd mixture of fascination and disdain that Brits hold for Americans. We are infrequently thought of, and when we are it is with minimal interest, even though a startling number would actually prefer to leave the sceptered isle and make a new home in Canada. The tourists thronging Trafalgar Square barely notice the stately mansion on the western side festooned with red maple leaf flags — Canada House, our diplomatic centre in the U.K.

But on July 1 of each year, Canada Day, the square was taken over by Canadians (a festival since cancelled after the private sector sponsor pulled out). The anniversary of Confederation was marked by ball hockey games (with teams largely composed of expatriate bank employees), long lineups for Alberta pancakes and maple syrup, as well as opportunities to have your picture taken with a Mountie dressed in traditional red serge.

We found it both silly and irresistible fun. Julia even talked me into getting a temporary tattoo of the flag on my cheek. We listened to Canadian bands, chowed down on pancakes, and generally enjoyed the novelty of it all. I resisted the opportunity to buy a Molson Canadian, given that it is a beer I never drink at home.

We scrambled back to the flat to pull together a supper for some friends, a rare hosting moment in which Isabella did not want to trust my sketchy barbecue skills and instead bought a lasagna from an Italian joint in the neighbourhood.

Julia was entering the last week of the school year and I struggled to convince her to finish her homework as we awaited the arrival of our guests. The final days of the Royal School were proving to be both frantic and bittersweet. Her friend Addie, with younger sister, Celia, were with us for the night, and after supper they performed the Royal School song, which would be sung for the last time in a matter of days. It was a poignant moment.

With two days left in the school year, the redoubtable and wonderful Miss Eisele organized a little graduation ceremony for Julia's class, where she thoughtfully said a few words about each girl. Although she had a plummy BBC announcer accent, she was actually born in the United States, and spoke about how difficult it had been for her when she arrived in the U.K. at age eight, a parallel to Julia's struggles in her early days. When she lauded Julia for all the progress she had made, a great big lump grew in my throat. Our little girl now was able to reproduce a perfect received pronunciation accent, though she proudly kept speaking like a Canadian, and no longer needed special assistance from the sympathetic Cockney cafeteria cook, Christine, to navigate unfamiliar food choices.

There are too few teachers like Miss Eisele. Too few people like Christine, with big hearts for kids. If you have young children struggling to adjust in a new environment I hope you are lucky enough to meet similar saviours.

The girls gathered around the piano in their classroom, now a portable in the schoolyard thanks to the new corporate owners, and raised their voices in song. Another tear-jerker pulled from the pages of sentimental English boarding school stories.

In reality, British private education was now thoroughly a business, and we were seeing the symptoms as the Royal School prepared to pass into history. Some staff were being let go; others did not wait for the axe and lined up other jobs.

On the second-last day, I snuck out of work for an hour to catch a gymnastics performance by the girls. Julia's flexibility and strength had grown dramatically. She could now do a bridge that was impossible when she landed in London. Our daughter had grown in so many ways. She had also taken up guitar at the school. The resourceful gym teacher, Ms. Lada, had gently coached her into becoming a much-improved swimmer.

None of this seemed to mean much for the corporation responsible for the regime change. In the final week of school, Julia's judo teacher, the ebullient, inspiring, and chiselled Winnie, was told he would not be able to offer his courses in the fall.

For all the aggravations, the school was invaluable to us, bringing a couple of friendships that had quickly solidified and deepened — fellow expatriates facing similar challenges who made common cause and joined together in an essential mutual support society. We thought it would be ephemeral, but some relationships turned out to be lasting and profound. Almost like we had been through a war together.

Julia's best friends were now settled: classmates Zoë from Calgary and Addie from New Jersey. Collectively, they formed the JAZ club, an ingenious name they dreamed up themselves. Zoë, reserved but mischievous; Addie, deep but fun-loving; Julia, ebullient yet sensitive. Brilliant, beautiful, happy girls. Their shared love for Harry Potter meant that their playtimes were filled with Hogwarts wizardry.

And then it was the last day of the Royal School Hampstead. After 157 years of educating girls, the name was passing into history. I took the day off work. A tent was set up in the playground with chairs inside. The official ceremonies focused on the girls who were graduating, but in many ways it was also a wake for all.

Over the years, the Royal had evolved, the military link as a school for soldier's daughters withering to a distant memory, even if it was still officially part of the mandate. It was now dominated by international students. The valedictorian for the final graduation service was an Australian girl.

Awards were handed out for each level. Addie, she of the remarkable reading ability, was given a citation.

Then the girls gathered at the front for one final rendition of the "Royal School Song." Here is where I lost it. It was a gentle, traditional lilt, made all the more touching by the voices of little girls.

Up on the hills of Hampstead
Our school awaits each day.
The sun rising on the hill and heath
And the girls who make their way.
London awaits before us
And enriches all our schemes.
At home on the hill girls from round the world
Work together to find their dreams.

My little girl, now seven, was transformed in the nine months since she had arrived. On her first day, she was weeping and inconsolable. On her second week, she wailed that her life was ruined because she could not navigate the exotic food choices at the cafeteria. But over the course of the school year, with the help of wonderful teachers, staff, and classmates, Julia adapted, grew, and, on this final day, triumphantly prevailed.

On her own initiative she wrote an extra line to conclude the "Royal Song," which our extraordinary daughter now stepped forward and delivered with assured conviction:

There will never be a school as great as you!

I swallowed hard.

Ceremonies concluded, there was a luncheon for all. Julia, such a poised performer, was now gushing tears — not because of the passing of the Royal but because Addie had been awarded a prize and not her.

"How could she do that to me?" she sniffled. I tried in vain to argue that she had been honoured with a solo line in the singing of the song, but it took some time for her to calm down.

I took her into the kitchen, determined to have a picture with the heroic Christine, who took her into her fleshy arms for an embrace that was true and lasting. Then the girls in Julia's class gathered around Miss Eisele for a group hug and photo.

Although the lunch was done and our belongings gathered up, we lingered in the yard with our friends.

"I don't want it to end," said Isabella, she who had been so traumatized when I was appointed to the London job. She pressed her body close and we slipped our arms around each other's waists. I owed her. Big time. My Foreign Correspondent adventure was a massive sacrifice for her, but she adapted, carved out her own way, and made our journey immeasurably richer. She did not want London, but London won her over.

Little Celia, younger sister of Addie, took matters into her own hands. She led several people to the front of the seating area in the tent and told us to take a chair. There would be one more show. She figured out how to turn on the electric piano and started to tap out "Jingle Bells."

Teachers and parents filtered back into the tent and before long everyone was belting out Christmas carols in the June heat and dancing with abandon.

Finally the party petered out, with final hugs and goodbyes. It was time.

I searched for Julia and found her with her pals Addie and Zoë off in a corner of the yard. The JAZ club. Addie's mom, Carolyn, was with them and as I approached I could hear that they were trying to figure out a way of writing their initials on a wall.

Carolyn gently advised them that "writing in blood is not a great idea."

My eyes widened. Seven-year-old girls from Toronto, New Jersey, and Calgary had become blood sisters mere months after meeting in London.

I grabbed a small, sharp stone and suggested that it would work well as an instrument for scratching their initials into the wall. Zoë and Addie were content to do so, and Julia followed suit.

I started to walk toward the exit with our friends and saw that Julia had lingered behind. As I walked back I could see that she was pressing her knuckle into her cheek and biting.

"Sweetie, what are you doing?"

She stuck one finger in her mouth, drew out one tiny drop of blood, and smeared it on the wall over her initials and those of her friends.

She looked at me gravely.

"Don't tell Mommy."

Acknowledgements

I t starts and ends with Isabella and Julia. Isabella's gift of the journal was both inspiration and a vote of confidence as a writer, and I will be forever grateful. She did not seek this adventure, but she made it special.

Julia just happens to be a funny, fabulous, and perceptive kid; she has brightened our lives every day since she arrived on the scene and she constantly astonishes with unexpected insights. She not only adapted to London, she prevailed and sparkled.

I hope I have done our collective story justice. Any failings are mine. I also hope I have conveyed to readers exactly how much Isabella and Julia gave up and how much they contributed to making our London experience extraordinary. The Trailing Spouses and Kids of London are a remarkable breed.

Terry Fallis was generous with advice and insight about the publishing game, and his story of how he launched his first book was an inspiration.

The folks at Dundurn Press had the faith to publish my little book and I will be forever grateful. Thanks to Scott Fraser for saying yes to my pitch, to Dominic Farrell for his perceptive editing advice, and to the whole Dundurn team for their support in trying to get readers to buy it.

I was a reporter at Global News for just short of thirty years, where I made countless friends, who greatly outnumbered the scoundrels, lunatics, and jerks. Thanks to all of them, the friends, that is — particularly the *Global National* team who were tremendous collaborators throughout my time in London. Kenton Boston picked me for the Europe Bureau Chief job and I am in his debt. Dan Hodgson and Stuart Greer were terrific colleagues, who gave such unfailing support that I'm willing to forgive them for getting me addicted to Twitter and an iPhone.

I still get choked up when I think of how the people at the late, much-missed Royal School helped our little girl with unfailing kindness and wisdom — Miss Eisele and Christine in particular.

And lastly, our London friends, who are friends still. They are numerous and all are valued, but I must give special thanks to (in alphabetical order) Addie, Carolyn, Celia, Dave, Jon, Kayla, Roxane, and Zoë.

What a time we had! Your friendship made and makes our lives so much richer.

OF RELATED INTEREST

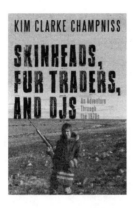

Skinheads, Fur Traders, and DJs: An Adventure Through the 1970s
Kim Clarke Champniss

A true story of an adventurous pop-loving teenager who, in the early 1970s, went from London's discotheques to the Canadian sub-arctic to work for the Hudson's Bay Company. His job? Buying furs and helping run the trading post in the settlement of Arviat (then known as Eskimo Point), Northwest Territories (population: 750).

That young man is Kim Clarke Champniss, who would later become a VJ on MuchMusic. His extraordinary adventures unfolded in a chain of *On the Road* experiences across Canada. His mind-boggling journey, from London to the far Canadian North and then to the spotlight, is the stuff of music and TV legends. Kim brings his incredible knowledge of music, pop culture, and the history of disco music, weaving them into this wild story of his exciting and uniquely crazy 1970s.

The 4 Year Olympian: From First Stroke to Olympic Medallist
Jeremiah Brown

After nearly being incarcerated at age seventeen and becoming a father at nineteen, Jeremiah Brown manages to grow up into a responsible young adult. But while juggling the demands of a long-term relationship, fatherhood, mortgage payments, and a nine-to-five banking career, he feels something is missing. A new goal captures his imagination: What would it take to become an Olympian?

Guided by a polarizing coach, Brown and his teammates plumb the depths of physical and mental exertion in pursuit of a singular goal. *The 4 Year Olympian* is a story of courage, perseverance, and overcoming self-doubt, told from the perspective of an unlikely competitor.

Whatever It Takes: Life Lessons from Degrassi and Elsewhere in the World of Music and Television
Stephen Stohn
with Christopher Ward

Producer of television's iconic *Degrassi* franchise Stephen Stohn tells stories from behind the scenes and of making it in the music and television world in this star-studded, rock 'n' roll trip through a Canadian show business explosion. Stohn, who has been at the heart of the entertainment industry for over forty years, shares a lifetime of experience and unique insights into how dreams are turned into reality.

"Whatever It Takes" — both a mantra and *Degrassi*'s theme song — has been heard millions of times all over the world. It embodies a philosophy of struggle and self-belief leading to accomplishment, as well as the story of an exploring mind, an adventurous pursuit of experience, ringing failures, and the willingness to see things in a different way.

Book Credits

Acquiring Editor: Scott Fraser

Editor: Dominic Farrell

Project Editor: Elena Radic

Proofreader: Ashley Hisson

Designer: Laura Boyle

Publicist: Michelle Melski

Dundurn

Publisher: J. Kirk Howard

Vice-President: Carl A. Brand

Editorial Director: Kathryn Lane

Artistic Director: Laura Boyle

Director of Sales and Marketing: Synora Van Drine

Publicity Manager: Michelle Melski

Editorial: Allison Hirst, Dominic Farrell, Jenny McWha, Rachel Spence, Elena Radic

Marketing and Publicity: Kendra Martin, Kathryn Bassett, Elham Ali

dundurn.com   dundurnpress

@dundurnpress   dundurnpress

dundurnpress   info@dundurn.com

FIND US ON NETGALLEY & GOODREADS TOO!

DUNDURN